NORTH DAKOTA
CENTENNIAL
1889~1989
100th ANNIVERSARY

The Prairie Collection Cookbook
Centennial Edition

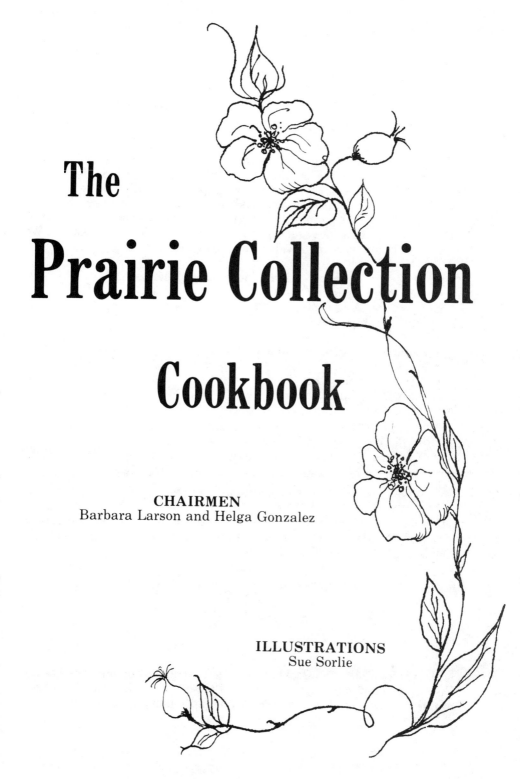

The
Prairie Collection
Cookbook

CHAIRMEN
Barbara Larson and Helga Gonzalez

ILLUSTRATIONS
Sue Sorlie

This prized collection of 400 tested recipes comes from members and friends of the Bismarck-Mandan Symphony League. It includes family favorites, ethnic specialties and party recipes not readily found in other cookbooks. The Prairie Collection cookbook has been endorsed by the North Dakota Centennial Commission as a special Centennial project. We do not claim that all the recipes are original, only that they are our favorites. We sincerely thank everyone involved in producing it.

Some of the uncommonly fine recipes included here are:
- The Original Smith and Curran
- Norwegian Egg Coffee
- Danish Pastry
- Wild Rice Soup
- Badlands Pitchfork Fondue
- Pit Roast
- Wild Game Des Lacs
- German Custard Kuchen
- Icelandic Vinarterta
- Dakota Bread
- Dandelion Wine

Copyright 1983
Bismarck-Mandan Symphony League, Bismarck, North Dakota 58501
2nd Edition November 1983 3,000
Centennial Edition April 1988 3,000
2nd Centennial Edition May 1989 3,000

Copies of The Prairie Collection Cookbook may be obtained from Bismarck-Mandan Symphony League c/o The Prairie Collection Cookbook, P.O. Box 131, Bismarck, N.D. 58502.

The Prairie Collection Cookbook has been compiled and published by the Bismarck-Mandan Symphony League. Proceeds from the sale of the book are used to support the Bismarck-Mandan Symphony Orchestra.

THE COMMITTEE

TYPING AND EDITING:
Helen Peterson

TESTING:
Alane Brosseau
Sigrid Bucklin
Jan Doerner
Lorraine Gregware
Mary Golden
Marilyn Grotewold
Joyce Sauer
Melva Weber
Rita Willer

CLERICAL:
Ruth Watson
Gail Wachter

INDEX:
Cindy Nelson

PROOF READING:
Alice Hjelle
Margaret Fiechtner

SALES AND MARKETING
Lorraine Anderson

SPECIAL ASSISTANCE:
Judi Adams
Barbara Glore
Harvey Larson
Liz Lucas
Susanne Mattheis
Pat Nelson
Bonnie Rothenberger
Bob Saueressig

SECOND EDITION EDITOR
Janet Barbie

MEADOWLARK

INTRODUCTION

The recipes collected in this cookbook are a reflection of the wonderful variety of foods that are proudly presented over and over again, and have come to be thought of as our favorites. They are a testimony to the creativity of our cooks. Also, the artwork in our cookbook is a reflection of the natural easiness of the life that surrounds us: the plants, the flowers, the meadowlark, the prairie dog. We think it is symbolic of the way man has chosen to live on the prairie in harmony with all the creations of nature.

THE ARTIST

Sue Sorlie is a native North Dakota artist. Her sensitive illustrations of native wild flowers, grasses, birds and animals reflect the unique beauty of the prairie.

TABLE OF CONTENTS

Longbilled Curlew

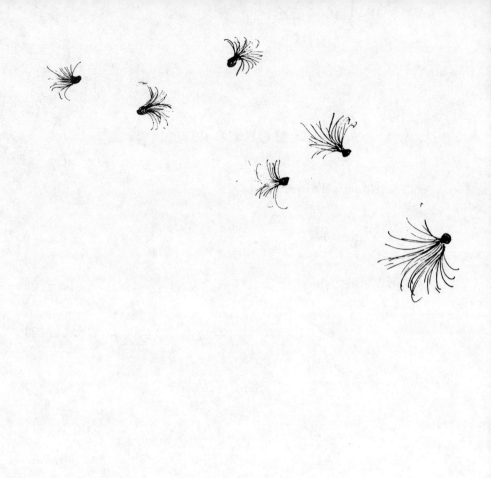

BEVERAGES,
APPETIZERS AND SOUPS

BEVERAGES

Smith and Curran

The Smith and Curran was first mixed in the Blue Blazer Lounge of the Prince Hotel in Bismarck, North Dakota, about 1952. Oilman James P. Curran recalls that he and his partner, Wendell Smith, "were in the saloon one night trying to figure out something to get down".

2 ounces creme de cacao
1 ounce sweet cream

Club soda
Ice cubes

Mix creme de cacao and cream in a tall glass. Add ice cubes and fill glass with club soda. A refreshing after dinner drink.

Champagne Punch

2 bottles champagne
1 fifth Rhine wine
1 quart club soda

1 quart ginger ale
1 cup brandy
½ cup Triple Sec

Mix and pour into a punch bowl containing an ice mold. Yield: 1½ gallons.

Kir

½ gallon white wine   ½ cup creme de cassis

Mix, chill and serve in stemmed glasses. A small strip of lemon peel may be added to each glass. Yield: ½ gallon

Raspberry Apéritif

1 (10 ounce) package frozen
    raspberries

3 ounces orange liqueur
1 bottle champagne, chilled

Puree and strain raspberries. Save juice and discard seeds. Chill until very cold. Add liqueur and champagne. Serve in stemmed glasses.

For punch, add ginger ale or club soda.

May Bowle

4 cups strawberries, sliced
1 cup sugar
1 pint cognac
1 bottle white wine

3 bottles Moselle
2 bottles champagne
1 pint whole strawberries

Combine sliced strawberries and sugar and let stand one hour. Add cognac and the one bottle white wine and let marinate overnight. Strain and pour into punch bowl over ice ring which has been frozen with whole strawberries in it. Add 3 bottles of Moselle and champagne. Float whole strawberries. Yield: 36 half cup servings

Sangria

2 cups sugar
1 cup water
½ gallon red wine
2 cups brandy
1 lime

1 lemon
1 orange
1 banana, peeled (optional)
2 quarts chilled club soda

Boil sugar and water 5 minutes and cool. Combine with wine and brandy. Cut fruit into thin slices and add. Refrigerate overnight. Before serving add club soda.

Orange or Lemon Frappé

1 (12 ounce) can frozen
  lemonade concentrate or
  frozen orange concentrate
12 ounces water
12 ounces vodka (optional)

6 ounces milk
6 ounces cream
1 ounce grenadine
Juice from one lemon

Combine concentrate, water and vodka in a blender and mix well. With blender running, add milk, cream, grenadine and lemon juice. Transfer to a plastic container and freeze at least 24 hours. Just before using, remove from freezer and blend until smooth. Serve in stemmed cocktail glasses.

To make without vodka, follow above directions but do not freeze.

Strawberry Daiquiri

4 cups fresh or frozen whole
strawberries — or more if
you like.
1 fifth white rum
1 (12 ounce) can pink lemonade
concentrate

1 (46 ounce) can unsweetened
pineapple juice
1 quart 7-Up
Powdered sugar and
grenadine to taste

Puree berries. Add other ingredients. Mix well and freeze in a 5 quart container. Spoon slush into glasses and serve.

Holiday Eggnog

4 eggs, separated
½ cup sugar
⅛ teaspoon salt
1 teaspoon vanilla or
1 teaspoon rum flavoring

2 cups cream, whipped
Freshly grated nutmeg

Beat egg yolks, sugar and salt until thick and lemon colored. Stir in flavoring. Fold egg yolk mixture into whipped cream. Beat egg whites until stiff. Fold into egg-cream mixture. Chill well and serve in punch cups. Grate a little nutmeg over each serving. Note: This eggnog is very thick and may be eaten with a spoon. Dilute with a little milk if a thinner eggnog is desired. 1½ ounces of white rum may be added to each serving if desired.

Tom and Jerry Batter

12 eggs, room temperature
2 cups granulated sugar
2 cups powdered sugar

1 (14 ounce) can sweetened
condensed milk
1 teaspoon vanilla extract

Separate eggs. In a large mixing bowl, beat egg whites on low speed until frothy. Turn to high and beat until stiff peaks form. Add granulated sugar very slowly, then add one cup of the powdered sugar slowly. Beat until mixed and set aside. In another bowl, beat egg yolks until thick. Add the other cup of powdered sugar, milk and vanilla. Fold egg white mixture into yolk mixture. Servings: 12

 Serving suggestion: Place one tablespoon batter into a mug. Add one ounce whiskey and fill mug with boiling water. Stir and top with grated nutmeg.

Glog (Swedish)

8 cups sugar
7½ cups water
1½ ounces whole cloves
1 tablespoon cardamon seeds

1 quarter-sized piece whole ginger
Raisins
Almonds, blanched

Simmer above ingredients for 2 hours. Let stand overnight. Strain and bottle syrup. Store in refrigerator.

To serve: Mix 1 part syrup to 4 parts red wine. Add raisins and almonds to taste. Heat almost to boiling; do not boil. Serve hot.

Spectacular Irish Coffee

½ cup milk
¼ cup Irish whiskey
1 quart coffee ice cream
1 teaspoon instant coffee
  powder

½ pint whipping cream,
  whipped
Cinnamon sticks

Blend milk and whiskey in blender. Spoon in ice cream and coffee powder. Blend until smooth. Pour in tall chilled glasses and top with whipped cream. Add cinnamon stick as a stirrer.

Perfect for after dinner.

Egg Coffee (Norwegian)

16 cups water
1 large egg

1 cup regular grind coffee

Bring water to boiling in a large coffee pot. Mix whole egg, shell included, in a measuring cup. Add enough water to make ½ cup. Combine with coffee. When water is boiling, turn off burner and add coffee mixture. Let coffee pot remain on turned-off burner for 45 minutes or until grounds settle to bottom of pot. Pour through a strainer before serving. The coffee will be very clear and aromatic.

APPETIZERS

Spinach Dip

1 (10 ounce) package frozen chopped spinach, thawed and squeezed dry
1 package Knorr's vegetable soup mix
1 (8 ounce) can water chestnuts, chopped and drained
1 small onion, finely chopped
1 cup sour cream
½ cup mayonnaise

Mix and refrigerate overnight. Serve with crackers or fresh crusty bread. Yield: 2 cups

Green Goddess Dip

1 clove garlic, minced
2 tablespoons anchovy paste
3 tablespoons chives, finely chopped
1 tablespoon lemon juice
1 tablespoon tarragon wine vinegar
½ cup sour cream
1 cup mayonnaise
⅓ cup parsley, minced
Salt and coarsely ground pepper to taste

Mix above ingredients until well blended. Serve with fresh vegetables. Yield: Approximately 2 cups

Hot Cheese Dip

1 package (8 ounce) cream cheese
1 package (3 ounces) dried beef, chopped
2 tablespoons onion flakes
¼ cup chopped green pepper
2 tablespoons milk
4 ounces sour cream
½ cup pecans, chopped

Soften cream cheese with milk. Gradually add beef, onion, green pepper. Fold in sour cream. Place ingredients in greased 8-inch pie pan. Spread top with pecans. Bake at 350 degrees for 20 minutes or until slightly brown on top. Yield: 8-inch dish

Hot Broccoli Dip

2 (6 ounce) rolls garlic cheese
2 (10 ounce) packages frozen
   chopped broccoli, lightly
   cooked and well drained
1 medium onion, chopped
   and sautéed in butter

1 (10¾ ounce) can cream of
   mushroom soup
10 to 12 shakes red pepper

Melt cheese over low heat. Add other ingredients. Serve hot in a casserole. Accompany with corn or potato chips.

This recipe can easily be doubled or tripled to serve a large group.

Cream Cheese with Jezebel Sauce

1 (18 ounce) jar pineapple
   preserves or apricot
   preserves
1 (18 ounce) jar apple jelly
1 (5 ounce) jar horseradish,
   drained

1 (1.1 ounce) small can dry
   mustard
1 tablespoon cracked black
   pepper
1 (8 ounce) package cream
   cheese

Combine pineapple preserve, apple jelly, horseradish, mustard and black pepper in a bowl. Mix well with a wire whisk. Spoon 1 cup sauce over a block of cream cheese. Serve with crackers. Yield: 5 cups

Chutney Ball

¼ cup chutney, drained and
   chopped
8 ounces cream cheese

2 teaspoons curry powder
   Salted peanuts, chopped

Mix chutney, cream cheese and curry. Form into ball. Roll in chopped peanuts. Can be frozen. Serve with Triscuits. Yields: 1 chutney ball

Stilton Spread

1 cup Stilton cheese,
   coarsely crumbled
½ cup unsalted butter

½ cup cream cheese
¼ cup Macadamia nuts

Put cheeses and butter in a food processor and process until smooth. Add nuts and process just until coarsely chopped. Put in a small crock and refrigerate.

Serve with crackers or celery sticks. Yield: 2 cups

Note: If Stilton cheese is unavailable, Gorgonzola may be used instead.

13

Herbed Cheese Spread Chablis

½ pound Monterey Jack cheese

2 (8 ounce) packages cream cheese

1 (2½ ounce) jar shredded Parmesan cheese

½ teaspoon crumbled marjoram

½ teaspoon dill weed

½ teaspoon hickory smoke salt or seasoned salt

3 tablespoons soft butter

½ cup Chablis or dry white wine

Crisp crackers and fresh grapes.

Finely grate the jack cheese; soften the cream cheese. Combine all cheese with herbs, salt and soft butter. Beat until well blended. Stir in wine until mixture is smooth. Pack into lightly oiled 3 cup mold. Cover and chill in refrigerator overnight, so mold firms and flavors mellow. Turn out on serving platter; surround with crackers and tiny bunches of fresh grapes. Can be served as a dessert or appetizer. Yield: 3 cups

Mushrooms á la Grecque

(Prepare one day in advance)

1 pound fresh mushrooms, about 1½ inches diameter

1½ cups water

¾ cup olive oil

2 tablespoons lemon juice

1 small garlic clove, minced

1 stalk celery, finely diced

1 tablespoon white wine vinegar

¼ teaspoon fennel seed

¼ teaspoon oregano

¾ teaspoon ground coriander

½ bay leaf

¼ teaspoon whole peppercorns

¼ teaspoon salt

Clean mushrooms, discarding stems. In a pan combine all ingredients, except mushrooms, and simmer for 15 minutes. Add whole mushrooms and cook another 5 minutes. Chill for at least 24 hours. Drain and serve.

Chilled Dilled Peas

1 (10 ounce) box tiny frozen green peas or (8 ounce) can tiny peas

½ cup mayonnaise

½ cup sour cream

1 bunch green onions, finely sliced

¼ cup fresh snipped dill or tablespoon dried dill weed

1 teaspoon curry powder

Salt and pepper to taste

Barely cook peas. Drain well. Combine with all other ingredients and chill for at least 2 hours before serving with crackers. Yields: 2½ cups

Taramosalata (Greek)

6 slices homemade, white
   bread, crusts trimmed
1 cup cold water
½ cup tarama (salted carp roe)

¼ cup lemon juice
¼ cup onion, finely grated
¾ cup olive oil

Soak bread in water for 5 minutes. Squeeze dry and mash until smooth. Add the tarama, 1 teaspoon at a time, mashing and stirring constantly. Beat in the lemon juice and grated onion, continuing the mashing process until mixture becomes a smooth paste. Beat in the oil, 1 tablespoon at a time, making certain the oil is absorbed before adding more. Adjust seasoning and refrigerate until ready to serve.

Serve spread on toast or crackers.

Artichoke Spread

1 (16 ounce) can artichoke
   hearts
1 cup mayonnaise

1 cup Parmesan cheese,
   grated

Drain artichokes thoroughly. Chop into small pieces. Add mayonnaise and cheese. Mix ingredients well and chill. Serve with crackers.

Variation: Place in an oven-proof quiche dish or casserole and bake at 350 degrees until bubbly around edges and thoroughly heated in center.

Hot Mushroom Appetizer

4 slices bacon
8 ounces mushrooms, chopped
4 green onions, finely chopped
1 garlic clove, minced
2 tablespoons flour
½ teaspoon fresh ground pepper
1 (8 ounce) package cream cheese, cubed
2 teaspoons Worcestershire sauce
1 teaspoon soy sauce
½ cup sour cream
1 teaspoon lemon juice
Cocktail rye or assorted crackers

Cook bacon until crisp. Crumble in a small bowl. Pour off all but 2 tablespoons fat. Add mushrooms, onion, garlic and saute until liquid evaporates. Stir in flour and pepper. Add cream cheese, Worcestershire, soy sauce, and cook until cheese melts. Blend in sour cream, lemon juice and bacon. Cook until heated through, but do not boil.

Serve warm with cocktail rye or crackers.

Sauerkraut Balls

½ pound cooked ham
½ cup chopped onion
1 tablespoon oil
¼ cup bulk sausage
1 cup flour
½ teaspoon salt
½ teaspoon dry mustard
1 cup milk
1 pound canned sauerkraut, well drained and finely chopped
Flour to coat balls
2 eggs, slightly beaten
1 ⅓ cup milk
½ teaspoon salt
Bread crumbs to coat balls
Oil for deep frying

Grind ham and onion together. In a large skillet, heat oil and brown sausage, breaking it into small pieces as it cooks. Add ham and onion; cook until heated. Sift flour, salt and mustard together. Add all at once to meat mixture and stir. Add 1 cup milk while stirring. Cook and stir for 2 to 5 minutes until mixture thickens. Add sauerkraut. Cook and stir for a few minutes until ingredients are well mixed. Cool. Form into one inch balls; roll in flour. Combine egg, milk and salt. Dip balls in this mixture, then roll them in bread crumbs. Deep fry in hot, 360 degree oil until browned. Drain on absorbent paper. Serve hot.

Note: Balls can be prepared in advance and frozen uncooked. Thaw for thirty minutes before deep frying.

Spinach Balls

2 (10 ounce) packages frozen
  chopped spinach
3 cups herb-seasoned
  stuffing mix
1 large onion, finely chopped
6 eggs, well beaten

¾ cup melted butter or
  margarine
½ cup Parmesan cheese
1 teaspoon garlic salt
½ teaspoon thyme

Cook spinach according to directions on box. Squeeze spinach to remove all moisture. Combine spinach with remaining ingredients. Shape into ¾ inch balls and place on lightly greased cooky sheet. Bake at 325 degrees for 15-20 minutes. Yield: 11 dozen

Note: Can be frozen before baking. Bake 20-25 minutes.

Spanakopita
(Greek Spinach Pie)

½ package (1 pound size)
  prepared phyllo or strudel
  pastry leaves
¼ cup butter
½ cup finely chopped onion
3 packages (10 ounce size)
  frozen spinach, thawed and
  well drained
4 eggs

½ pound feta cheese,
  crumbled
¼ cup chopped parsley
2 tablespoons chopped fresh
  dill or 1½ teaspoons
  dillweed
1 teaspoon salt
⅛ teaspoon pepper
1 cup butter, melted

Preheat oven to 350°. Let pastry leaves warm to room temperature, according to directions on package label.

In ¼ cup hot butter, sauté onion until golden, about 5 minutes. Add spinach; stir to combine with onion. Remove from heat. In large bowl, beat eggs. Stir in cheese, parsley, dill, salt, pepper and spinach-onion mixture. Mix well.

Brush a 13x9x2-inch baking pan with 2 tablespoons melted butter. In bottom of baking pan, layer 8 phyllo-pastry leaves, brushing top of each with melted butter. Spread evenly with spinach mixture. Cover with 8 more leaves, brushing each with butter; pour any remaining melted butter over top.

Using scissors, trim off any uneven edges of pastry. Cut through top pastry layer to form 18 rectangles, about 3 by 2 inches. Cut them smaller for appetizers. Bake 30 to 35 minutes, or until top crust is puffy and golden. Serve warm.

Note: Keep unused pastry leaves covered with damp towel to prevent drying out.

Salmon Mousse

2 envelopes unflavored gelatin
¼ cup cold water
¾ cup boiling water
1 cup mayonnaise
¼ cup finely chopped onion
⅛ to ¼ teaspoon cayenne pepper

1 teaspoon salt
2 teaspoons dried dill weed
2 cups poached fresh salmon, or canned salmon with skin and bones removed
1 cup heavy cream, whipped

Soften gelatin in cold water. Add boiling water and stir until gelatin dissolves and mixture cools to room temperature. Stir in mayonnaise, lemon juice, onion, cayenne, salt and dill. Refrigerate until mixture begins to thicken. Fold in salmon and whipped cream. Spoon into a decorative 6 to 8 cup mold. Chill several hours or overnight. Turn out onto a platter and garnish with any fresh greens. Serve with cocktail rye bread or crackers. Makes at least 12 appetizer portions.

Shrimp Mold

1 (10½ ounce) can tomato soup
3 (8 ounce) packages of cream cheese
1½ envelopes gelatin
⅓ cup water

¾ cup celery, chopped
¾ cup onion, chopped
1 cup mayonnaise
2 (4½ ounce) cans shrimp, drained

In a double boiler, over simmering water, mix soup and cream cheese. Soften gelatin in cold water. Add to soup and cheese mixture. Cool. Add celery, onion, mayonnaise and shrimp. Pour in lightly greased mold. Chill in refrigerator until set. Serve with crackers.

Stuffed Grape Leaves (Greek)

6 tablespoons olive oil
1 cup onions, finely chopped
⅓ cup long-grain rice, uncooked
¾ cup water
½ teaspoon salt
Freshly ground black pepper, to taste

2 tablespoons pine nuts
2 tablespoons currants
40 preserved grape leaves
2 tablespoons cold water
Lemon wedges

In a heavy skillet, heat 3 tablespoons olive oil until light haze forms. Add the onions and sauté for 5 minutes. Add rice, stirring constantly for 3 minutes. Do not let rice brown. Pour in water. Add salt and pepper and bring to a boil over high heat. Reduce heat to low, cover and simmer for about 15 minutes.

In a small skillet, heat 1 tablespoon oil and sauté pine nuts until a delicate brown. Add them to rice and stir in currants.

In a large pot, bring 2 quarts of water to a boil over high heat. Drop in the grape leaves and immediately turn off the heat. Let leaves soak for 1 minute; drain and plunge them into a bowl of cold water to cool quickly. Gently separate the leaves and spread them, dull sides up, on paper towels to drain.

Layer the bottom of a heavy casserole with 10 leaves. Stuff the remaining leaves: Place 1 tablespoon filling on leaf, fold in sides, and roll into a tight cylinder. Stack stuffed leaves, side by side, seam sides down, in layers in the casserole. Sprinkle with remaining 2 tablespoons oil and cold water. Place the casserole over high heat for 3 minutes. Reduce heat to low and simmer, tightly covered, for 50 minutes. Uncover and cool to room temperature. Serve on a platter with lemon wedges.

Hot Taco Pie

1 pound lean ground beef
1 package dry taco mix
1 (16 ounce) can refried beans
½ cup sour cream

½ cup green chili sauce
¾ cup Cheddar cheese, shredded

Brown beef in large skillet and drain excess fat. Mix the taco mix and refried beans with the ground beef. Pat into 10 inch pie plate. Mix sour cream and chili sauce and spread on top of meat mixture. Cover with the shredded cheese and bake in 350 degree oven until bubbly, 15-20 minutes. Serve with Doritos. Yield: 10 inch pie

Mexican Taco Pie

1 (16 ounce) can refried beans
1 (8 ounce) carton avocado dip
1 (8 ounce) carton green chili dip
1 pound sharp Cheddar cheese, grated

1 (16 ounce) can pitted ripe olives, sliced
1 green pepper, finely chopped
1 bunch green onions, sliced
1 tomato, seeded and chopped

Spread beans on a 12-inch serving plate. Layer the avocado and green chili dips. Sprinkle the cheese on top. Arrange olives, pepper and onions in a decorative pattern over the cheese layer. Chill in the refrigerator for 2-3 hours. Serve with tortilla chips.

Mushrooms with Spinach and Ham Stuffing

½ cup green onions, finely chopped
3 tablespoons butter
1 (10 ounce) package drained, defrosted, frozen spinach
¾ cup ham, finely chopped

1 cup bechamel sauce
Salt and freshly ground pepper, to taste
18-24 two-inch mushroom caps
2 tablespoons butter, cut in small pieces

Preheat oven to 350 degrees. Sauté onions in butter for 2 minutes. Add spinach, mix and cook for 4 minutes. Transfer mixture to bowl. Stir in ham and bechamel sauce. Season with salt and pepper to taste. Butter large, shallow baking dish. Sprinkle caps with salt and spoon filling into them. Arrange in baking dish and dot with butter. Bake for 10-15 minutes or until tender and filling is lightly browned. Serve hot as an appetizer on toast points, or as a luncheon dish with rice.

Béchamel Sauce:

2 tablespoons butter
3 tablespoons flour

1 cup hot milk
Salt and white pepper, to taste

Melt butter in saucepan over medium heat. Stir in flour and cook for 1 minute, stirring constantly. Remove from heat and blend in milk. Return to high heat until sauce comes to a boil, stirring vigorously. Reduce heat and simmer for 2-3 minutes until sauce thickens. Season to taste with salt and white pepper.

Bacon and Water Chestnuts

2 (8 ounce) cans whole water
   chestnuts
1 pound bacon, sliced in half
1 (one pound) package brown
   sugar

2 cups hot tangy
   ketchup

Drain chestnuts. Wrap with bacon strips and secure with toothpicks. Arrange in a 9x13 inch pan. Mix together brown sugar and ketchup and pour over chestnuts.

Bake 35 to 45 minutes in 350 degree oven.

Antipasto

1 (12 ounce) bottle chili sauce
1 cup hot ketchup
   Juice of one lemon
1 teaspoon horseradish
1 tablespoon brown sugar
1 (6 or 7 ounce) jar sweet
   mixed pickles and liquid
3 (8 ounce) jars sliced
   mushrooms, drained
1 (16 ounce) can pitted ripe
   olives, drained
1 (16 ounce) jar pimento
   stuffed green olives, drained

2 carrots, slivered and in
   2-inch pieces
3 (7 ounce) cans albacore
   tuna, drained
1 (8 ounce) jar pickled onions
   drained
1 (4 or 5 ounce) jar pickled
   cauliflower, drained
1 (16 ounce) can artichoke
   hearts, quartered

Put chili sauce, catsup, lemon juice, horseradish, brown sugar, pickles and their liquid in a large pot. Simmer until sugar dissolves, stirring constantly. Add all other ingredients except artichoke hearts. Simmer for 10 minutes. Stir in artichoke hearts. Remove from heat, cool and refrigerate.

Serve as an appetizer with crackers, or as a first course in individual clam shells. The recipe makes about 3 quarts and freezes very well.

Note: The pickles and olives may be sliced in half if desired.

Artichoke Appetizers

1 large artichoke
1 teaspoon salad oil
1 bay leaf, crushed
½ teaspoon salt
3 ounces cream cheese, softened
¼ teaspoon Tabasco
½ teaspoon garlic powder
Salt to taste
2 tablespoons light cream
4 ounces small shrimp, canned or frozen
Paprika

Cook artichoke in water to cover. Add the oil, bay leaf and salt. Simmer until tender, about 30 minutes. Cool and remove the leaves. Use the leaves that are firm and have a good edible portion on the ends.

Blend the cream cheese with Tabasco, garlic powder, additional salt to taste and cream to make smooth paste. Spread on base of each leaf. Place a small shrimp on top of filling and sprinkle with paprika.

Arrange on a round plate or tray in the shape of a sunflower so each leaf is easy to pick up.

Herring Salad

22 ounces pickled herring cutlets, drained and diced
2 cold boiled potatoes, peeled and diced
8 ounces canned beets, diced
2 dill pickles, diced
1 tart apple (raw) pared and diced
2 or 3 green onions, minced
3 tablespoons oil
1 tablespoon white wine vinegar
Salt and pepper to taste
½ cup sour cream
2 hard-boiled eggs, chopped

Mix all ingredients and serve on a large lettuce leaf as an appetizer or first course.

Second Method: Put all ingredients through a food grinder (omit hard-boiled eggs and sour cream). Shape mixture to resemble a fish. Press the tip of a spoon over the fish to resemble fish scales. A small end piece of a black olive can be used for the eye and the green part of the scallions can be shaped as the tail.

Serve with buttered pumpernickel bread. Serves: 6-8

Marinated Shrimp Appetizer

¼ cup olive oil
2 tablespoons fresh lemon juice
2 tablespoons liquid from jar of Spanish green olives
½ teaspoon salt
½ teaspoon dry mustard
⅛ teaspoon cayenne pepper
Dash of black pepper, about ¹⁄₁₆ teaspoon
½ bay leaf
1 garlic clove, halved
2 pounds shrimp, peeled, deveined and cooked
1 cup Spanish stuffed, green olives, halved
1 small lemon, thinly sliced
1 medium onion, thinly sliced

Combine oil, lemon juice, olive liquid, salt, mustard, cayenne pepper, bay leaf and garlic. Place shrimp, olives, lemon slices and onion in shallow container. Pour dressing over the ingredients. Stir and mix well. Cover tightly and refrigerate overnight. Serve cold. Serves: 6-8

Shrimp and Artichoke Heart Appetizers

1 (10 ounce) package frozen artichoke hearts
4 tablespoons oil
1 pound fresh or frozen shrimp
1¼ pounds whole mushrooms
2 cloves garlic, finely minced
½ teaspoon salt
Pepper to taste
½ teaspoon oregano
2 tablespoons lemon juice
¼ cup finely chopped fresh parsley

Blanch artichoke hearts according to package directions. Heat oil in frying pan; add shrimp and mushrooms. Cook, stirring frequently, until shrimp turns pink. Add artichoke hearts, garlic, salt, pepper and oregano; stir. Add lemon juice and parsley; stir to combine. Serve warm in chafing dish. About 30 appetizers.

BEAVER

Shrimp in Tomato, Wine and Feta Cheese (Greek)

4 medium ripe tomatoes (or 1½ cups chopped, drained canned tomatoes)

1½ pounds raw shrimp in shell (25-30 shrimp, medium-sized)

6 tablespoons olive oil

¼ cup onions, chopped

½ cup dry white wine

2 tablespoons parsley, chopped

½ teaspoon oregano

1 teaspoon salt
Freshly ground black pepper, to taste

2 ounces feta cheese, cut into small cubes

Drop fresh tomatoes into boiling water for 15-30 seconds. Remove and skin with sharp knife. Cut out the stem and slice in half crosswise. Squeeze to remove seeds and juices. Chop coarsely. (Canned tomatoes need only to be drained and chopped.)

Shell the shrimp but leave the tail intact. Remove dark vein with point of a knife. Wash under cold water; pat dry and set aside.

In a large skillet, heat oil until light haze forms. Add the onions; sauté for 5 minutes until soft and golden. Stir in tomatoes, wine, 1 tablespoon parsley, oregano, salt and a few grinds of fresh peppercorn. Bring to a boil. Reduce heat and cook uncovered until the mixture thickens to a light puree. Add the shrimp and cook over moderate heat for 5 minutes or until the shrimp turn pink. Stir in cheese; adjust seasoning and sprinkle the top with remaining tablespoon of parsley.

Valley Street Chicken Wings

3-4 pounds chicken wings, tips removed

¼ cup soy sauce

¼ cup honey

¼ cup bottled barbecue sauce

¼ cup ketchup
Horseradish to taste

Arrange chicken wings on a flat baking pan. Mix other ingredients. Pour over chicken. Bake at 275 degrees for 2 hours, or until all the sauce is absorbed and the wings are glazed. Turn wings occasionally. Serves: 8

NUTALLS VIOLET

Grand Soufflé Torte

Souffle layers:
4 tablespoons butter
½ cup flour
2 cups milk
1 teaspoon sugar
4 egg yolks
4 egg whites
1/16 teaspoon cream of tartar
Dash salt

Salmon Cream Cheese Filling:
1 (8 ounce) package cream
cheese, room temperature
½ cup sour cream

2 tablespoons lemon juice
4 tablespoons green onions,
minced
¼ pound smoked salmon

Sour Cream Frosting:
4 tablespoons sour cream
1 tablespoon green onion,
chopped
1 tablespoon lemon juice
1½ tablespoons parsley,
minced
1 lemon, sliced

For soufflé layers, mix butter and flour together in saucepan. Add milk and cook until thickened. Beat in sugar and egg yolks with whisk. Beat egg whites until stiff. Fold into milk mixture. Generously butter 2 9-inch layer pans, lined with wax paper. Pour in batter. Bake 350 degrees for 35 minutes. Cool in pans.

For the filling, beat all ingredients together.

For the frosting, mix all ingredients together.

To assemble place one layer on platter. Spread with salmon mixture. Place second layer on top and spread with cream frosting. Sprinkle with parsley and decorate with lemon slices. The appetizer can be entirely prepared and decorated 1 day early and refrigerated. Cut in small wedges to serve. Serves: 12

Wolf Trap Pâté

1 cup butter
1 large onion, chopped
1 pound chicken livers
½ cup chicken broth
½ teaspoon paprika

½ teaspoon salt
⅛ teaspoon pepper
1 large clove garlic, crushed
2 tablespoons wine

In a skillet, heat butter and sauté onion. Add chicken livers and cook for 10 minutes. Add chicken broth, paprika, salt, pepper, garlic and wine. Cook 5 minutes. Pureé mixture in food processor. Chill thoroughly. Serve with crackers or French bread. Yield: 3 cups

Ranch House Pâté with Cognac

2 green onions, chopped
¼ cup butter
10 ounces chicken livers
1 teaspoon salt
1 teaspoon dry mustard
¼ teaspoon nutmeg

⅛ teaspoon ground cloves
4 ounces cream cheese
2 ounces cognac or brandy
Chopped fresh mushroom for garnish

Sauté green onions in 2 tablespoons butter. Add chicken livers and cook covered for 10 minutes. Puree liver mixture and remaining ingredients, except mushrooms, in food processor. Turn into clean bowl and chill at least 24 hours before serving as a spread for rye bread. Garnish with sliced or chopped mushrooms, if desired. Yield: 2 cups

Pâté Maison

1½ pounds chicken livers
2 tablespoons butter
½ cup onion, chopped
1 clove garlic, minced
1½ pounds ground fresh pork
2 tablespoons parsley, chopped

1 teaspoon salt
¼ teaspoon poultry seasoning
¼ teaspoon pepper
1 egg, slightly beaten
2 tablespoons brandy
2 bay leaves

Preheat oven to 400 degrees. Pat chicken livers dry with paper towels and cut each in half. Sauté the livers in butter 5 minutes. Remove from skillet with slotted spoon to a cutting board. Add onion and garlic to the fat left in the pan and cook, stirring constantly, 1 minute. Set aside. Chop the chicken livers finely. Mix all ingredients, except bay leaf, in a large bowl. Pack the mixture into a 1¼ quart terrine or a 9x5x3 inch loaf pan. Put bay leaves on top. Cover. Place terrine in a pan of hot water and bake 1 hour. Remove from oven and cool pate. Refrigerate 2 hours. Serves: 12

Bobolink

Beef Tartare

2½ pounds finely ground beef,
(sirloin or round steak)
½ tube anchovy paste
(1 tablespoon)
1 large onion, finely chopped
3 teaspoons Dijon mustard

2 teaspoons salt
Coarsely ground pepper, to
taste
3 tablespoons cognac
Dash Worcestershire
sauce
6 drops Tabasco sauce

Mix above ingredients well and mold into a round shape. Serve with party rye bread. Should be eaten immediately after preparing. Yield: 3 cups

Hawaiian Beef Sticks

2 inch piece of fresh
ginger, sliced
2 cloves garlic, mashed
2 small onions, chopped
1 cup soy sauce
4 tablespoons sugar
8 small, dried hot chili
peppers

2 tablespoons red wine
vinegar
4 teaspoons cornstarch
½ cup water
2 pounds beef sirloin

In a small pan, combine fresh ginger, garlic, onions, soy sauce, sugar, chili peppers, and vinegar. Cook over medium heat until slightly thick, about 20 minutes. Combine cornstarch with water. Gradually stir into sauce and cook stirring until clear and thickened. Pour mixture through wire strainer, pressing out all juices and discard the pulp. Cool. (Marinade may be made a day ahead.) Cut beef into bite-sized pieces; add to marinade and allow to stand, covered, for 2 hours. Thread 2 or 3 pieces of meat on a skewer; barbecue over hot coals or broil.

Sweet and Sour Meat Balls

1½ pounds ground beef
⅔ cups cracker crumbs, finely crushed
½ cup chopped onion
⅔ cups evaporated milk or half & half
1 teaspoon seasoned salt
⅓ cup flour

Mix together ground beef, cracker crumbs, onion, evaporated milk and seasoned salt. Shape into at least 30 balls. Roll in flour and brown in 3 tablespoons shortening. Drain excess oil.

Sweet-Sour Sauce:
1 can (13 ounce) pineapple chunks
2 tablespoons cornstarch
½ cup vinegar
½ cup brown sugar
2 tablespoons soy sauce
2 tablespoons lemon juice
1 cup green pepper, coarsely chopped
1 tablespoon pimento, chopped

Drain pineapple chunks; reserve pineapple. Measure syrup and add water to make 1 cup liquid. Blend together pineapple liquid and cornstarch until smooth. Stir in vinegar, brown sugar, soy sauce, and lemon juice. Cook until thickened and clear. Add pineapple, green pepper and pimento. Mix well, cover and simmer 15 minutes.

Pour over meat balls, simmer covered 15 minutes and serve. Yield: approximately 30 meatballs

Feta, Cream Cheese and Ham in Puff Pastry

1 tablespoon oil
2 scallions, chopped
1 cup ham, cubed
1 medium tomato, peeled and chopped
¼ teaspoon Italian herb seasoning
Dash of pepper
8 ounces cream cheese
2 ounces feta cheese
1 egg, beaten
1 box puff pastry dough (frozen)

Sauté scallions and ham in the oil for about 2-3 minutes. Add tomato, Italian herb seasoning and pepper. Cook uncovered on medium heat for about 5 minutes. Remove from heat and cool.

Beat the cream cheese, feta cheese and egg until creamy. Season with pepper.

Thaw pastry dough; roll it out on floured surface to measure 12" x 11". Spread cheese mixture evenly on pastry. Place ham mixture evenly on top of cheese. Roll the pastry, jelly roll fashion. Crimp edges to seal. Brush pastry with beaten egg. Poke holes in top to let steam escape. Bake on ungreased baking sheet in 375 degree oven for 30-35 minutes. Serves: 4 as a first course or luncheon dish; 8 as an appetizer.

Bourbon Hot Dogs

½ cup brown sugar
¾ cup bourbon
1 tablespoon onion, grated
½ cup ketchup

1 cup barbecue sauce
2 pounds miniature smokie hot dogs

Combine all ingredients, except the hot dogs, in large sauce pan. Add the hot dogs and simmer in sauce for 1 hour or more. Serve hot in chafing dish with toothpicks on the side for easy handling. Serves: 10-20 people

Hot Ryes

1 cup Swiss cheese, finely grated
¼ cup bacon, cooked and crumbled
1 can (4½ ounces) ripe olives, chopped

¼ cup green onions, minced
1 teaspoon Worcestershire sauce
¼ cup mayonnaise
Party rye bread

Combine all ingredients, except bread. Spread on party rye or pumpernickel. Bake at 375 degrees for 10 to 15 minutes or until browned. These may be frozen after baking and reheated. Yield: 36

Cheese Wafers

1 pound sharp Cheddar cheese, grated
1 stick, less 1 tablespoon butter
1 cup flour

½ teaspoon salt
½ teaspoon red pepper
1 cup chopped pecans (optional)

Knead cheese with butter, flour, salt and pepper. Add pecans. Shape into roll; refrigerate overnight. Slice thin; place on cookie sheet. Bake at 325 degrees to 350 degrees for about 10 minutes or until golden and crisp.

Gougere

½ cup hot water
¼ cup butter
⅛ teaspoon salt
⅛ teaspoon sugar
½ cup flour

¾ teaspoon dry mustard
Dash cayenne pepper
2 eggs
½ cup (2 ounces) shredded Swiss cheese

In small saucepan, combine water, butter, salt and sugar. Heat until butter melts and mixture boils. Vigorously mix in flour, dry mustard and cayenne all at once. Stir over medium heat until mixture leaves side of pan. Remove from heat. Beat in eggs, one at a time, until blended. Stir in cheese. Drop from teaspoon onto greased baking sheet forming 30 small puffs.

Bake in 450 degree oven for 8 minutes; then bake at 375 degrees for 12 minutes until puffed and golden. Turn off oven. Let puffs remain in oven for 3 minutes.

Serve hot or at room temperature.

Note: May be split and filled with a variety of savory fillings just before serving.

Flatbread

1 cup butter
¾ cup sugar
3 cups buttermilk
1½ teaspoons soda
1 cup oatmeal
3 cups graham flour

2 teaspoons baking powder
1 cup all bran cereal
1 teaspoon salt
Add white flour to form a firm dough for rolling

Cream butter and sugar. Add buttermilk, in which soda has been dissolved. Stir in oatmeal, graham flour, baking powder, all bran, salt and white flour.

Preheat oven to 350 degrees. Form walnut-size balls of dough; roll on a pastry board, as with pie crust, into large, round, thin sheets. The thinner the better. Preheat cookie sheet. Place the rolled-out flat bread on a cookie sheet and bake for 3-4 minutes.

A thin, crisp stack of these sheets placed on a large tray will keep 3-4 weeks. Yield: 60 pieces

Note: The recipe requires a lot of rolling but is well worth the effort. Use as you would crackers. The flavor is exceptional.

Cheese Walnuts

Sweet butter
Roquefort cheese

Walnut halves

Mash equal amounts of butter and cheese together. Spread a small amount of mixture between 2 walnut halves. Chill before serving.

30

SOUPS

Chilled Broccoli Bisque

2 (10 ounce) packages frozen
   broccoli
2 (10 ounce) cans chicken broth
2 tablespoons butter
1 medium onion, quartered
1 teaspoon salt

1-2 teaspoons curry
   Dash black pepper
2 tablespoons lime juice
¼ cup sour cream
   Lime slices
   Chives, chopped

Place broccoli in pan with broth, butter, onion, salt, curry and pepper. Bring to boil, reduce heat, cover and simmer 10 minutes.

Purée half of mixture in blender. Repeat with remaining half. Stir in lime juice, cover and refrigerate 4 hours or more.

Garnish with lime slices, sour cream and chives. Serves: 6

Cold Cream of Spinach Soup

½ cup onions, sliced
2 tablespoons butter
1 (10 ounce) package frozen
   spinach
5 cups chicken stock
⅓ cup raw white rice

1/16 teaspoon nutmeg
   Salt and pepper, to taste
1 cup light cream
2 egg yolks
1 tablespoon lemon juice
½-¾ cup sour cream

Sauté onions slowly in butter until golden. Thaw the spinach, drain and squeeze dry. Stir spinach into onions. Cover and cook over low heat for 5 minutes. Stir to prevent scorching.

Add chicken stock, rice, nutmeg, salt and pepper to taste. Simmer covered for 20 minutes or until rice is tender. Purée in blender in small batches. Bring again to simmer and thin the soup with more stock, if necessary. Remove from heat. Whisk in a mixture of egg yolks and cream. Adjust seasonings. Add lemon juice to taste. Refrigerate.

Serve each cup with a dollop of sour cream.

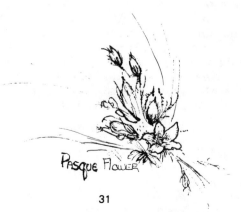

PASQUE FLOWER

Gazpacho

1 cup fresh tomatoes, peeled and chopped
½ cup cucumber, chopped
½ cup green pepper, chopped
½ cup celery, finely chopped
¼ cup onion, finely chopped
2 tablespoons parsley, chopped
1 tablespoon chives, chopped
1 clove garlic, minced
2-3 tablespoons vinegar
2 tablespoons oil
½ teaspoon Worcestershire sauce
½ teaspoon salt
Pepper to taste
2 cups tomato juice

Mix all ingredients in a large bowl. Cover and chill at least 4 hours or overnight. Serve with garlic croutons. Serves: 6

Consommé Madrilène

4 cups well seasoned chicken stock
3 ripe tomatoes, quartered and seeded
4 tablespoons sherry
Salt and pepper

Put tomatoes in large pot. Add 2 tablespoons sherry and stock. Cover and simmer 10 to 15 minutes. Remove from heat. Let stand 10 to 20 minutes. Taste and season. Strain through several layers of cheese cloth. Reheat but do not boil. Add remaining sherry and serve.

Almond Soup with Sherry and Vinegar

4 tablespoons butter
1 large carrot peeled and chopped
1-2 cups of chopped onion
2 stalks celery, chopped
4 cups chicken broth
1 teaspoon thyme
1 bay leaf
6 sprigs parsley
¼ cup white wine vinegar
2 tablespoons sherry
¼ pound coarsely chopped whole almonds (about a cup)
¼-½ cup heavy cream

Melt the butter in a soup pan and add the carrot, celery, onion. Cook covered stirring occasionally over low heat for 25 minutes, or until vegetables are lightly colored. Add the chicken broth, herbs, vinegar, and sherry and almonds. Bring to a boil, reduce heat and simmer 45 minutes to 1 hour or until almonds are soft and tender. Pour soup through a strainer, reserving liquid, and transfer solids to food processor. Add 1 cup of reserved liquid and process until smooth. Return soup to pan, add reserved liquid and thin soup to taste with heavy cream. Reheat gently to steaming and serve immediately. Serves: 4-6

Note: This can be made early in the day with the cream added at the last minute.

Greek Lemon Soup

2 quarts chicken stock
1 carrot, peeled
1 whole onion
1 stalk celery
4-5 peppercorns

¾ teaspoon salt
2 chicken bouillon cubes
½ cup rice (optional)
3 egg yolks
  Juice of 1 lemon, strained

Bring chicken stock to a boil. Add carrot, onion, celery, peppercorns, salt and bouillon cubes. Gently boil for 1 hour. Remove vegetables. Skim off fat. Add rice; boil 15-20 minutes, uncovered.

Beat egg yolks. Stir in the lemon juice. Add about 2 cups of the hot broth; blend well. Carefully stir this mixture into remaining broth. Cook over low to medium heat, stirring constantly, until hot. Do not boil as soup will curdle. Do not cover. Serve immediately.

Little Dumpling Soup

¼ cup water
2 tablespoons butter or margarine
½ cup less 1 tablespoon of flour
A pinch of salt

1 large egg
4-5 cups of good chicken or beef
  broth, simmering
1 tablespoon parsley, chopped

In a small saucepan, bring water, butter and salt to a boil. When the butter is completely melted, remove pan from heat and add the flour all at once. Mix rapidly with a spoon. Place the mixture on low heat and let it dry out a little. Transfer it to a small mixing bowl and beat in the egg until it is incorporated and the batter looks smooth. Drop the batter by small teaspoonsfull into the simmering broth. Partially cover the pot and let it simmer for 12-15 minutes. Garnish with chopped parsley. Serves 4 to 6.

French Onion Soup

4-5 cups thinly sliced onions
½ cup butter
2 cloves garlic, minced
1 tablespoon flour
6 cups beef stock
1 cup white wine
¼ cup cognac
4 cups Gruyere and/or Parmesan cheese, grated
8 slices crusty French bread
Salt and freshly ground pepper, to taste

Lightly brown sliced onions in butter. Add the garlic and sprinkle flour over this mixture. Gradually add stock, stirring constantly, until soup begins to boil. Lower the heat and simmer for 1 hour. Add wine, cognac, salt and pepper to taste. Simmer gently.

Sprinkle bread slices with half grated cheese and bake until cheese is melted in a 325 degree oven.

When soup is ready to serve, ladle into ovenproof bowls. Add bread slice, cheese side down. Sprinkle additional cheese over bread and soup. Bake at 450 degrees until cheese bubbles. Serves: 8

Wild Rice Soup

½ cup wild rice
10 cups chicken stock or chicken broth
¼ cup butter or margarine
1 medium onion, finely chopped
8 ounces mushrooms, sliced
½ cup celery, thinly sliced
½ cup flour
1 teaspoon salt
½ teaspoon curry powder
½ teaspoon dry mustard
½ teaspoon chervil
¼ teaspoon white pepper
2 cups half and half cream
⅔ cups sherry
Parsley

Soak raw wild rice, preferably overnight, rinsing a few times. Pour off water and cook in 4 cups chicken stock or broth for 30 to 45 minutes, or until absorbed and fluffy.

In large 4 or 5 quart pan, melt butter over medium heat; sauté onion until golden. Add mushrooms and celery and cook 2 to 3 minutes. Stir in flour. Slowly add 6 cups broth, stirring constantly until slightly thickened. Add rice, salt, curry, mustard, chervil, and pepper until thoroughly blended. Reduce heat to low, slowly stirring in half and half cream and sherry. Simmer until ready to serve.

Garnish with parsley. Makes 3 quarts.

Scottish Oyster Stew

Broth:
- 3 quarts whole milk
- 1 pint half and half
- 1 medium onion chopped, large pieces
- 3 stalks celery with tops on
- 2 teaspoons parsley
- ¼ teaspoon nutmeg
- 1 bay leaf
- 1 quart oysters

Roux:
- ½ cup butter
- ½ cup flour
- ½ teaspoon cayenne pepper
- Salt to taste

Drain the oysters and reserve the liquor. Combine all the broth ingredients and oyster liquor in a large soup pot. Simmer 20 minutes, then strain. Add oysters and simmer 15 minutes more. In a sauce pan melt the butter, stir in the flour and cook 3 minutes. Slowly add 2 cups of the broth and cook until thick and smooth. Stir the thickened roux into the pot. Add cayenne pepper and salt to taste. Serves: 15

Tortilla Soup

- 2 quarts chicken stock
- 1½ pounds chicken wings
- 10 corn tortillas
- 2 tomatoes
- 1 (3 ounce) can green chilies
- 1 can salsa verde sauce
- 8 ounces Monterey Jack cheese, grated
- Chopped parsley

Gently simmer the chicken wings in the chicken stock until tender. Remove bones and skin and return meat to broth. Cut tortillas into ½ inch strips and fry in hot fat until crisp, golden but not browned. Peel and dice tomatoes. Remove seeds from chilies and cut into thin strips. Add tomatoes, chilies and salsa verda sauce to soup. Heat thoroughly. Fill individual soup bowls, top with tortilla strips, and pass the cheese and parsley. Yield: 2 quarts

...MALLARD.....

Knepfla Soup (Germans from Russia)

5 raw potatoes, diced
1 medium onion, finely
  chopped
1 stalk celery, finely chopped
1 gallon water
2 tablespoons chicken base
2 cups flour
2 teaspoons baking powder

1 teaspoon salt
2 eggs
½ cup water
1 (10½ ounce) can cream of
  chicken soup
1 cup cream
3 tablespoons butter

In large soup pot combine potatoes, onion, celery, water and chicken base. Cook until potatoes are soft.

Knepfla dough: Combine flour, baking powder, salt, eggs with ½ cup water. Roll dough into log shapes approximately ½ inch in diameter and cut ½ inch pieces of the log into hot soup mixture. Add cream of chicken soup, cream and butter. Simmer. Soup is finished when the knepflas are soft. (12-15 minutes). Yield: 1 gallon

Green Borscht

This is a popular soup among Germans from Russia, not nearly as well known as red borscht, and completely different in taste and appearance. Green borscht utilizes various greens from the spring or summer garden.

2-3 quarts ham or chicken stock
1 potato, diced
1 carrot, diced
1 rib of celery, diced
3 green onions and tops,
  minced
¼ cup rice, uncooked
1 bay leaf
10 peppercorns
10 ounce package frozen
  chopped spinach or fresh
  spinach

2 cups red beet leaves,
  chopped
½ cup fresh dill, minced, or 2
  tablespoons dry dill weed
¼ cup parsley, minced
Juice from 1 or 2 lemons
Salt to taste
Sour cream, 1 tablespoon
per serving

In large soup pot bring the stock to a boil and add potato, carrot, celery, green onion, rice, peppercorns and bay leaf. Reduce heat, cover pot and simmer 20 minutes. Add spinach, beet leaves, dill and parsley and simmer 5-10 minutes. Remove from heat. Add lemon juice and salt to taste. (Borscht is best made 1-2 days in advance.) Serve hot with sour cream. Yield: 8-10 servings

Variations: Cooked, cubed ham may be added. If beet leaves are not available, double the amount of spinach.

Red Borscht

2 quarts beef stock
1 potato, cubed
1 carrot, diced
1 parsnip, diced
1 rib celery, sliced
1 onion, chopped
3-4 red beets, diced or 2 (16 ounce) cans diced or match-stick beets and juice
1 bay leaf
10 black peppercorns
6 cups shredded cabbage
1 (6 ounce) can tomato paste
1 (8 ounce) can tomato sauce
2 cups stewed canned tomatoes or 2 cups sliced fresh tomatoes
½ cup fresh dill, minced or 2 tablespoons dried dill weed
¼ cup fresh parsley, minced
Juice from 1 or 2 lemons or vinegar to taste
Salt to taste
Sour cream — 1 tablespoon per serving

In a large pot (6 quart) combine the first 9 ingredients and simmer, covered for 20 minutes. Add cabbage and simmer 10 minutes. Add the next 6 ingredients; bring to boil and simmer 5 minutes. Remove from heat. Add lemon juice and salt. (Borscht is best made 1-2 days in advance.) Serve with sour cream. Yield: 8-10 servings

Variations: Cooked, cubed beef may be added. The soup may be strained and the liquid served hot or cold with sour cream.

Cookbook Committee Pea Soup

2 pounds dried peas
10 cups water
6 (10¾ ounce) cans of chicken consommé, undiluted
2 (2-inch) squares salt pork, scalded, or ham bone
2 garlic cloves
1 teaspoon dried thyme
1 tablespoon chopped parsley
2 leeks, chopped
2 carrots, chopped
2 turnips, chopped
2 potatoes, chopped
¼ teaspoon cayenne pepper (optional)
10 whole peppercorns
1 teaspoon ground cumin
¼ teaspoon ground coriander
1 quart half and half

Wash peas and soak overnight in the water. In the morning add consommé, scalded salt pork, vegetables and seasonings. Bring to a boil and simmer for 2 hours. Remove salt pork and discard. Put soup through a food processor by batches. Return processed soup to pot and heat through. Stir in half and half and correct seasoning. Makes 24 one cup servings. Extra chicken consomme may be added to "stretch" the number of servings.

German Bean Soup

2 cups dried great northern beans (1 pound)	2-2½ teaspoons salt
¼ pound bacon, diced	½ teaspoon pepper
2 medium onions, sliced	½ teaspoon dried thyme
2 medium carrots, sliced	2 bay leaves
2 quarts water	1 large potato, peeled
1 cup celery, sliced	1 ham bone or shank
	2 tablespoons lemon juice

Evening before: Wash beans, cover with water and soak overnight.

Next morning: Sauté bacon. When golden add onions and carrots, cooking until onions are tender. Drain beans, add to bacon with 2 quarts water, celery, salt, pepper, thyme and bay leaves. Grate potato into pot. Add ham bone. Simmer 3-5 hours until beans are tender. Remove bay leaves and ham bone. Chop any meat on ham bone and return to soup. Before serving add lemon juice. Yield: 9½ cups soup

SALADS
AND
VEGETABLES

Cardinal Salad

1 (3 ounce) package lemon gelatin
1 cup hot water
¾ cup beet juice
3 tablespoons vinegar
½ teaspoon salt
2 teaspoons onion juice or grated onion
1 tablespoon prepared horseradish
1 cup cooked beets, diced
¾ cup celery, diced

Dissolve gelatin in hot water. Add beet juice, vinegar, salt, onion juice or grated onion and horseradish. Chill. When slightly thickened, fold in celery and beets. Turn into mold or 8 small molds. Chill until firm. Unmold on crisp lettuce. Garnish with mayonnaise. Serves: 8

Cranberry-Orange Salad

2 (3 ounce) packages raspberry gelatin
1 envelope unflavored gelatin
2 cups boiling water
½ cup cold water
1 (12 ounce) bag of fresh or frozen cranberries
2 medium oranges, unpeeled
1¾ cups sugar

Combine raspberry gelatin, unflavored gelatin and boiling water; stir and add cold water. Mix well. Set in refrigerator until slightly thickened.

In a food processor or blender, grind cranberries and cut-up oranges. Stir in sugar. Add to gelatin mixture. Mix well. Pour into favorite mold or a 13x9-inch baking dish. Chill. Serves: 10-12

Note: ½ cup chopped celery and ½ cup chopped walnuts may be added, if desired. To add tartness, substitute 1 (3 ounce) box of lemon gelatin for raspberry gelatin.

Tomato-Horseradish Ring

2 envelopes gelatin
½ cup cold water
½ cup milk
2 (10¾-ounce) cans tomato
   soup
½ cup horseradish
3 tablespoons vinegar
1 can black olives, chopped
1 (8 ounce) can pineapple
   tidbits, drained

Soften gelatin in cold water. In a saucepan mix milk, tomato soup, horseradish and vinegar and bring to a boil. Add gelatin. Stir well. Add olives and pineapple. Place in lightly greased mold. Chill in refrigerator until set. Serve with mayonnaise.

Tomato Aspic

2 envelopes unflavored
   gelatin
½ cup cold water
2½ cups tomato juice
1 teaspoon onion salt
1 teaspoon celery salt
⅛ teaspoon salt
Dash of pepper
½ bay leaf
2 tablespoons lemon juice

Soften gelatin in cold water. Cook tomato juice and seasonings 5-10 minutes. Remove bay leaf. Add gelatin and lemon juice. Pour into ring mold or individual molds. Chill. Serves: 6

Aspic Dressing:
1 (12 ounce) carton cottage
   cheese
1 tablespoon onion, chopped
1 tablespoon green pepper,
   chopped
1 tablespoon celery, chopped
1 cup green olives, chopped or
   sliced
1 tablespoon pimento,
   chopped
½ cup mayonnaise
⅛ teaspoon salt
Dash of pepper

Stir all ingredients together. Cover and marinate overnight. Serve with tomato aspic.

Prairie Ragwort

Vegetable Salad Vinaigrette

1 head cauliflower	8 ounces fresh mushrooms,
4 medium carrots, cut into	sliced
julienne strips (1½x4-inch)	2 medium tomatoes, cut into
2 (10 ounce) packages frozen	wedges
asparagus (or fresh)	1 (14 ounce) can artichoke
8 ounces fresh green beans	hearts, drained

Cook cauliflower until tender, yet crisp, about 6 minutes in salted boiling water. Cook carrots about 3 minutes. Cook asparagus and beans until tender, yet crisp. Drain and rinse vegetables in cold water to prevent overcooking.

Place cauliflower in center of large, round serving platter. Arrange other vegetables around cauliflower. Coat with vinaigrette dressing and cover with plastic wrap. Refrigerate at least 4 hours.

Vinaigrette Dressing:

1 cup oil	1 tablespoon Dijon mustard
½ cup white wine vinegar	1 tablespoon pimento,
1 tablespoon sugar	chopped
1 tablespoon horseradish	1 teaspoon celery salt
1 tablespoon onion, grated	½ teaspoon pepper

Combine all ingredients in a jar and shake well.

Broccoli Vinaigrette

2 pounds fresh broccoli,	½ cup dill pickle, finely
stems trimmed and peeled	chopped
2 cups bottled oil and	½ cup green pepper, minced
vinegar dressing with	¼ cup parsley, snipped
herbs and spices	¼ cup capers

Cook broccoli in about 1-inch salted water until barely tender. Drain.

In screw-top jar, combine the bottled salad dressing, pickle, green pepper, parsley and capers. Shake vigorously to blend. Pour dressing over broccoli. Chill several hours or overnight.

Serve on lettuce-lined platter. Garnish with pimento strips, if desired. Serves: 12

Mushroom Salad

2-3 green peppers, cored,
    seeded and thinly sliced
⅔ cup olive oil
⅓ cup red wine vinegar
1 teaspoon Dijon mustard
¼ teaspoon salt
¼ teaspoon pepper

1 small red onion, sliced
    thinly and in rings
½ can ripe olives, sliced
1 pound fresh mushrooms,
    sliced
1 (11 ounce) can mandarin
    oranges

In small covered jar blend olive oil, vinegar, mustard, salt and pepper. Shake well. In large mixing bowl combine pepper slices, red onion rings, olives and mushrooms. Pour the dressing over the mushroom-pepper mixture and allow to marinate about 4 hours in refrigerator. Serve on lettuce leaves. Sprinkle a few mandarin oranges on top of each serving.

Rickshaw Salad

	8 Servings	45 Servings
vermicelli	10-ounces	2 pounds
mayonnaise	¾ cup	1 quart
soy sauce	2 tablespoons	¾cup
Chinese oyster sauce (optional)	2 tablespoons	¾ cup
Chinese hot mustard	1 teaspoon	2 tablespoons
salt	1 teaspoon	1 tablespoons
garlic powder	¼ teaspoon	1 teaspoon
white pepper	dash	¼ to ½ teaspoon
bean sprouts, drained	1 (16 ounce) can	1 (No. 10) can
frozen peas, thawed	1 cup	2 pounds
celery, diced	½ cup	1½ quarts
green pepper, diced	⅓ cup	1 pint
onion, chopped	⅓ cup	1 pint
water chestnuts, drained and sliced	⅓ cup	12 ounces
canned mushrooms, drained	1 (2 ounce) can	12 ounces

Break vermicelli into 3-inch lengths. Cook in boiling, salted water (1 gallon water plus 2 tablespoons salt per pound) until tender, yet firm, about 6-7 minutes. Drain. Rinse with cold water to cool. Drain.

Combine mayonnaise, soy sauce, oyster sauce, mustard and seasonings.

Stir in all remaining ingredients, including vermicelli. Cover and chill thoroughly, at least several hours or overnight.

COW
PARSNIP

California Salad

1 (10 ounce) package frozen California blend vegetables
12 cherry tomatoes, halved
¼ cup lemon juice
¼ cup oil
¾ teaspoon garlic salt
½ teaspoon oregano leaves
⅛ teaspoon pepper

1½ cups (6 ounces dry) macaroni, cooked
2 cups Swiss cheese, slivered (½ pound)
¾ cup celery, chopped
¼ cup ripe olives, finely cut
½ cup mayonnaise
12 salad greens (lettuce leaves)

Cook California blend vegetables until tender-crisp. Drain and cool. Combine with tomatoes, lemon juice, oil, garlic salt, oregano and pepper. Marinate 1 hour, stirring occasionally.

Cook macaroni, as directed on the package, until tender yet firm. Drain, rinse with cold water and drain.

Add macaroni, cheese, celery and olives to vegetable mixture. Toss lightly. Chill. Stir in mayonnaise, just before serving. Serve on salad greens. Garnish, as desired. Serves: 6

Seafood Vinaigrette

2 cups boiled potatoes, diced
1-1½ cups peas, cooked
1 apple, diced
1 small dill pickle, diced
2-3 green onions, minced
2-3 cups cooked seafood (shrimp, crab, lobster, scallops)
Salt and pepper, to taste

3 tablespoons oil
2 tablespoons white wine vinegar
1-1¼ cups mayonnaise (homemade preferred)
1½ cups beets, cooked and diced
3 hard-boiled eggs, quartered

Place all vegetables, except beets, and seafood into a large bowl. Shake oil and wine vinegar together in a jar and pour over mixture. Gently mix. Fold in mayonnaise and adjust seasonings. Add beets last and gently mix again.

Chill in refrigerator 1-2 hours before serving. Serve with quartered hard-boiled eggs. Serves: 8

Variations: Diced cooked chicken, ham or beef may be used in place of seafood.

Blue Grotto Salad

½ cup olive oil
3 tablespoons red wine vinegar
1 teaspoon Dijon mustard
½ teaspoon salt
¼ teaspoon dry mustard
⅛ teaspoon fresh-ground pepper
1 garlic clove, crushed
4 large mushrooms, thinly sliced
1 small red onion, thinly sliced
4 ounces fresh spinach, stems removed

1 head romaine, torn into bite-size pieces
1 (6½ ounce) can albacore tuna, drained and flaked or 1 small tin flat anchovy fillets
2 whole pimentos, cut in ¼-inch slices
8 large pitted ripe olives, sliced
8 radishes, thinly sliced
1 (16 ounce) can artichoke hearts, quartered

Mix oil, vinegar, mustards, salt, pepper and garlic in a large salad bowl and whisk until smooth. Add remaining ingredients in the order listed. Do not toss. Refrigerate for 3-4 hours. Toss just before serving. Serves: 8

Curried Shrimp Salad

3 cups uncooked shell macaroni
2 (4½ ounce) cans tiny shrimp, rinsed and drained
2 green onions, finely chopped
½ green pepper, finely chopped

3 stalks celery, finely chopped
½ teaspoon seasoned salt
½ teaspoon celery salt
1 teaspoon curry powder
1½ cups mayonnaise

Prepare macaroni according to instructions on box. Set aside. Mix shrimp, onion, green pepper and celery and add to cooked macaroni. Combine spices with mayonnaise. Add to shrimp mixture and refrigerate overnight, allowing flavors to blend. Serves: 8

ARNICA

Hot Shrimp and Crab Salad

1 (6 ounce) can crab
1 (4½ ounce) can shrimp
1 small onion, minced
1 cup celery, diced
4 sprigs parsley, finely cut
Juice of ½ lemon
½ teaspoon salt
Dash of cayenne
2 teaspoons Worcestershire sauce
1 cup mayonnaise
¾ cup soft bread crumbs
2 tablespoons oil

Drain crab meat and clean shrimp, rinse both and drain. Mix all ingredients lightly, except for crumbs and oil.

Pile mixture into 4 large custard cups or shells.

Mix crumbs and oil. Sprinkle on top of the 4 cups or shells. Bake at 350 degrees for about 25 minutes. Serve while hot. Serves: 4

Exotic Chicken Almond Salad

4½ to 5 pounds chicken breasts
½ cup butter, melted
½ teaspoon salt
⅛ teaspoon pepper
3 (3½ ounce) packages slivered almonds
2 cups mayonnaise
½ teaspoon curry
2 teaspoons soy sauce
2 cups celery, sliced
3 (6 ounce) cans sliced water chestnuts, drained
2 pounds green seedless grapes
2 heads Boston or bibb lettuce, washed and dried, refrigerated
1 small can litchi nuts or pineapple tidbits

Brush chicken breasts with melted butter, salt and pepper to taste. Wrap in heavy foil and seal edges tightly. Bake at 350 degrees for 1 hour. Strip chicken from bone when cooled and cut in bite-size pieces.

Coat almonds with melted butter and spread on cooky sheet. Roast at 350 degrees for about 15 minutes until a soft golden color. Watch carefully. Spread on paper towels and sprinkle with salt. Set aside until just before serving.

Both the chicken and almonds may be done the day before and refrigerated.

A few hours before serving, mix mayonnaise with curry powder and soy sauce. If the mayonnaise is not homemade, add 2 tablespoons of lemon juice. Combine with chicken, celery, water chestnuts and grapes. Chill.

Arrange lettuce leaves around edge of large platter. Either mound chicken salad in center and sprinkle almonds over top, or spoon chicken salad into nests of lettuce or pineapple boats. Garnish with litchi nuts or pineapple tidbits. Serves: 12 for a luncheon.

Note: Mandarin oranges may be substituted for grapes, turkey for chicken.

Celestial Chicken Salad

2 chicken breasts, cooked, skinned, deboned and diced
1 head lettuce, sliced thinly
4-5 green onions, thinly sliced, tops included
2 tablespoons almonds, slivered and toasted
2 tablespoons sesame seeds, toasted
4 ounces Chinese rice stick noodles deep fried and drained

Mix chicken, lettuce and onions. Toss to mix. Just before serving, add almonds, sesame seeds and rice sticks.

Pour dressing over all and toss.

Dressing:
1 tablespoon sesame oil
2 tablespoons sugar
1 teaspoon salt
1 teaspoon monosodium glutamate (optional)
½ teaspoon freshly ground pepper
¼ cup oil
3 tablespoons rice wine vinegar

Combine all ingredients and mix well. Serves: 12

Variation: Use romaine lettuce, add ½ cup chopped celery and ¼ pound fresh mushrooms.

Note: Rice sticks are found in the speciality food sections of most supermarkets, labeled as "Dynasty" brand Maifun Rice Sticks.

Pear Duckling Salad

1 (4 to 5 pound) domestic duckling, cooked, skinned and boned
½ teaspoon salt
3 fresh pears, peeled and sliced
1 tablespoon fresh lemon juice
1 cup mayonnaise
¼ cup sliced ripe pitted olives
¼ cup sliced green pimento olives
¼ cup slivered almonds
Watercress or parsley
Leaf lettuce

Sliver meat and sprinkle with salt. Add pears and other ingredients. Toss lightly. Serve on a bed of leaf lettuce. Garnish with watercress or parsley. Serves: 4

Variation: Dark meat of turkey or chicken may be substituted for duck.

Spinach Salad

Dressing:
½ cup sugar
1 cup oil
⅓ cup ketchup
¼ cup wine vinegar
1 small onion, grated
2 tablespoons
  Worcestershire sauce
¼ teaspoon salt
  Seasoned pepper, to taste

1 pound fresh spinach,
  washed, drained and torn
  into pieces, stems removed
1 (8 ounce) can water
  chestnuts, drained and
  sliced
1 (16 ounce) can bean sprouts,
  drained (or 8-ounces fresh)
2 hard boiled eggs, chopped
5 slices bacon, cooked and
  crumbled

Mix dressing in blender and chill. Toss the 5 salad ingredients with dressing to taste.

Greek Salad

Herb Dressing:
½ cup olive oil
½ cup lemon juice
1 teaspoon salt
¼ teaspoon seasoned pepper
¼ teaspoon oregano
½ teaspoon marjoram

2 cups cooked shrimp
2 tablespoons parsley
2 tablespoons chives or
  green onions, sliced

Mix ingredients for herb dressing. Marinate shrimp with parsley and chives or green onions in herb dressing. Set aside.

1 cup walnuts or pecans
2 tablespoons butter

½ teaspoon rosemary

Lightly toast walnuts or pecans in a small frying pan with butter and rosemary, stirring constantly. Cool and set aside.

6-8 cups lettuce or greens of
  choice
6 radishes, sliced
½ cup stuffed green olives,
  sliced

½ cup small, pickled onions
3 tomatoes, chopped
¾ cup feta cheese

Toss greens, radishes, olives, onions, tomatoes and feta cheese with shrimp and herb dressing. Add nuts just before serving.

Pea-Nut Salad

1 (10 ounce) package frozen
  peas
1 cup cashews, chopped
6 slices bacon, cooked and
  crumbled

¼ cup onions, chopped
½ cup celery, chopped
½ cup sour cream
½ teaspoon salt
½ teaspoon dill weed

Combine all ingredients. Chill.

Variation: Add ½ cup mayonnaise and 6 ounces small cooked shrimp. Omit bacon and sour cream.

Broccoli-Cauliflower Salad

1 bunch of broccoli
1 head of cauliflower
½ cup onions, chopped
⅓ cup green pepper, chopped
1 cup mayonnaise
1 cup sour cream
¼ cup sugar
1½ cups Cheddar cheese,
  grated

½ to 1 pound bacon, fried or
  broiled and crumbled
½ cup water chestnuts, sliced
  (optional)
1 cup fresh mushrooms,
  sliced (optional)

Separate broccoli and cauliflower into small pieces. Add onion and green pepper. Mix mayonnaise, sour cream and sugar. Add to the vegetables. Fold in the grated cheese. Crisp-fry or broil bacon. Crumble into small pieces and fold in, saving a few to sprinkle over the top. Chill well. Serves: 10-12

Beef Spinach Salad

3 cups cooked roast beef,
  thinly sliced
3 cups cooked, long grain
  white and wild rice mixture
1 cup Italian dressing
1 tablespoon soy sauce
½ teaspoon sugar

2 cups raw spinach, torn in
  bite-size pieces, stems
  removed
1 medium zucchini, sliced
¾ cup celery, thinly sliced
½ cup dry-roasted sunflower
  seeds

Combine ½ cup dressing, soy sauce and sugar with cooled rice, blending well. Add roast beef and remaining dressing. Refrigerate for 1-2 hours.

Add spinach, zucchini, celery and seeds just before serving. Toss gently. Serves: 6-8

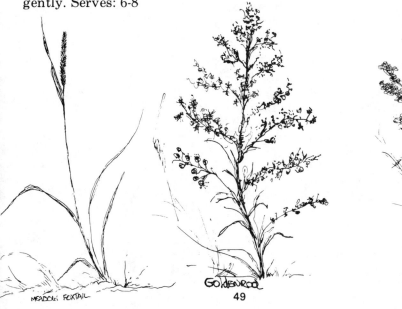

MEADOW FOXTAIL

GOLDENROD

YARROW

Vegetable Lasagna

Bake this lasagna the day before you serve it. It will be even better.

¼ cup olive oil
4 garlic cloves, minced
4 shallots, minced
1 large onion, chopped
½ cup parsley, chopped
1 teaspoon dried basil or
 ¼ cup fresh leaves, chopped
1 teaspoon dried thyme or 1 fresh
 sprig
2 (35 ounce) cans Italian plum
 tomatoes, very well drained
1 tablespoon tomato paste

2 cups chicken broth
12 tablespoons butter
1 pound fresh mushrooms,
 sliced
⅓ cup flour
3 cups whole milk
salt and pepper to taste
1 parsley sprig
1 bay leaf
½ teaspoon dried thyme
8 ounces dry lasagna noodles
1 cup grated Parmesan cheese

Heat oil in a large saucepan. Cook garlic, shallots and onions over medium heat until the onion is soft but not browned. Add parsley, basil, thyme, tomatoes, tomato paste and broth. Partially cover and simmer until sauce thickens, about 30 minutes.

In a large skillet, melt 2 tablespoons butter over high heat. Saute mushrooms until they are nicely browned. Add the mushrooms to the tomato sauce and cook for 10 minutes. Taste and correct the seasoning.

Make a bechamel sauce by melting 6 tablespoons of butter in a 2-quart saucepan over medium heat. Whisk in the flour and cook for 1 minute, whisking constantly. Do not brown the mixture. Add the milk all at once, and whisk until the mixture bubbles and is quite thick. Season with salt and pepper. Add parsley, thyme and bay leaf, cover, and simmer 20 minutes, stirring often. Discard parsley and bay leaf and reserve sauce.

Cook the lasagna noodles, drain and rinse. Butter a 9x13 baking pan. Line the bottom with a single layer of lasagna noodles. Trim the noodles to fit evenly. Spread about 2 cups of the tomato sauce over the noodle layer. Top with about ½ cup of the bechamel sauce. Sprinkle with ½ cup Parmesan cheese and a large grinding of pepper. Repeat the layering procedure once more. Dot the final layer of Parmesan cheese with the remaining butter. Place the baking pan on a cookie sheet and bake at 350 degrees in the center of the oven until nicely browned, about 45 minutes. Remove from oven and cool about 20 minutes to settle the lasagna. Serve immediately, or refrigerate overnight and reheat, covered, for 35 minutes at 350 degrees.

Artichokes Florentine

6-8 cooked artichoke bottoms, use two cans, drained or frozen (thawed)

2-3 (10 ounce) packages frozen, chopped spinach thawed and drained

½ cup Swiss or Parmesan cheese, grated

Arrange artichoke bottoms side by side in a shallow 1½ quart casserole. Mix 1 cup Mornay sauce with spinach. Cover artichokes with spinach mixture. Spoon remaining Mornay sauce over top. Sprinkle with grated cheese. Bake uncovered in a 375 degree oven for 30 minutes or until bubbly.

Mornay Sauce:

4 tablespoons butter
4 tablespoons flour
1 cup chicken stock
1 cup light cream
4 tablespoons Swiss cheese, shredded

4 tablespoons Parmesan cheese, grated
Salt and cayenne pepper to taste
⅛ teaspoon nutmeg (optional)

Melt butter in pan. Mix in flour and cook, stirring until flour is light golden. Remove from heat and blend in broth and cream. Return to heat and bring to full rolling boil. Add cheese and seasonings. Stir until blended. Makes 2 cups.

Green Beans Almondine

¼ cup slivered blanched almonds
¼ cup butter
¼ teaspoon salt

1-2 teaspoons lemon juice
2 cups hot, cooked, drained julienne style green beans

Cook almonds in butter over low heat until golden, stirring occasionally. Remove from heat. Add the salt and lemon juice. Pour over the cooked beans. Serves: 4

Green Bean Casserole

1 (10 ounce) package frozen French-cut green beans
1 (10¾ ounce) can cream of mushroom soup
1 (8½ ounce) can water chestnuts, drained
1 (14 ounce) can French fried onion rings

Cook beans until just tender. Drain and mix with soup and thinly sliced water chestnuts.

Place in a shallow casserole. Top with onion rings.

Bake at 350 degrees for 30 minutes or until casserole bubbles.

Refried Beans

1 pound dried pinto beans
5 cups water (or more if needed)
4 tablespoons of cooking fat, bacon grease or oil (more if needed)
Salt and pepper, to taste

Pick over beans and discard any foreign material or bad beans. Wash thoroughly and drain beans. Soak beans, in water to cover, overnight in a 5-quart pan. Drain, fill pan with fresh water and bring to a boil. Reduce heat and simmer, covered, until beans are done, approximately 3 hours. (Add more water during the cooking process, if needed; beans should be covered with water. If beans were not previously soaked, the cooking time will be 5-6 hours.)

In a heavy skillet heat the fat (save fat from frying chicken, pork chops, roasts or bacon). Add beans and about 1 cup liquid from cooking pot. Mash the beans with a potato masher to a consistency of limp mashed potatoes. Over medium heat, cook and stir the mixture until some of the liquid has been absorbed (it is possible more liquid may be needed). Season with salt and pepper to taste.

Serve hot with any meat or poultry dishes. Serves: 8-10

Bourbon Baked Beans

2 (28 ounce) cans baked beans
½ cup strong black coffee
½ cup bourbon
⅓ cup chili sauce
1 tablespoon dry mustard
1 onion (chopped)

Mix well and place in bean pot. Bake uncovered 1 hour at 300 degrees. Stir occasionally.

Blazing Beets

¾ cup water
¾ cup orange juice
2 teaspoons orange rind, grated
¼ teaspoon salt
⅛ teaspoon pepper
2 teaspoons brown sugar
1½ tablespoons cornstarch
2 tablespoons butter
3 cups cooked beets, sliced
¼ cup brandy

Mix water, orange juice, orange rind, salt and pepper, sugar and cornstarch in a small bowl. Set aside.

Melt butter in a large skillet and gradually add juice mixture, stirring constantly until sauce is clear and smooth.

Add beets, lifting to coat with sauce. Simmer for about 10 minutes to heat through.

Add brandy, ignite. Have a cover handy to partially cover if flame leaps too high. Serve from a warmed bowl as soon as flame is out. Serves: 6

Note: Carrots may be substituted for beets.

Jade-Green Broccoli

1 bunch (2 pounds) broccoli
1 teaspoon sugar
1 teaspoon monosodium glutamate
1 tablespoon cornstarch
2 tablespoons soy sauce
½ cup water or chicken stock
⅛ teaspoon salt, or to taste
¼ cup vegetable oil
1 garlic clove, minced
2 tablespoons sherry

Separate broccoli into florets; peel stems and cut into ⅛ inch slices. Mix sugar, monosodium glutamate, cornstarch, soy sauce, chicken stock and salt in pitcher and set aside. Heat the oil in frying pan or wok over medium heat. Add broccoli and garlic and stir fry 2 minutes. Add sherry. Cover pan and cook 2 minutes more. Remove cover and add ingredients from pitcher. Stir and cook until done. Remove from pan and serve immediately.

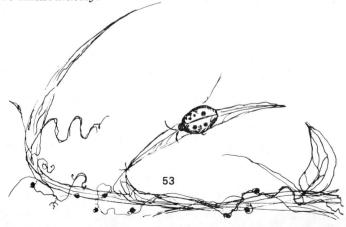

53

Swiss Broccoli

1 pound frozen or
  fresh broccoli, cooked and
  drained
1 teaspoon onion, minced
1 tablespoon butter
1 tablespoon flour

½ teaspoon sugar
½ teaspoon salt
  Freshly ground pepper
1 cup sour cream
  Slices of Swiss cheese
  Paprika

Place cooked and drained broccoli in shallow, greased baking dish. In separate pan sauté the onion in butter until golden. Stir in flour, sugar, salt and pepper. Remove from heat and blend in sour cream. Pour over broccoli. Place slices of Swiss cheese over broccoli and sauce. Sprinkle with paprika. Bake in 350 degree oven for 15 to 20 minues.
Serves: 4

Braised Carrots with
Artichoke Hearts and Mushrooms

1½ pounds carrots
1½ cups water
1 tablespoon sugar
1½ tablespoons butter
¼ teaspoon salt
  Dash of pepper
½ pound fresh mushrooms,
  quartered
1 tablespoon oil
2 tablespoons butter

2 tablespoons green onions,
  sliced
1 (10 ounce) box frozen
  artichoke hearts, cooked
  and quartered
⅓ cup canned beef consommé,
  undiluted
2 tablespoons chives or
  parsley, chopped

Peel carrots and slice diagonally into ¼-inch ovals. Place in a 2-quart saucepan with water, sugar and butter. Cover and simmer slowly until carrots are crisp-tender. Drain. Salt and pepper. Set aside.

Sauté mushrooms with oil and butter in a hot skillet until lightly brown. Stir in green onions and artichoke hearts, toss for a minute. Combine mushroom and artichoke mixture with carrots. Pour in consommé, cover saucepan, simmer 4-5 minutes until liquid has almost completely evaporated. Adjust seasoning.

Place in warmed serving dish and garnish with chives or parsley.
Serves: 6

Sweet-Sour Carrots

2 pounds carrots, pared
1 medium onion, thinly sliced
1 green pepper, slivered
¾ cup vinegar
1 (10¾ ounce) can tomato soup
1 cup sugar
10 drops Tabasco sauce
½ cup oil
1 teaspoon Worcestershire sauce
1 teaspoon prepared mustard

Slice carrots, cook in small amount of salted water until tender-crisp and drain.

In a saucepan mix vinegar, tomato soup, sugar, Tabasco, oil, Worcestershire and mustard. Cook 15-20 minutes over medium heat, stirring until slightly thickened.

Mix hot carrots, green pepper and onions in a medium serving bowl. While sauce is warm, pour over mixture. Serve hot or cold. Serves: 12

Celery Far East

4 cups celery, cut up
1 (10½ ounce) can cream of chicken soup
1 (2 ounce) jar chopped pimento
1 (8 ounce) can sliced water chestnuts
½ cup slivered almonds
½ cup dry bread crumbs
2 tablespoons butter

Cook celery in boiling salted water for 5 minutes. Drain. Add cream of chicken soup, pimento and water chestnuts. Place in 2 quart casserole. Sauté almonds and bread crumbs in butter. Sprinkle over celery in casserole. Bake uncovered for 35 minutes at 350 degrees. Serves: 4-6

Eggplant Casserole (Ratatouille or Gevetsch)

1 large eggplant (1½ to 2 pounds)
2-3 small zucchini (2 pounds)
1 teaspoon salt (or more if needed)
½ cup oil (or more if needed)
2 large onions, chopped
3-4 green peppers, cut into strips
2-3 garlic cloves, minced
4-5 ripe tomatoes (or 2 to 2½ cups canned tomatoes)
1 bay leaf
½ cup fresh parsley, minced
Pepper to taste

Peel eggplant and cut into ¼ inch slices. Salt the slices lightly and place in a colander to drain for 30 to 45 minutes. Cut the zucchini into ¼ inch slices. Salt lightly and place in another colander to drain 30 to 45 minutes. Dry eggplant slices with paper towels. Sauté in a hot skillet with a little oil, one layer at a time on both sides, until slightly brown. Remove to a bowl. Dry and sauté zucchini using the same method. In the same skillet, sauté onions and green peppers for about 15 minutes, stirring frequently until tender, but not browned. Slice tomatoes and drain in a colander for 10 to 15 minutes to remove excess liquid and seeds. Add to skillet with onion and green pepper. Add garlic, increase heat and allow liquid to evaporate, stirring constantly.

Layer all the vegetables into a 2 quart casserole. Sprinkle with parsley; season with salt and pepper and bay leaf. Bake uncovered for about 30 minutes at 350 degrees. Stir vegetables several times during baking time to prevent the top layer from drying out and help the moisture to evaporate.

Alternate method: Cook vegetables on top of the stove in a large skillet, stirring frequently.

Serve either hot or cold. This dish is best when prepared one day ahead of serving time.

Rosehips

Eggplant Parmesan with Tomato Sauce

2 medium eggplants or 1 large eggplant
3 eggs, well beaten
1 cup bread crumbs
1 cup olive oil
1 heaping cup Parmesan cheese
½ pound mozzarella cheese, grated
½ teaspoon salt

Peel and slice eggplant. Salt and let drain on toweling for 15 minutes.

Dip in beaten eggs, then bread crumbs and fry in hot oil. Brown on both sides. When browning is completed, layer eggplant, sauce and cheese in a 3 quart casserole. Repeat layers.

Bake 30-45 minutes at 350 degrees.

Sauce:
3 onions, chopped
2-3 garlic cloves, pressed
¼ cup olive oil
2 teaspoons salt
1 tablespoon sugar
1 teaspoon oregano
1 teaspoon basil
½ teaspoon anise seed
8 large ripe tomatoes, peeled and chopped
¾ cup chicken stock
¼ cup white wine
2 tablespoons parsley, chopped

Sauté onion and garlic in oil. Add seasonings, liquid and tomatoes. Simmer 25-30 minutes. Add chopped parsley and simmer 5 more minutes.

Mushrooms au Gratin

1 pound fresh mushrooms
3 tablespoons butter
½ cup sour cream
Salt and pepper to taste
Juice of ½ lemon, or to taste
1 tablespoon flour
4 ounces grated Swiss cheese
¼ cup chopped parsley

Sauté mushrooms in butter. Cover pan about 2 minutes to bring out the juices. Blend sour cream, salt, pepper, lemon juice and flour until smooth. Stir in mushrooms and heat, stirring until blended and beginning to boil. Pour into casserole and sprinkle with cheese and parsley. May be prepared in advance and refrigerated at this point. Bake uncovered at 425 degrees for 10 to 15 minutes.

Onions Malheur

1 loaf day-old French bread, sliced and buttered
2 tablespoons butter
2 large, sweet Spanish onions, sliced and separated into rings (6 cups)

½ pound Cheddar cheese, grated
¼ teaspoon pepper
2 (10¾ ounce) cans cream of chicken soup
1½ soup cans milk

Place French bread in a 9x13 inch pan. Melt butter in large frying pan. Add onion rings, cover and cook slowly over low heat until golden. Spoon onions over French bread. Spread cheese over top and sprinkle with pepper. Heat soup and milk in same frying pan used for onions, stirring until smooth. Pour over onion-cheese layer, lifting bread slices to coat bottom of pan. Bake at 350 degrees until golden brown. Serve as a side dish with grilled or roasted meat.

Soubise

¼ cup long grain white rice
4 tablespoons butter or margarine
1 pound yellow onions, thinly sliced

½ pound fresh mushrooms, sliced
½ teaspoon salt

Cook rice in 2 quarts salted, boiling water for 5 minutes; drain. Melt butter in 1½ or 2 quart casserole. Add cooked rice and other ingredients; mix thoroughly. Bake, covered, in 325 degree oven for 45 minutes. A nice accompaniment for beef.

French Fried Onion Rings

Cut onions in ⅛-inch slices and separate into rings. Soak the rings in a bowl of milk; dredge with flour and spread out to dry.

Dip the rings in milk again; roll in pancake flour, bread crumbs or ground corn flakes. The rings should be powder dry. They now can be used immediately or kept in the refrigerator for 2-3 days.

When ready to serve, fry in deep fat until brown.

Petits Pois

3 (10 ounce) packages tiny
  frozen peas
1 (10 ounce) package small
  frozen onions
5 tablespoons butter
5 tablespoons boiling water

1 tablespoon sugar
¼ teaspoon salt
⅛ teaspoon pepper
10-12 green onions, cut in 2-inch
  pieces
2 cups lettuce, shredded

Thaw peas 1 hour before preparing recipe. Set aside.

Cook onions according to package directions. Set aside.

Melt butter in a large saucepan or skillet. Add boiling water, sugar, salt, pepper and onions. Stir in peas and blend with seasonings. Gently stir in lettuce. Cover pan and cook over medium heat until peas are tender, about 6 minutes. Serves: 10-12

Jansson's Frestelse
(Jansson's Temptation)

2 large onions, thinly sliced
5 medium potatoes, cut in ¼
  inch julienne strips
1 can (2 ounce) flat fillets of
  anchovies, drained

3 tablespoons butter
  Pepper, to taste
1-1½ cups light cream

Sauté the onions with 2 tablespoons butter until onion is soft. In a shallow, buttered baking dish (9 x 9 x 2 inches) arrange the potatoes, onions and anchovies in layers — starting and ending with potatoes. Pour cream over all and dot top with the remaining butter. Bake in 375 degree oven for 1¼ to 1½ hours or until potatoes are tender. Serves: 4

Oven Fried Potatoes

4 large potatoes (about 2
  pounds), scrubbed but not
  peeled
¼ cup oil
1 tablespoon Parmesan
  cheese, grated

½ teaspoon salt
¼ teaspoon garlic powder
¼ teaspoon paprika
¼ teaspoon pepper

Preheat oven to 375 degrees.

Cut each potato, lengthwise, into 6 wedges. Place in shallow pan, skin-side down.

Mix oil, cheese, salt, garlic powder, paprika and pepper. Brush 2 tablespoons on potatoes.

Bake 45 minutes, brushing with more oil mixture every 15 minutes. Turn potatoes over and bake 15 minutes more or until tender and brown. Serves: 4

Baked German Potato Salad

¾ cup bacon, diced	1½ teaspoon salt
1 cup celery, chopped	½ teaspoon pepper
1 cup onion, chopped	8 cups cooked, cubed potatoes
3 tablespoons flour	(about 9 medium)
1⅓ cups water	1 cup radishes, sliced
2⅔ cup cider vinegar	(optional)
⅔ cup white sugar (or less)	½ cup dill pickle, chopped

Cook bacon in large skillet. Remove and combine with potatoes. Drain off fat; return ¼ cup to skillet. Add celery and onion; cook 1 minute. Blend in flour. Stir in water and vinegar, cooking until mixture is thick and bubbly. Stir in sugar, salt and pepper. Mix well.

Pour mixture over potatoes and bacon in a greased 3-quart casserole or Dutch oven. Mix lightly.

Cover and bake in a 350 degree oven for 30 minutes. Remove from oven and stir in radishes and dill pickle. Serve hot. Can be re-heated successfully. Serves: 10-12

Potato Casserole

½ pound cottage cheese	¼ teaspoon salt
2 cups potatoes, mashed	¼ teaspoon cayenne pepper
½ cup sour cream	3 tablespoons Parmesan
2 eggs, beaten	cheese
¼ cup parsley, chopped	
½ cup green onions, thinly sliced	

Put cottage cheese through sieve or food mill. Stir in potatoes, sour cream, eggs, parsley, onion, salt and pepper. Beat well.

Place in baking dish, 1½-quart casserole, lightly greased. Cover with Parmesan cheese.

Bake at 350 degrees for 30 minutes.

Note: May be prepared up to baking point and stored in refrigerator overnight or until needed.

Ruffed Grouse

60

Potato Casserole

1 (32 ounce) package frozen
   hash browns
1 (10¾ ounce) can potato soup
1 (10¾) can celery soup
8 ounces sour cream
¼ cup chopped onion

¼ cup chopped green pepper
1 (2 ounce) jar chopped pimento,
   drained
Salt and pepper
Parsley, chopped
Paprika, to taste

Mix and place all ingredients into an oven-proof greased casserole. Sprinkle top with chopped parsley and paprika and bake for 1 hour at 350 degrees. Serves: 8

Sweet Potato Casserole

1 (1 pound) can sweet potatoes
2 oranges, unpeeled
½ cup butter
   Salt and pepper, to taste

2 tablespoons brown sugar
½ cup honey

Cut potatoes into ¾-inch slices. Cut unpeeled oranges into very thin slices.

Lightly oil a 2-quart Pyrex casserole. Layer potatoes and orange slices, ending with oranges on top. Dot with butter. Add salt and pepper, to taste. Sprinkle with brown sugar and pour honey over all.

Bake uncovered at 350 degrees for 45 minutes. Serves: 4-6

Red Cabbage Casserole

1 head red cabbage, shredded
1 cup cranberry juice
1 tablespoon sugar
2 tablespoons butter

3 tablespoons red currant
   jelly
¼ teaspoon salt
½ cup vinegar

In a large saucepan mix all ingredients, except vinegar, cover and simmer for 1½ hours. Stir occasionally. Add vinegar during last 15 minutes of cooking time.

Baked Sauerkraut with Apples

1 quart sauerkraut
¼ cup onion, sliced
2 tablespoons butter or bacon fat
2-3 apples, peeled and sliced

1 cup white wine
1 cup chicken broth (homemade) or consommé, undiluted

Drain sauerkraut. Sauté onion in butter or fat until soft and golden. Stir in sauerkraut and apples. Add wine and broth or consomme. Simmer uncovered for 30 minutes. Cover and cook on top of stove or bake at 325 degrees in the oven for 1 hour. If there is too much liquid left in the bottom of the cooking pot, simmer or bake uncovered for another 30 minutes.

Spinach Stuffed Zucchini

3 medium zucchini
1 (10 ounce) package frozen, chopped spinach, cooked and drained
2 tablespoons flour

½ cup milk
⅓ cup Cheddar cheese, grated
4 slices bacon, cooked crisp and crumbled

Clean zucchini, cut in half lengthwise and blanch until tender-crisp. Drain thoroughly. Scoop out centers and chop.

Combine chopped zucchini, spinach and flour in saucepan; add milk. Cook and stir until thickened.

Place zucchini halves on lightly greased jellyroll pan. Fill with spinach mixture and top with cheese and bacon.

Bake at 350 degrees for 15-20 minutes. Serves: 6

Spinach Casserole

5 (10 ounce) packages frozen chopped spinach
16 ounces cream cheese
1 pound bacon

2½ cups sour cream
5 tablespoons onion flakes
4 teaspoons horseradish

Cook spinach according to directions on package. Drain well. Mix rest of ingredients, except the bacon, with the spinach. (It can be prepared to this point several days before use.) Cook and crumble bacon and add to mixture just before heating.

Bake 1 hour at 350 degrees in a well-greased 9x13 inch pan. Serves: 20-30

Baked Tomatoes and Onions

1 (No. 2½) can whole tomatoes
½ teaspoon salt
¼ teaspoon pepper
4 medium onions, cut in slices

1 cup bread crumbs
¾ cup brown sugar
3 tablespoons butter

Mix tomatoes, salt and pepper, onions and ½ cup bread crumbs together in a baking dish. Cover with brown sugar then cover with remaining bread crumbs. Dot with butter.

Bake, uncovered, about 3 hours at 325 degrees. Top will become very brown.

Note: Especially good with beef.

Tomatoes Svengali

2 (1 pound) cans tomatoes
1 cup orange-cranberry relish
¼ cup golden raisins
1 teaspoon each salt and ginger

2 tablespoons sugar
½ teaspoon cayenne pepper

Cut up tomatoes. Combine all ingredients and simmer about 10 or 15 minutes. Chill and serve as a side dish with roast meats.

Whipped Turnip Puff

4 cups turnips, cooked and mashed
2 cups soft bread crumbs
2 tablespoons sugar

½ cup butter, melted
¼ teaspoon pepper
4 eggs, slightly beaten

Mix all ingredients together. Spoon into greased 6-cup casserole. Brush the top with a little additional butter.

Bake at 375 degrees for 1 hour. Serves: 8

OATGRASS & JACKRABBIT

Vegetable Casserole

1 small eggplant, thinly sliced
2 tomatoes, thinly sliced
2 zucchini, thinly sliced
3 medium carrots, thinly sliced
½ bunch broccoli, thinly sliced
2 green onions, sliced

½ pound mozzarella cheese, thinly sliced
½ cup Italian bread crumbs
1 garlic clove, minced
Freshly ground pepper, to taste
½ tablespoon lemon juice
½ teaspoon oregano
10 green olives, sliced

Make layers of vegetables and cheese with bread crumbs and seasonings in a baking pan.

Cover by making a tent with foil. Bake 1½ hours at 350 degrees. Serves: 6-8

Vegetable Curry

6 tablespoons oil
1 large onion, thinly sliced
2 garlic cloves, minced
1 tablespoon fresh ginger, minced
1 tablespoon curry powder
1 teaspoon salt
½ teaspoon cumin, ground
½ teaspoon coriander, ground
⅛ teaspoon cayenne
2 large tomatoes, peeled and cut in ½-inch wedges

½ cup plain yogurt
½ pound mushrooms, sliced
1 large green pepper, cut in thin strips
2 medium carrots, thinly sliced
4 medium zucchini, cut in ½-inch slices
2 (1 pound) cans garbanzo beans, drained
2 tablespoons fresh coriander

Pour oil into a heavy 5-quart Dutch oven and place over medium heat. Add onion, garlic and ginger. Cook, stirring frequently, until onion is tender. Add curry powder, salt, cumin, coriander, cayenne and tomatoes. Cook, stirring mixture occasionally, until both onions and tomatoes are very soft (about 10 minutes).

Stir in yogurt. Add mushrooms, green peppers, carrots and zucchini. Stir to coat. Cover and simmer, stirring occasionally, until vegetables are barely tender (about 10 minutes). Add garbanzos. Cover and simmer until beans are hot (about 5 minutes).

Turn into serving dish and sprinkle with coriander.

For accompaniment, offer salted roasted peanuts, plain yogurt mixed with coriander and chopped hard-boiled eggs. Serves: 6

Spicy Zucchini

1 medium onion, finely chopped
1 garlic clove, minced
⅓ cup parsley, chopped
2 tablespoons oil (olive oil, if desired)
1 pound zucchini
1 (8 ounce) can tomato sauce
¼ cup dry white wine
1 tablespoon sugar
¼ teaspoon nutmeg
¼ teaspoon cinnamon
¼ teaspoon pepper
½ teaspoon salt
½ cup Parmesan cheese, grated

Sauté onion, garlic and parsley in oil in a large frying pan until onions are limp. Slice zucchini into ⅛ to ¼-inch ovals; add to pan and simmer on low heat, covered, for 5 minutes.

Stir in tomato sauce, wine, sugar, nutmeg, cinnamon, pepper and salt.

Cover and simmer until zucchini is tender (3-5 minutes), stirring frequently. Stir in cheese just before serving. Serves: 4

GRASSHOPPER IN BUFFALO BURR

Zucchini Pie

4 cups thinly sliced zucchini
1 cup chopped onion
½ cup margarine
½ cup chopped parsley
½ teaspoon each salt & pepper
¼ teaspoon garlic powder
¼ teaspoon basil

¼ teaspoon oregano
2 eggs, well beaten
8 ounces shredded mozzarella
1 (8 ounce) can refrigerator crescent rolls (optional)
2 teaspoons Dijon mustard

Preheat oven to 375 degrees. Sauté zucchini and onion in melted butter 10 minutes. Stir in parsley and other seasonings. In a large bowl blend eggs and cheese well. Stir in vegetable mixture. Separate dough and place triangles into and up the sides of a 10-inch (ungreased) pie plate to form crust. Spread bottom with Dijon mustard. Pour vegetable mixture into crust evenly and bake 20 minutes or until a knife inserted in the middle comes out clean.

Note: May be baked in a buttered baking dish without crust.

MEATS
AND
MAIN DISHES

Cheese Soufflé

8 slices white bread, crusts removed, coarsely crumbled
¾ pound Cheddar cheese
4 eggs, beaten

2 cups milk
½ teaspoon dry mustard
½ teaspoon salt
Paprika for garnish

Mix bread and grated cheese. Spread evenly in a 9 by 13 inch pan. Beat eggs, milk, mustard and salt together and pour evenly over bread and cheese. Sprinkle with paprika. Soufflé may be refrigerated over night at this point. Bake for 1 hour at 350 degrees. Serve with a cheese sauce, creamed crabmeat sauce or creamed shrimp sauce.

Variation: Add 1 cup chopped broccoli and 1 teaspoon chicken stock crystals to soufflé mixture. Serves: 6.

Golden Shrimp Puff

10 slices white bread (crusts removed)
6 eggs
3 cups milk
2 tablespoons minced parsley

¾ teaspoon dry mustard
½ teaspoon salt
2 cups shredded sharp Cheddar cheese (8 ounces)
2 cups cooked shrimp

Heat oven to 325 degrees. Remove crusts from bread; cut slices into cubes. Beat eggs, milk and seasonings. Stir in bread cubes, cheese and shrimp. Pour into oblong buttered baking dish, 11½ x 7½ x 1½ inches. Bake uncovered one hour or until center is set. Serves: 4-6

Note: Serve with asparagus spears, fresh fruit salad and hot rolls.

24 Hour Wine and Cheese Omelet

1 large loaf day old French or Italian bread, crusts removed, broken into small pieces
6 tablespoons melted butter
¾ cup shredded Swiss cheese
½ cup shredded Monterey Jack cheese
1 pound cooked, drained, crumbled bacon or ½ pound cooked ham, coarsely chopped

16 eggs
3¼ cups milk
½ cup dry white wine
4 green onions, chopped
1 tablespoon prepared mustard
¼ teaspoon coarsely ground pepper
⅛ teaspoon cayenne
1½ cups sour cream
1 cup shredded Parmesan cheese

Butter two 9 x 13 inch pans. Spread bread over bottom of pans. Drizzle bread with butter. Sprinkle cheeses (Swiss and Monterey Jack), and meat on top of bread. Beat eggs, milk, wine, onion, mustard, pepper and cayenne until foamy. Pour over cheeses. Cover with foil and refrigerate overnight. Bake at 325 degrees, covered, for 1 hour. Uncover, spread with sour cream and sprinkle with Parmesan cheese. Bake uncovered for 10 minutes. Serves: 16-20

Mushroom and Sausage Pie

½ pound Italian sausage
1½ pounds small whole
    mushrooms
½ cup parsley, minced
2 eggs
1 cup light cream

½ cup Parmesan cheese,
    grated
¼-½ teaspoon salt
9-10 inch pastry shell unbaked
    (pre-bake 5-8 minutes)

Crumble sausage in a frying pan and add mushrooms. Cook over high heat, stirring frequently, until mushrooms and meat are lightly browned and all liquid has evaporated, about 15 minutes. Remove 3 tablespoons of the sausage drippings from the pan and discard. Add parsley to mushroom mixture, return to heat and cook for 2-3 minutes more.

Beat eggs with light cream and cheese, blend in the mushroom mixture and add salt to taste. Pour in to pastry shell. Arrange mushrooms so that any stems showing are turned down into the liquid and push the mushrooms down so the pie is evenly filled.

Bake at 375 degrees for 30 minutes, or until crust is well browned. Let pie stand about 10 minutes before cutting. Serves: 4-6

Basic Quiche with Variations

1 (9 inch) pre-baked pie shell
¾ pound grated Swiss and/or
    Gruyere cheese
2 tablespoons chopped
    parsley
¼ teaspoon pepper
2 tablespoons flour (rounded)
1 small diced onion
4-6 beaten eggs

½ cup mayonnaise or sour
    cream
½ cup milk or cream
¾ cup ham, turkey, chicken
    or bacon (optional)
1 cup sliced mushrooms
    (optional)

Line bottom of pie shell with grated cheese. Mix remaining ingredients. Pour the mixture into pie shell. Bake at 350 degrees for 40 minutes or until center is set. Serves: 6

BLOODROOT

69

Zucchini Quiche

Basic Shortcrust Pastry:
2 cups flour
½ teaspoon salt
½ teaspoon sugar

¾ cup butter
1 teaspoon lemon juice
1-3 tablespoons ice water

Mix flour, salt and sugar; cut in butter, sprinkle in lemon juice and water.

Quiche:
1 recipe basic shortcrust pastry
¼ cup Parmesan cheese, grated
¼ cup Cheddar cheese, grated
½ cup dry bread crumbs
2 eggs, separated

4 small zucchini
1½ cups sour cream
2 tablespoons chives, chopped
2 tablespoons flour
⅛ teaspoon cream of tartar
Salt and pepper, to taste
1 tablespoon butter

Combine the cheeses. Add ½ of the cheese mixture to the pie crust dough. Form into a ball. Chill. Press into a 10-inch quiche dish. Chill again.

Mix the remaining cheeses with bread crumbs. Set aside.

Wash zucchini and cut into ¼-inch slices. Drop in boiling, salted water for 5 minutes. Drain.

Beat the egg yolks and sour cream together. Add chives, flour, salt and pepper. Beat egg whites with cream of tartar until stiff but not dry. Fold into sour cream mixture.

Arrange a layer of zucchini slices on bottom of pie crust, placing them edge to edge. Cover with small amount of sour cream mixture. Continue layers until all zucchini is used. Cover with sour cream mixture. Sprinkle with cheese-bread crumb mixture. Dot with butter. Bake 10 minutes at 450 degrees. Turn heat down to 325 degrees and bake for 40 minutes longer. Serves: 8-10

Confetti Wheat Pilaf

⅓ cup sliced celery
⅓ cup chopped celery leaves
⅓ cup sliced green onions
with tops
2 tablespoons butter
2 tablespoons vegetable oil
2 cups bulgur wheat
2 (13½ ounce) cans chicken
broth

1 teaspoon seasoned salt
¼ teaspoon freshly ground
pepper
1 (4 ounce) jar chopped,
drained pimento
3 tablespoons snipped, fresh
parsley

Sauté celery, celery leaves and onions in butter and oil in a large skillet for 2 minutes. Add bulgur; sauté until golden, 5-8 minutes. Stir in broth, salt and pepper. Heat to boiling; reduce heat; simmer, covered, 15 minutes. Let stand 5 minutes. At serving time, stir in pimento and parsley. Serves: 8

Wild Rice

1 cup wild rice   1 teaspoon salt
4 cups water

Wash the rice several times and drain. Stir it slowly into boiling water. Reduce heat to simmer. Cover and cook until tender (40 to 50 minutes). Drain rice in a colander and rinse with warm water.

In a 3 or 4 quart saucepan   1 tablespoon chives (or green
combine: onion) minced
  4 ounces butter   2 teaspoons chicken base or
  4 ounces mushrooms, finely   2 chicken bouillon cubes
    chopped

Stir this over low heat until butter melts and chicken base is dissolved. Then add the cooked rice and heat over low heat. Stir mixture to combine ingredients. Serves: 8 to 10.

North Dakota Noodle Bake

8 ounces wide noodles   ¼ teaspoon pepper
2 tablespoons butter   2 cups cottage cheese
½ cup finely chopped onion   2 cups sour cream
½ cup finely chopped celery   1 cup shredded brick cheese
1 teaspoon salt   3 eggs, beaten
1 teaspoon caraway seed
  (optional)

Cook noodles; drain. Melt butter in skillet; sauté onion and celery. Stir in salt, caraway seed and pepper. Arrange ⅓ of the noodles in buttered 2 quart casserole; add one-half of the vegetable mixture. Spread one-half of the cottage cheese and sour cream over noodles. Repeat, ending with noodles. Sprinkle with brick cheese; top with eggs. Bake in 350 degree oven for 30-45 minutes. Let stand for 10 minutes before serving. Yield: 8 servings

Spinach-Noodle Casserole

1 (8 ounce) package wide   1 cup sour cream
  noodles   ½ cup butter
2 (10 ounce) packages frozen,   1 medium onion, chopped
  chopped spinach, thawed   3 eggs, slightly beaten
  and drained   Salt and pepper, to taste

According to package directions, boil noodles but for only ½ the time.

In a large skillet, melt butter and sauté onion. Mix all ingredients together and pour into large, greased casserole. Bake 30 minutes at 350 degrees. Serves: 4-6

Fettucine Alfredo

12 ounces of fettucine
2 teaspoons salt
5 quarts boiling water
1 egg yolk

⅔ cup cream
¼ pound butter, melted
½ cup grated Parmesan cheese

Place fettucine noodles and salt into 5 quarts of boiling water. Boil 9-12 minutes. Beat egg yolk lightly with fork and add to cream. Place drained hot noodles in warm serving bowl. Pour egg and cream mixture over noodles. Add melted butter and about half of grated cheese. Toss noodles with fork and spoon until well blended. Add remainder of cheese a little at a time while tossing. Top with additional grated cheese, if desired. Serve immediately. Serves: 6

Cheese Manicotti

¼ cup chopped onion
1 clove garlic, crushed
2 tablespoons cooking oil
1 (16 ounce) can tomatoes, cut up
1 (8 ounce) can tomato sauce
1 teaspoon dried oregano, crushed
½ teaspoon dried thyme, crushed

1 small bay leaf
¼ teaspoon salt
12 manicotti shells
2 beaten eggs
1½ cups ricotta cheese
1 (8 ounce) package shredded mozzarella cheese
½ cup grated Parmesan cheese
¼ cup snipped parsley

In saucepan cook onion and garlic in oil until tender, but not browned. Add tomatoes, tomato sauce, sugar, oregano, thyme, bay leaf and salt. Bring to boiling; simmer, uncovered, for 45 minutes. Remove bay leaf.

Cook manicotti shells in boiling, salted water just until tender. Drain. Rinse in cold water. Combine eggs, ricotta, one-half the mozzarella, Parmesan, parsley, ¼ teaspoon salt, and dash of pepper. Spoon cheese mixture into shells. Pour one-half the tomato mixture into a 13x9x2 inch baking dish; top with stuffed shells. Pour remaining sauce over shells. Sprinkle with remaining mozzarella. Bake, covered, at 350 degrees for 30 minutes. (If desired, refrigerate casserole up to 24 hours. Bake, covered, 45 minutes.) Serves: 6

Quick Manicotti

Pasta: 8 manicotti shells

Filling:
- 1 pound ground beef
- 8 ounces mozzarella cheese, diced
- ¼ cup grated Parmesan cheese
- 1 tablespoon chopped parsley
- 1 teaspoon seasoned salt
- ¼ teaspoon white pepper
- ¼ teaspoon garlic powder

Sauce:
- 1 (15 ounce) can tomato sauce
- 1 cup water
- 2 tablespoons onion flakes
- 1½ teaspoons brown sugar, packed
- ¾ teaspoon oregano
- ½ teaspoon basil
- ½ garlic salt

Place manicotti shells in 7½ x 12 x 1½ inch baking dish, cover with boiling water; let stand 5 minutes; rinse with cold water, drain thoroughly. Brown beef and combine with other filling ingredients; mix well. Combine sauce ingredients in sauce pan over medium heat until warm. Stuff drained shells with filling and return to baking dish. Pour sauce over filled shells. Bake, covered, at 375 degrees for 45 minutes or until al dente. Serve with additional Parmesan.

Pasta with Vegetable Sauce

- 20 ounces California blend vegetables, frozen
- ½ cup chopped onion
- 3 tablespoons butter or margarine
- 5 ounce can evaporated milk
- 1 teaspoon dried basil
- ⅛ teaspoon each salt and pepper
- ¾ cup shredded Monterey Jack cheese
- ⅓ cup parsley
- 8 ounces hot cooked pasta

Cook vegetables to crisp-tender; drain, reserve. In a medium saucepan, cook onion in 1 tablespoon butter until tender, not brown. Add milk, basil, ⅛ teaspoon salt, ⅛ teaspoon pepper. Boil 1 minute. Lower heat, stir in cheese, stir until melted. Mix in parsley and vegetables. Toss pasta with remaining 2 tablespoons butter. Pour sauce over pasta and toss until coated. Serve with grated Parmesan if desired. Serves: 6

Linguine with Clam Sauce

½ cup butter
1 tablespoon olive oil
5 large cloves garlic, pressed or crushed
2 heaping tablespoons flour
2 cups clam juice
½ cup parsley, chopped
½ teaspoon dried thyme
½ cup vermouth (or any dry white wine)
2 cups canned minced clams, drained (two 7 ounce cans)
8-12 ounces linguine noodles

Heat butter and olive oil in a sauce pan and add the garlic. Stir 2-3 minutes. Add flour and cook, stirring, for 2-3 minutes. Add clam juice. (If reserved clam juice is not enough, bottled clam juice is available.) Cook, stirring, until sauce thickens. The sauce will be thin. Add parsley, thyme and vermouth. Cook a few minutes. Add clams and heat through. Boil linguine according to package instructions. Drain well and place in a warm serving bowl. Pour clam sauce over the pasta. If desired, Parmesan cheese may be sprinkled over each serving. Serves: 4-6

Briani
(Indian Chicken Curry)

4 pounds chicken or turkey
2 cups plain yogurt
1 tablespoon salt
2 teaspoons saffron
2 tablespoons hot water
2 cups long grain rice
1 cup chopped onions
½ cup butter
2-3 teaspoons curry powder
1 teaspoon ginger, ground
6 whole cloves
2 cinnamon sticks
Dash cardamom, ground
2 teaspoons garlic powder
1 teaspoon cumin, ground
½ teaspoon salt
1 cup golden raisins
2 apples, pared, cored and chopped

Poach chicken in salted water until tender. Remove chicken, reserving 4 cups broth for saffron rice. Remove meat from bones and mix with yogurt and salt. Set aside.

Make saffron rice: Soak saffron in 2 tablespoons of hot water. Mix with chicken broth and add rice. Bring to a boil, cover, and simmer for 15 minutes or until rice is fluffy and liquid is absorbed.

Meanwhile, saute onion in butter over low heat. Add spices and cook for 3 minutes. Add chicken mixture and simmer 10 minutes. Add apple and raisins. Spoon curry over saffron rice. Top with a variety of condiments such as: Chutney, coconut (grated), sliced almonds, chopped tomatoes. Serves: 6-8

Moussaka
(Eggplant Casserole)

Meat Sauce:
2 tablespoons butter
1 cup onion, finely chopped
1½ pounds ground beef or lamb
1 clove garlic, crushed
½ teaspoon dried oregano
  leaves
1 teaspoon dried basil leaves
½ teaspoon cinnamon
1 teaspoon salt
  Dash pepper
2 (8 ounce) cans tomato sauce

Cream Sauce:
2 tablespoons butter
2 tablespoons flour
½ teaspoon salt
  Dash pepper
2 cups milk
2 eggs

2 eggplants (approximately
  2½ pounds total)
  Salt
½ cup butter, melted
½ cup Parmesan cheese,
  grated
½ cup Cheddar cheese, grated
2 tablespoons dry bread
  crumbs

Meat sauce: In hot butter in 3½ quart Dutch oven, saute onion, beef and garlic, stirring until brown, about 10 minutes. Add herbs, spices, tomato sauce and bring to boil, stirring. Reduce heat, simmer, uncovered for ½ hour.

Halve unpared eggplant lengthwise. Slice crosswise, ½ inch thick, like half moons. Place in bottom of broiler pan, sprinkle lightly with salt and brush lightly with melted butter. Broil, 4 inches from heat, 4 minutes per side, or until golden. Set aside.

Cream sauce: In medium saucepan, melt butter. Remove from heat, stir in flour, salt and pepper. Add milk gradually. Bring to boil, stirring until mixture is thickened. Remove from heat. In small bowl, beat eggs with wire whisk. Beat in some hot cream sauce mixture, return mixture to saucepan and mix well. Set aside.

To assemble casserole, layer half of eggplant, slightly overlapping, in a shallow 2 quart baking dish, 12 x 7½ x 2 inches. Sprinkle with 2 tablespoons each grated Parmesan and Cheddar cheeses. Stir bread crumbs into meat sauce. Spoon evenly over eggplant in casserole, then sprinkle with 2 tablespoons each Parmesan and Cheddar cheeses. Layer rest of eggplant slices, overlapping, as before. Pour cream sauce over all. Sprinkle top with remaining cheese. Bake in preheated oven at 350 degrees for 35-40 minutes or until golden brown and top is set. If desired, brown top a little more under broiler, about 1 minute. Cool slightly to serve. Garnish with sprigs of parsley. Cut in squares. Serves: 12

Cannelloni

The crepes:

1 cup cold water	½ teaspoon salt
1 cup milk	2 cups flour
4 eggs	4 tablespoons melted butter

Combine all ingredients in a blender and mix well. Refrigerate at least 2 hours. Strain batter before frying crepes. Heat an 8-inch crepe pan and coat lightly with oil. Spoon in 2 to 3 tablespoons batter or just enough to cover the bottom of the pan. Tilt to spread evenly. When batter loses its wet look, turn crepe and cook briefly. Turn out on a kitchen towel. When cool, stack one on top of the other. Keep lightly covered until ready to fill and roll. Makes 24 crepes.

The sauce:

⅓ cup olive oil	2 teaspoons salt
1½ cups finely chopped onion	2 teaspoons sugar
1 garlic clove, minced	1 teaspoon dried oregano
1 (35 ounce) can Italian plum tomatoes, not drained	1 teaspoon dried basil
	½ teaspoon fennel seeds (optional)
1 (6 ounce) can tomato paste	
2 tablespoons chopped parsley	1 pound lean ground beef, browned (optional)

Heat olive oil in a large saucepan. Saute onion and garlic until soft but not browned. Add remaining ingredients and simmer, partially covered, until sauce thickens, about 20 minutes.

The filling:

2 eggs, slightly beaten	1 tablespoon chopped parsley
2 pounds ricotta cheese	salt and pepper to taste
8 ounces Mozarella or Swiss cheese, grated	½ cup grated Parmesan cheese for topping

Combine all ingredients in a bowl, except the Parmesan cheese.

To assemble: Butter two 11x7 baking dishes. Spoon about ¼ cup filling down the center of each crepe and roll it up. Into each dish, spoon 1½ cups sauce. Place 12 filled crepes on top and cover with 1 more cup sauce. Sprinkle each dish with ¼ cup Parmesan cheese. Bake uncovered for 30 minutes at 350 degrees.

Vegetable Burritos

2 tablespoons oil
1 large onion, thinly sliced
2 garlic cloves, minced
½ pound mushrooms, sliced
1 large green pepper, thinly sliced
2 medium carrots, thinly sliced
4 medium zucchini, cut in ½-inch slices
2 large tomatoes, peeled and cut in ½-inch wedges
1 (7 ounce) can green chilies, chopped and drained
1 (2¼ ounce) can dark olives, sliced and drained
1 teaspoon chili powder
1 teaspoon salt
½ teaspoon cumin
½ teaspoon oregano
1½ cups Monterey Jack cheese (with japapeno pepper, if desired), grated
1½ cups Cheddar cheese,
12 flour tortillas

Heat oil in 12-inch skillet. Sauté onion and garlic until tender. Add the next 11 ingredients and bring to a boil. Lower heat, cover and simmer until the vegetables are tender, about 10 minutes. Mix the two cheeses together. Add 2 cups of cheese to vegetable mixture. Turn into a shallow casserole and sprinkle with remaining cheese. Broil, 6 inches from heat, until cheese is melted and bubbly, about 3 minutes.

Wrap tortillas in foil. Heat in a 350 degree oven for 20 minutes.

Condiments:
1 cup taco sauce
1 cup guacumole
1 cup sour cream
1 cup chopped green onions
1 cup sunflower seeds

For each burrito, spoon a little vegetable mixture down the center of a warm tortilla; top with condiments to taste, and roll. Serves: 4-6

Stuffed Cabbage Rolls
(Ukrainian, Germans from Russia)

1 large head of cabbage, (3-4 pounds)
3-4 strips lean bacon, diced
1 medium onion, chopped
1 pound lean beef, ground
1 cup cooked rice
1 egg
¾ teaspoon salt
⅛ teaspoon pepper
1 can (14½ ounces) whole tomatoes
1 can (15 ounces) tomato sauce
1 cup water
1 cup sauerkraut (optional)
Sour cream

Place the cabbage in a large kettle of boiling water. Boil 3-5 minutes. Drain cabbage and rinse in cold water. With a small, sharp knife loosen and remove 12-15 large outer leaves. Cut out lower portion of thick inner vein from each cabbage leaf.

Filling: In a heavy saucepan, over moderate heat, sauté bacon and onion until the onion is golden but not brown. Add to ground meat and mix. Add rice, egg, salt and pepper. Mix well.

Put 2-3 tablespoons of filling on the stem end of each leaf and fold sides of leaf over filling. Roll up from thick end of the cabbage leaf. Place rolls, seam side down, into a large baking dish. Mix canned tomatoes, tomato sauce, sauerkraut and water. Pour mixture over cabbage rolls. Cover tightly. Bake at 350 degrees for 1½ hours. Add more water, if needed.

Serve with a heaping spoonful of sour cream for each serving.

Hot Taco Salad

1½ pounds ground beef
1 teaspoon salt
¼ teaspoon pepper
1 tablespoon chili powder

Brown and simmer together 20 minutes.

½ cup sour cream
½ cup mayonnaise
½ head finely chopped lettuce
1-2 tomatoes, chopped
½ cup colby or other cheese, grated
½ grated mozzarella cheese
½ cup onion, chopped
2 cups taco or nacho chips, crushed

Make dressing by mixing sour cream and mayonnaise.

Layer in baking dish: ½ of the meat, cheese, lettuce, onions, tomatoes, dressing and chips; repeat layers. Bake at 400 degrees for 20-25 minutes.

Jean's Beans

1 pound dried navy beans
½ cup dark molasses
½ cup brown sugar
4-5 medium onions (chopped)
½ (46 ounce) can tomato juice
½ (14 ounce) bottle catsup
3 tablespoons prepared
   mustard
10 drops Tabasco sauce
   Garlic salt
   Salt and pepper

1 tablespoon white vinegar
1 tablespoon white sugar
1 tablespoon lemon juice
1 can beer
  Pinch of soda
1 pound bacon, cut in small
   pieces
2 pounds ham, cut in cubes
2 pounds pork, cut in cubes

Soak beans overnight and drain. Place everything together in a medium size roaster. Bake at 350 degrees until bubbling. Turn oven to 200 degrees. Bake all day (8-10 hours), stirring occasionally.

Calico Beans

2 (16 ounce) cans butter
  beans
2 (16 ounce) cans pork and
  beans
2 (16 ounce) cans kidney
  beans
2 (16 ounce) cans lima beans
¾ cup brown sugar

½ cup catsup
1 tablespoon prepared
   mustard
½ pound fried bacon, crumbled
1 pound ground beef,
   browned
1 large onion, chopped and
   browned with ground beef.

Mix all ingredients. Place in baking dish. Bake at 350 degrees for 2 hours. Freezes well.

Mexican Casserole

4 pounds ground beef
2 large onions, chopped
2 cloves garlic, minced
¼ cup chili powder
6 cups tomato sauce
1 teaspoon sugar
1½ tablespoons salt (or less)
2 cups sliced black olives
2 (4 ounce) cans green chilies, diced
24 corn tortillas, fried a few seconds in hot oil and cut into quarters

4 cups small curd cottage cheese
1 pound Monterey Jack cheese, grated
2 cups grated Cheddar cheese

Garnish:
1 cup sour cream
1 cup chopped green onions

Brown the meat with onions and garlic. Add spices, tomato sauce, sugar, olives and green chilies; simmer 15 minutes.

Spread one-third of the meat mixture into a 6-quart casserole (or use two 9x13 inch baking pans). Cover meat mixture with half of the grated Monterey Jack cheese, half of the cottage cheese and half of the tortillas. Repeat. Finish final layer with meat mixture and top with grated Cheddar cheese.

Bake uncovered in a 350 degree oven for 30 minutes. To serve, spread sour cream over casserole and sprinkle with chopped green onions. Serves: 12-24

Fleischkuechla

Dough:
5 cups flour
2 teaspoons salt
1 cup sour cream, scant
2 cups milk, scant

Filling:
2 pounds lean ground beef (if meat is dry, a little ground pork may be added)
1 medium onion, finely minced
Salt and pepper to taste
Fat for deep frying

Mix ingredients for dough. If dough is sticky add more flour. Take half of the dough and roll it on a floured surface to ⅛ inch thickness. Cut out 4-inch circles with a sauce dish or cookie cutter, or cut into squares.

Fill each with 1 to 2 tablespoons of meat mixture. Enclose meat mixture by pinching dough edges tightly together into half moon or triangle shapes.

Deep fat fry at 375 degrees until golden brown on both sides.

Serve with a tossed salad or with soup. Good with beer. Serves: 8-12.

Remarks: Fleischkuechla are popular with Germans from Russia.

Pancit

1 package rice noodles
¼-½ cup peanut or corn oil
1 medium onion, chopped
3 garlic cloves, minced
½ pound lean pork, cut in strips
1 chicken breast, cut in strips
½ pound shelled shrimp
1½ cups sliced or julienne celery
1½ cups carrots, julienne
1 cup cabbage, shredded
5 tablespoons soy sauce

Soak noodles in water. Sauté garlic and onions in oil in wok or fry pan. Add meats and shrimp; stir until pink color disappears. Add vegetables; stir-fry to crisp-tender. Add noodles which have been drained; mix thoroughly. Add soy sauce. Adjust salt and pepper to taste. Serves: 4

North Dakota Chili

1 tablespoon butter
1 tablespoon oil
2 pounds lean ground or diced beef
2 cups onion, thinly sliced
1 cup celery, finely chopped
1 (15 ounce) can tomato sauce
1 (15 ounce) Italian plum tomatoes
1 cup beer
1 cup water
½ cup tomato ketchup
4 whole cloves
4 whole allspice
3 large garlic cloves, chopped
¼ teaspoon baking cocoa
¼ teaspoon cinnamon
½ teaspoon Worcestershire sauce
⅛-¼ teaspoon cayenne pepper
1 teaspoon cumin
2-4 tablespoons chili powder
2 tablespoons masa harina

Heat butter and oil in large, deep pot. Brown meat; add onion and cook until transparent. Add all other ingredients except masa harina. Simmer partially covered for 1 hour. Add more water if mixture becomes too thick.

Just before serving, mix a little chili with the masa harina in a small bowl. Turn off burner and add masa mixture to chili pot. Let stand 15 minutes. Stir once and serve with the following condiments, each arranged in separate bowls: chopped green onion, sliced green, pimento olives, sliced ripe olives, sour cream, shredded Cheddar cheese and hot, cooked pinto beans. Serves: 8

PRAIRIE VETCH.

Aristocrat Open-Face Sandwich

Blue Cheese Sauce:
- 8 ounces sour cream
- 4 ounces blue cheese
- ¼ teaspoon garlic powder
- Splash of milk

- 8 slices white bread
- 8 thin slices turkey breast, cooked
- 8 thin slices boiled ham
- 8 slices mozzarella cheese
- Parmesan cheese
- 8 slices tomatoes
- Alfalfa sprouts

Mix ingredients for blue cheese sauce and set aside. Sauce is at its best when made a day in advance.

Toast bread. Trim crusts, butter and cut each slice diagonally into 2 toast triangles. For each serving, place 4 toast triangles on a broiler-proof plate; arrange in a row with center points overlapping. Take 2 slices of ham and 2 of turkey and fold each in half. Insert a folded piece of meat between each triangle, alternating ham and turkey. Spread with blue cheese sauce. Top with 2 mozzarella slices and sprinkle with Parmesan. Repeat assembly for 3 other sandwiches. Broil until the cheese melts. Remove from oven and garnish with tomato slices and sprouts. Serve immediately. Serves: 4

Pizza Meat Loaf

- 2 pounds ground chuck
- 1 cup dry bread crumbs
- 2 eggs
- ½ cup Parmesan cheese
- 3 teaspoons diced onion

- 1 teaspoon oregano
- 1 cup tomato juice
- 1 (8 ounce) can pizza sauce
- 1 cup shredded mozzarella cheese

Combine meat, crumbs, eggs, Parmesan cheese, onion, oregano and tomato juice. Place in a 8 inch x 8 inch baking pan. Bake at 350 degrees for 45 minutes. Remove from the oven and spread the pizza sauce over the loaf. Sprinkle the mozzarella cheese on top. Return to the oven and bake 10 minutes longer. Cut into squares. Serves: 9

Swedish Meatballs with Mushrooms and Gravy

¼ cup fine bread crumbs
½ cup milk
1 pound lean ground beef
1 egg, beaten
1 small onion, chopped
1 tablespoon chopped
  parsley
½ teaspoon salt
¼ teaspoon pepper
⅛ teaspoon each: basil,
  marjoram, rosemary,
  and thyme
6 ounces fresh mushrooms

Sour Cream Gravy:
¼ cup water
⅛ teaspoon pepper
2 teaspoons soy sauce
  A pinch of: rosemary, basil,
  marjoram, thyme
1 cup sour cream

Soak bread crumbs in milk. Mix remaining ingredients except mushrooms. Form into 1 inch balls. Over medium heat, brown meatballs on all sides, keeping them rounded. Remove to baking dish with cover.

Sauté mushrooms in frying pan. Place on meatballs. Loosen drippings from bottom of frying pan. Stir in ¼ cup water, soy sauce, and remaining spices. Stir in sour cream, heat and stir until smooth. Pour over mushrooms and meatballs. Bake 20 minutes at 350 degrees. Serves: 6

Shrimp Stroganoff

¼ cup minced onion
5 tablespoons butter, divided
1½ pound shelled raw shrimp
½ pound fresh mushrooms,
  quartered
1 tablespoon flour

1½ cups sour cream,
  room temperature
1¼ teaspoon salt
  Pepper to taste
  Cooked saffron rice
1 (1 pound) can artichoke
  hearts, quartered

In large skillet sauté onion in ½ cup butter until softened. Add shrimp and sauté 3-5 minutes or until pink in color. Transfer mixture to heated dish and keep warm. In same skillet sauté mushrooms in remaining butter over moderately high heat until browned. Sprinkle mushrooms with flour and cook, stirring for 2 minutes. Reduce heat to moderate to low and stir in the shrimp mixture, sour cream, salt and pepper. Cook stirring for 2-3 minutes until shrimp are thoroughly heated. Do not boil. Serve immediately over saffron rice tossed with quartered artichoke hearts. Serves: 4-6

Scalloped Oysters

1 pint fresh oysters
2 cups medium-coarse cracker crumbs
½ cup butter, melted
¾ cup light cream
¼ cup oyster liquor
¼ teaspoon Worcestershire sauce
½ teaspoon salt

Drain oysters, reserving ¼ cup liquor. Combine crumbs and butter. Spread ⅓ of crumbs in greased 8 x 11 inch pan. Cover with half of the oysters. Sprinkle with pepper. Using another ⅓ of the crumbs, spread a second layer; cover with remaining oysters. Sprinkle with pepper. Combine cream, oyster liquor, Worcestershire sauce and salt. Pour over the oysters. Top with last of crumbs. Bake in moderate oven 350 degrees about 40 minutes. Serves: 4

Cy's Seafood Special

5 tablespoons unsalted butter
2 tablespoons green onions and tops
1½ cups clam juice
1 pound shrimp in shell (or fish of choice)
¼ cup dry vermouth
1½ cups heavy cream
1 teaspoon flour
2 tablespoons fresh dill or dried dill weed
2 tablespoons chives
Salt and freshly ground pepper, to taste
Parsley

Heat 2 tablespoons butter in heavy pan over medium heat. When foam subsides, add onions and sauté 2 minutes. Add clam juice; heat to boiling. Add shrimp; boil until bright pink and opaque in center, about 2 minues. Remove shrimp and reserve liquid in pan. Shell, leaving tail intact, and devein. Split shrimp in half lengthwise, stopping before tail.

Bring reserved liquid in pan to boiling. Add vermouth; boil to reduce by half, 10 minutes. Add cream; boil to reduce by half, 15 minutes. Mix 1 tablespoon butter and 1 teaspoon flour. When liquid in pan is reduced, whisk in flour mixture until sauce thickens. Whisk in remaining butter, dill, chives, salt and pepper. Place shrimp back into sauce until warmed. Garnish with parsley. Serve over rice or pasta. Serves: 4

Note: Poached walleye pike may be substituted for shrimp.

Walleye or Trout Stuffed with Shrimp

6 walleye or trout fillets
2 tablespoons slivered
  almonds
2 green onions chopped
8 mushrooms, sliced

2 cups Mornay sauce (see
  below)
6 ounces cooked shrimp
Bread crumbs
Salt and pepper
Lemon wedges

Sauté chopped onions and almonds in butter. Chop shrimp and mushrooms and add to skillet. Cook, stirring, for several minutes. Add 2 tablespoons Mornay sauce.

Mornay Sauce: Over low heat blend 2 tablespoons flour and 2 tablespoons butter, then add, stirring, 1 cup clear chicken broth and 1 cup light cream. Cook to thicken slightly. Add and stir until melted 2 tablespoons grated Swiss cheese.

Spread walleye or trout fillets with shrimp mixture. Salt and pepper. Roll fillets and secure with toothpicks; arrange in buttered casserole and cover with the remaining Mornay sauce. Sprinkle with bread crumbs and bake in 350 degree pre-heated oven for 20 minutes, or until brown. Serve with lemon wedges.

Salmon Stuffed Sole

8 small sole fillets
¾ pound salmon fillet,
  skinned
Salt and white pepper
1 lemon, cut in halves
½ cup dry white wine
2 tablespoons butter
1 tablespoon flour

2 egg yolks
¼ cup whipping cream
1 package (10 ounce) frozen
  spinach, cooked, drained
2 small tomatoes, halved
  and broiled
½ pound mushrooms, sliced
  and sauteed in butter

Sprinkle sole and salmon with salt and pepper on all sides. Cut salmon into 8 chunks about the width of the sole fillets. Roll sole around salmon and place the rolls in a buttered baking dish. Squeeze lemon over fish rolls, then slice the lemon and place on top of the fish. Pour ½ cup wine over the fish.

Bake, covered, in a 400 degree oven for 25 minutes, until fish separates into flakes when tested with a fork. Discard lemon slices; keep fish warm. Measure pan juices and add more wine, if necessary, to make 1 cup liquid.

In a saucepan melt butter. Stir in flour and cook until bubbly. Gradually add fish liquid, stirring over medium heat until thickened. Beat egg yolks with cream. Stir in a little of the hot liquid. Smoothly blend egg mixture into sauce and cook, stirring constantly, until thickened. Do not boil.

Place sole rolls on a warm serving dish.

Stir any remaining fish juices into sauce. Pour sauce over fish rolls. Place a bed of spinach at either end of serving dish. Place tomato slices on top of spinach. Spoon mushrooms over all.

Salmon Baked in Pastry

1 bunch fresh spinach or (10 ounce) package of frozen spinach
½ medium onion, diced
Pinch of dill weed and thyme
1 tablespoon grated lemon rind
1 cup basic thick white sauce
3 hard boiled eggs, chopped
1 cup cooked wild rice
8 ounces crab meat
Salt and pepper to taste
1 (17¼ ounce) package puff pastry
2 pounds fresh salmon fillet
1 cup hollandaise sauce
1 egg yolk with a tablespoon of water, beaten

Cook spinach and drain thoroughly. Squeeze dry.

Sauté onion 5 minutes, add dill weed, thyme and sauté another 5 minutes. Add spinach, lemon rind and white sauce. Mix well. Add chopped egg, rice and crab. Salt and pepper to taste.

Roll out puff pastry until large enough to encase salmon.

Place ½ of the spinach mixture on puff pastry. Then place salmon on top of it. Spread the remaining ½ of the spinach mixture on the salmon. Fold pastry around the salmon until it is encased. Place fold side down on baking sheet, brush with the beaten egg yolk.

Bake at 350 degrees for 45 minutes or until golden brown.

Serve each cut of salmon with a dollop of hollandaise sauce.

North Dakota Fish Boil

1 cup salt (yes, one cup of salt)
5 quarts water
Peeled potatoes
Peeled small onions
Walleye or northern pike fillets
1 cup melted butter
Parsley

Put water, salt, and vegetables in large container, such as a canner, and boil until vegetables are nearly done. Add fish fillets and continue boiling 5-6 minutes until fish flakes and is opaque. Remove fish and vegetables to heated platter. Garnish with parsley and serve with melted butter.

The amount of the water and salt is constant. The other ingredients may be varied according to the number of servings desired or the number of fish caught.

Great for a large group at the lake.

Baked Marinated Chicken

The Marinade:

½ cup red wine vinegar
½ cup olive oil
1 tablespoon dried oregano leaves
8 cloves of garlic, mashed
1½ cups pitted prunes

½ cup salad olives (green stuf
olives)
3 bay leaves
salt and pepper to taste

Mix marinade ingredients in a large non-aluminum bowl.

3 chickens cut up into 24 pieces
1 cup white wine
1 cup brown sugar

Add chicken pieces to the marinade and refrigerate 3 to 4 hours or overnight.

Arrange chicken in a single layer in one or two large, shallow non-aluminum baking pans. Do not crowd chicken pieces. Add white wine to the marinade and spoon the marinade over the chicken. Sprinkle with the brown sugar. Bake in a pre-heated 350 degree oven for about 1 hour or until the chicken is done. Baste chicken several times while it is baking.

To serve, remove the chicken with a slotted spoon to a heated serving dish. Pour the pan juices into a saucepan, degrease as much as possible, simmer a few minutes and spoon over the chicken. Good hot or at room temperature. Serves 8 to 12.

Chicken Lemonese

4 whole chicken breasts, halved, skinned and boned (8 pieces)
⅓ cup flour
1½ teaspon salt
¼ teaspoon pepper
1 large egg
1 tablespoon water
½ cup grated Parmesan cheese
½ cup seasoned Italian bread crumbs

3-4 tablespoons butter or margarine
3-4 tablespoons corn oil
¼-⅓ cup lemon juice
2 lemons peeled and thinly sliced
2 tablespoons chopped parsley

Put chicken breasts between wax paper. Pound to flatten.

Combine flour, salt and pepper in one dish. Beat egg with water in a second dish. Combine cheese and bread crumbs in a third dish.

Dredge chicken breasts with flour, coating well. Dip floured breasts into egg mixture, then roll in cheese and crumb mixture. Pat firmly. Place on waxpaper and let set in refrigerator 15 minutes to 2 hours.

Heat 1 tablespoon butter and 1 tablespoon oil in large skillet. Sauté cutlets of chicken, 2 or 3 at a time, on both sides until browned and cooked through. Remove, drain and keep warm on platter. Add remaining butter and oil to skillet as needed for remaining breasts. Remove brown bits from drippings.

Heat any remaining butter or oil in pan. Stir in lemon juice (amount depends on individual taste) and sliced lemons into pan drippings. Heat but do not boil. Spoon over the chicken, sprinkle with parsley and serve. Serves: 6-8

Chicken Olé

4 whole chicken breasts, skinned, boned and halved
¼ cup flour
⅓ cup olive oil
1 medium onion, sliced
1 cup tomato sauce
½ teaspoon oregano

½ teaspoon sugar
1 tablespoon parsley, chopped
Salt and pepper to taste
1 cup seedless raisins
½ cup green olives, chopped
2 medium tomatoes, sliced

Coat chicken breasts with flour. Brown chicken on all sides over medium heat in oil. Remove chicken to casserole. Sauté onions in drippings in skillet until lightly brown. Add tomato sauce, oregano, sugar and parsley. Mix well. Salt and pepper to taste.

Add tomato mixture to chicken and cover. Bake in preheated oven at 375 degrees for 40 minutes. Add raisins and olives. Bake for 5 minutes. Add sliced tomatoes and return to oven for 5 minutes. Serves: 8

Chicken Cacciatore

2 (3 pound) chickens, cut in serving pieces
½ cup olive oil
½ cup butter
8 ounces fresh mushrooms, sliced
2 large onions, chopped
1 green pepper, chopped
5 garlic cloves, minced
1 teaspoon dried basil
1 (16½ ounces) can Italian plum tomatoes
¼ cup dry red wine
1 pound bay scallops (optional)
¼ teaspoon salt
⅛ teaspoon pepper
8 ounces medium egg noodles, boiled and drained

Preheat oven to 350 degrees.

Sauté chicken in olive oil and butter until brown. Remove to a shallow 9x13 inch baking dish. In the oil and butter, sauté mushrooms, onions, pepper and garlic until soft. Add basil, tomatoes, red wine and scallops. Bring to a boil. Add salt and pepper. Taste to adjust seasonings. Pour mixture over chicken and bake uncovered for 30 minutes or until tender. Place chicken on a serving platter. Mix noodles in the baking dish with the sauce and toss well. Arrange sauce and noodles around chicken on platter. Serves: 6-8

Easy Barbecue Chicken

2 fryer chickens, cut in pieces
2 medium onions, sliced
1 cup tomato ketchup
1 (16 ounce) bottle hickory smoked barbecue sauce
¾ cup maple syrup
¼ cup corn oil
½ teaspoon Tabasco sauce
Salt to taste
2 tablespoons flour
¼ cup water

Place chicken skin side up in large shallow pan. Tuck onion slices between the chicken pieces. Mix other ingredients excluding the flour and water. Pour over the chicken and onions. Bake uncovered in 350 degree oven for 1½ hours or until tender.

Remove chicken from pan. Mix flour and water; stir into sauce. Cook 2-3 minutes stirring constantly until it thickens. Pour over chicken and serve. Serves: 6-8

Chicken in French Apricot Sauce

1 (8 ounce) jar apricot
   preserves
1 envelope onion soup mix

1 (8 ounce) jar French
   dressing
2 chickens, quartered

Mix first 3 ingredients and spread over chicken. Bake at 350 degrees for 1½ hours. Garnish with fresh parsley. Serves: 8

Chicken Curry

8 chicken thighs
4 tablespoons butter
½ cup chopped onions
⅛ teaspoon ground cloves
⅛ teaspoon ground cinnamon
⅛ teaspoon ground black
   pepper

¼ teaspoon ground cumin
⅛ teaspoon paprika
½ teaspoon salt
½ teaspoon grated garlic
½ teaspoon grated ginger
3 tablespoons tomato paste

Melt butter in a 10 inch fry pan, add onions and brown. Place thighs in the same pan and brown lightly. Mix dry ingredients, garlic, fresh ginger and tomato paste with a little water to form a sauce. Pour over chicken. Stir well. Reduce heat to low and cook for 1 hour or until chicken is tender.

Garnish with parsley and slivered almonds. Serves: 4

Indonesian Chicken Wings and Szechwan Noodles

3-4 dozen chicken wings
 1 cup honey
 ¾ cup soy sauce
 ¼ cup pureed garlic
 ½ cup fresh grated ginger

Sauce for Noodles:
13 garlic cloves
 1 inch-long piece fresh
   ginger
 ½ cup rice vinegar
 ¼ cup sesame seed oil

 1 teaspoon Szechwan
   peppercorns, ground to a
   fine powder
 5 tablespoons sesame paste
   (optional Taheeni, sold in
   most health food stores)
 1 cup soy sauce
 2 teaspoons sugar
 1 pound Chinese rice noodles
   or whole wheat noodles
A few whole scallions or
   green onions for garnish

Discard wing tips and separate wing sections. Heat honey, mix in other ingredients (listed under chicken wings), and pour over chicken wings. Place in large shallow pan. Cover tightly with foil and bake at 325 degrees for 1½ hours. Remove foil and bake 15 minutes at 375 degrees.

Meanwhile, prepare sauce. Using processor, make a paste of the garlic and ginger, then add all sauce ingredients, mixing thoroughly. Set aside. Boil noodles according to package directions. Drain well. Toss together with the sauce until they glisten. Top with the chicken wings and garnish with scallions or green onions. Serves: 8-10

Note: Sesame paste may be made by roasting the seeds and blending them in the processor with the addition of a small amount of oil.

KILLDEER

Coq au Vin

4 tablespoons butter
2 tablespoons olive oil
¼ pound bacon, cubed
12 small onions, peeled
3 pound chicken, cut up
½ cup flour
12 small mushrooms
½ teaspoon salt
⅛ teaspoon pepper
2 cloves garlic

1 sprig thyme or ½ teaspoon dried thyme
2 bay leaves
2 sprigs parsley
4 tablespoons cognac, warmed
1½ cups good red wine
1 teaspoon sugar
1 tablespoon flour
Chopped parsley for garnish

Heat 3 tablespoons butter and 2 tablespoons oil with bacon cubes in a heat-proof casserole. Add onions when bacon begins to turn golden. Cook together 1 to 2 minutes. Remove bacon and onions.

Roll chicken in flour. Sauté in drippings, 5 minutes per side, or until golden. Return onions and bacon to the casserole. Add mushrooms, salt, pepper, garlic, thyme, bay leaves and parsley. Cover and bake in 350 degree oven until tender, about 1½ hours.

Remove chicken, vegetables and bacon from casserole. Skim excess fat from pan juices. Pour in cognac and ignite. Have cover available if flames shoot too high. Flame for 1 to 2 minutes. Add wine and sugar; bring to a boil and reduce sauce by ½. Thicken with a mixture of 1 tablespoon flour and 1 tablespoon butter. Strain sauce into serving casserole. Add chicken and vegetables. Simmer, covered, in a very slow oven until ready to serve. Garnish with finely chopped parsley.

Ballottine of Chicken

1 large roasting chicken (5 to 7 pounds) or two 3 pound chickens
5 ounces (approximately) boiled ham, cut into ½ inch strips
3 tablespoons brandy or sherry
1 large onion, finely chopped and sautéed
½ pound ground pork (bulk pork sausage)
1 pound ground chuck
1 teaspoon salt
½ teaspoon black pepper
1 clove garlic, mashed
¼ teaspoon dried tarragon
¼ teaspoon dried thyme
2 eggs, slightly beaten
¾ cup yogurt
¾ cup bread crumbs (from day-old bread)
½ cup minced parsley
½ cup minced chives (or green onions)
2 tablespoons clarified butter
½ cup white wine
½ to 1 cup chicken stock

Skin the chicken; Chop off wings and ball joints at the ends of the drumsticks. Make a cut down the back bone; ease skin off carcass, keeping skin in one, untorn piece.

Carefully remove the breast meat from the carcass and slice it into one-half inch strips. Place the chicken skin, the sliced breast strips and ham strips into a small bowl. Sprinkle with brandy. Cover and refrigerate until ready to use.

Remove remaining meat from the chicken carcass and chop in a food processor. Add the sautéed onions, pork sausage, ground chuck, spices, beaten eggs, yogurt, bread crumbs, parsley and chives; mix everything in the food processor.

Lay the reserved chicken skin, boned side up on a piece of waxed paper.   Spread ⅓ of the ground meat mixture over the skin leaving a ¾ inch border. Then place the reserved chicken and ham strips in alternating layers with the remaining ground meat. With a large strong needle and heavy thread, sew the chicken up to resemble its original shape or a plump roll. Tie the chicken roll with kitchen string in several places.

To cook the chicken: Brown the chicken on all sides in clarified butter. Place it in an oval shaped roasting pan. Bring wine and chicken stock to a boil and pour over chicken. Cover tightly. Bake in a preheated 350 degree oven for 1½ to 2 hours. The chicken is done at a thermometer reading of 170 degrees. Cut in slices; serve either hot or cold. Make gravy, if desired, with the pan juices.

Note: Chicken bundle may be prepared and frozen before baking. If frozen, defrost in refrigerator for 12 hours.

Badlands Pitchfork Fondue

Pitchfork fondues are prepared every Saturday night during the summer months in Medora, North Dakota.

1 (50 gallon) cast iron hog-scalding kettle, jacketed in steel to create a "firebox" with damper control. This may be placed on a grate over an open fire or a gas burner.
Beef tallow, enough to nearly fill your kettle when melted, (15-20 pounds), available from your butcher shop
Big bundle of dry ash or similar hot-burning firewood.
3-4-5-tong pitchforks, seasoned by normal farmyard use, cleaned.
8, 10 or 12 ounce rib eye steaks (other cuts will work, but Teddy Roosevelt loved RIB EYES.)
Season with Lawry's Salt

Several hours before "eat'n" time, build a roaring fire under the kettle. Desired temperature of melted tallow or oil should be 375 degrees. Place steaks on the pitchfork with at least 2, preferably 3, tines used. Plan 8-10 steaks per fork. Immerse in kettle and hold 3-4 minutes depending on thickness of steak and desired "doneness".

Note: If this sounds like too much work, the Wranglers in Medora love to do it for you.

BIG BLUESTEM GRASS

Pit Roast

This method of roasting meat for a large group is a favorite at summertime family reunions and Fourth of July picnics.

6-pound beef roast: sirloin tip, rump or rolled roast
Favorite seasonings: salt, onions, Worcestershire sauce, Tabasco,
chili powder, bay leaves, oregano

The Meat

Each roast should weigh about 6 pounds. Use as many roasts as determined by the size of the guest list, figuring approximately ½ pound per person. Use favorite seasonings or depend on an experienced butcher to flavor your roast or roasts.

The Pit

The pit should be about 3-feet deep and large enough to spread the meat out on the coals in a single, uncrowded layer, allowing a little space around each roast. The width should be 3-feet while the length is determined by the quantity of meat.

The Fire

Start the fire with hard wood about 3-6 hours before cooking time. The fire needs to be replenished until the coals have built up to a depth of 1 to 2 feet. Rocks or scrap metal may be added to coals to help retain the heat.

The Roast

Wrap each roast, in heavy duty foil using a drugstore wrap (fold over meat from end and sides and tightly roll). Wrap in 2 thicknesses of burlap which have been soaked in water for 30 minutes. Burlap must be wet. Wrap with wire leaving a tail long enough to reach the surface after covering with dirt. (This wire will help locate the cooked roast.) Place wrapped meat on coals. Quickly cover with a piece of galvanized tin and pile on 1-2 feet of dirt, being careful not to lose the locater wire. There should be no steam escaping. If steam appears, continue to cover with dirt. After 8 hours, uncover. Remove the wrappings from the meat and serve.

Time table: 8 hours in the pit for a 6-pound roast or roasts.

Standing Rib Roast

It is generally agreed that a standing rib of beef makes the best roast. The meat should be graded Prime or Choice. The most desirable cut in the small end (nearest the loin) and corresponds to rib numbers 12, 11, 10, 9 and 8. Carving is facilitated if the butcher trims the roast properly, loosens the meat from the ribs and saws off the backbone. The meat (rib eye) is then securely tied to the ribs for roasting. Choose a roast that is at least 3 ribs in size (6-8 pounds) and estimate 1 pound per person.

Let the meat stand at room temperature at least 1½ hours before roasting. Pre-heat oven to 325 degrees. Place the roast, fat side up, in a shallow roasting pan. Season with salt and pepper before, during or after roasting. Insert a meat thermometer so the tip is in the center of the thickest part of the roast and does not touch bone or rest in fat. Roast the meat for about 2 to 2½ hours for medium. Use the meat thermometer as a final guide: 140 degrees for rare, 160 degrees for medium, 180 degrees for well done.

Remove roast from oven and let stand for 15 to 20 minutes before carving. Cut the string and remove the ribs. Carve the roast into thick or thin, delicate slices. Serve the meat on a hot platter. Spoon a little meat juice over the slices and pass the remainder in a sauce boat.

Meat Juice:
Remove the excess fat from the pan juices. Pour in 1 to 2 cups of beef stock. Heat to simmer while stirring and scraping the pan. Strain and correct seasoning before serving.

Standing Rib Roast of Beef (Alternate Method)

Select a 12-pound prime rib roast. Have your butcher loosen meat from rib bones and tie all together with string.

Let meat stand at room temperature for 1½ hours before roasting. Early in the day, preheat oven to 375 degrees. Place rib roast on a rack in roasting pan, rib side down. Roast 1 hour. Turn oven off. Do not open oven door all day. Roast must stay in oven, undisturbed, for at least 5 hours.

40 minutes before serving, turn oven on again to 375 degrees. After 40 minutes roast should be pink all the way through. Remove roast from oven. Cut strings and let stand for 15 minutes before cutting into serving slices.

Deviled Rib Bones
(Use with the Standing Rib Roast Recipe)

4 freshly roasted rib bones	3 tablespoons cream
Salt and pepper to taste	½ cup of fine dry bread crumbs
2 tablespoons prepared English mustard	3 tablespoons melted butter

Sprinkle ribs with salt and pepper. Make a paste of the mustard and cream and coat the ribs. Sprinkle generously with the bread crumbs and dot with the melted butter. Place under the broiler until crisp and crusty. Turn to brown on all sides.

Eat with fingers.

Marinated Beef Tenderloin

One (3-4 pound) beef tenderloin	2 tablespoons vinegar
½ cup oil	2 teaspoons salt
¼ cup lemon juice	2 tablespoons sugar
1 tablespoon paprika	2 garlic cloves, crushed
2 tablespoons Worcestershire sauce	3-4 bacon strips
⅟₁₆ teaspoon Tabasco	

Mix all ingredients except bacon strips in screw-top jar. Cover and shake vigorously. Pour over meat and marinate for 2 hours. Remove meat from marinade. Secure bacon strips on top of meat. Place on barbecue grill with a cover. Bake 11 minutes per pound. Serve with Béarnaise sauce.

Béarnaise Sauce for Tenderloin:	3 egg yolks
2 shallots or green onions, minced	½ teaspoon salt
½ cup white wine	½ cup butter, cut in pieces
2 teaspoons dried tarragon leaves	

Cook onion, wine and tarragon over medium-high heat until reduced to almost 1 tablespoon. Cool slightly. Place egg yolks and salt in processor. Process until thick, about 1 minute. Add cooled liquid and continue processing. Add butter, 2 tablespoons at a time, through feed tube. Makes 1 cup.

Beef Tenderloin with Mustard Caper Sauce

1 (4 pound) beef tenderloin
3 tablespoons olive oil

4 tablespoons dried oregano (or more of fresh)

Let tenderloin stand at room temperature for 30 minutes. Rub all sides with oil.

Prepare coals. Set grill three inches above coals.

Set beef on grill and cook about eight minutes. Turn and continue cooking, frequently sprinkling coals with oregano, until meat thermometer inserted in thickest part of meat registers 135 degrees for medium rare (or more for more well done meat). Remove and let cool.

When ready to serve, slice meat thinly and arrange on platter in overlapping pattern. Spoon mustard sauce down center and pass remainder.

Mustard Caper Sauce:
3 generous tablespoons of coarsely ground French mustard
2 egg yolks, room temperature
1 small green onion, chopped

¼ teaspoon marjoram
2 tablespoons lemon juice
1 cup light olive oil
¼-½ cup whipping cream
1½ tablespoons capers, rinsed and drained

Combine first five ingredients in processor and mix until pale and creamy. With machine running, gradually add oil through feed tube in thin stream. Add cream and capers.

Serves: 6-8

98   GREAT BLUE HERON

Grilled Stuffed Beef Tenderloin with Bordelaise Sauce

½ cup butter
¾ pound fresh mushrooms,
  finely chopped
6 ounces cooked ham, diced
½ cup green onions, minced
¼ teaspoon salt

¼ teaspoon pepper
3 cups white bread, cubed
2 tablespoons water
2 beef tenderloin roasts (1½
  pounds each)
1½ pound bacon

About 1½ hours before serving, or early in the day, prepare the mushroom stuffing: In a large skillet over medium heat, melt butter. Add mushrooms, ham, green onions, salt and pepper. Cook until vegetables are tender, stirring frequently. Remove skillet from heat. Add bread cubes and water. Toss gently to mix well. Set aside until you are ready to stuff the tenderloin roasts.

Preparing the roasts: Make a lengthwise cut about 1½ inches deep along center of each roast. Spoon half the mushroom mixture into each roast, packing mixture firmly. Wrap one slice of bacon at a time around each roast, overlapping each slice. Secure bacon with poultry skewers.

Roast over hot coals on the grill 15 minutes each side for medium to rare or longer for desired doneness. Let stand 10 minutes before slicing. Serve with a Bordelaise sauce. Keep roasts on warm platter before serving.

Bordelaise Sauce:
4 shallots, minced
3 tablespoons butter
1½ cups red wine
½ teaspoon thyme
½ teaspoon marjoram

1½ cups beef bouillon
½ teaspoon lemon juice
2 tablespoons parsley,
  chopped
2 tablespoons flour
  Salt
  Pepper

Sauté shallots in two tablespoons of the butter until they are transparent. Do not brown. Add the wine, thyme, and marjoram and simmer rapidly until it is reduced to half its quantity. Add bouillon and simmer for about 5-10 minutes. Add lemon juice and parsley and simmer again for 5 minutes. Add remaining 1 tablespoon butter.

Thicken with 2 tablespoons flour mixed with a little water to make a medium paste. Add to sauce very slowly to avoid lumps. Salt and pepper to taste. Pour over beef tenderloins and serve. Serves: 8

Pizzaiola Steak

4 (6-8 ounce) tenderloin
   steaks, 1½-2 inches thick,
   fat trimmed
2 tablespoons butter
½ cup sliced green pimento
   olives
¾ teaspoon salt
¼ teaspoon freshly ground
   pepper
¼ cup dry vermouth
¼ cup heavy whipping cream
   Sliced pimento

Melt butter in heavy skillet, add fillets and olives. Add salt and pepper. Cook over high heat until brown on all sides (about two minutes on each side).

Add vermouth to pan. Spoon in heavy cream and add pimento.

The above can be done in mid-afternoon, if desired, or just continue to cook over low heat four minutes or more to the degree of rareness desired. Arrange on slightly toasted English muffins or buttered toast rounds. Pour sauce over steak with olives and pimento on top.

Use more vermouth and whipping cream for additional sauce. A baked Italian vegetable dish is just right with the steak. Serves: 4.

Nuernberger Sauerbraten
(Marinated Beef Roast)

4-5 pound beef roast
  3 tablespoons bacon
    drippings
5 juniper berries
2 teaspoons salt
2 tablespoons sugar

Marinade:
  2 cups water
  2 cups wine vinegar (or 1 cup
    vinegar and 1 cup wine)
  2 onions, chopped
  1 carrot, diced
8-10 peppercorns
  2 whole cloves
  2 bayleaves

Gravy:
  1 cup sour cream
 ¼ cup flour
 ¼ cup butter
 ¼ cup red wine
  3 cups liquid (reserved
    cooking liquid and enough
    marinade to make 3 cups)
    Salt and pepper to taste

Put roast in large bowl. Combine all ingredients for marinade in saucepan, bring to boil and remove from heat immediately. Let cool. Pour over meat. Refrigerate tightly covered for 3-4 days, turning meat over daily. Remove from marinade and drain well. Save strained marinade.

Brown meat in 3 tablespoons bacon drippings on all sides. Add 2 cups marinade, bring to boil and reduce heat. Cover tightly and simmer 3 hours or until tender. Baste with marinade about every ½ hour, adding more if needed. Remove meat and keep warm. Make gravy. Brown flour in butter until golden brown. Add cooking liquid, cooking until thickened. Add sour cream. Stir until smooth. Salt and pepper to taste.

Best when served with Bavarian potato dumplings and red cabbage. Dumpling mix is available in supermarkets under the name of "Panni". Serves: 8

Russian Pot Roast

3-4 pound beef blade or round
    bone chuck roast about
    two inches thick
1 tablespoon fat
1 medium onion, chopped
1 bay leaf
¼ teaspoon salt

¾ cup water
1 tablespoon brown sugar
2 tablespoons cider vinegar
3 tablespoons ketchup
⅓ cup raisins
½ cup cool water
1 tablespoon cornstarch

Melt fat in heavy skillet or Dutch oven., Brown roast well on each side. Add onion, bay leaf, salt and ¾ cup water. Cover tightly and cook slowly on top of range or in a 325 to 350 degree oven for 1½ hours.

Mix together and add brown sugar, vinegar, ketchup and raisins. Cover and continue cooking about 1 hour, or until meat is tender. Remove roast to a hot platter.

To make gravy, skim excess fat from broth. Stir ½ cup cool water into cornstarch. Mix until smooth. Add to liquid, cook and stir until gravy is clear and thickened. Serve gravy over hot roast beef slices. Serve with cooked rice, cooked barley, or mashed potatoes.

Dona Lucia's Mexican Biftec

4 pound boneless beef top
    round, sirloin tip, or rump
2 tablespoons oil
2 tablespoons vinegar
5 medium tomatoes, peeled
    and chopped
1 large onion, chopped

3-5 cloves of garlic, minced
½ teaspoon leaf oregano,
    dried
1 bay leaf
5 whole cloves
    Salt and black pepper to
    taste

Have the butcher slice the meat ¼" thick across the grain. Cut the slices into smaller pieces (approximately 2x3x¼).

Film the bottom of a 5-6 quart roasting pan with one tablespoon of oil.

In a medium bowl, mix the vinegar, tomatoes, onions, garlic, oregano, cloves and bay leaf.

Place one layer of meat in the roasting pan. Sprinkle lightly with salt and pepper. Spread some of the onion-tomato mixture over the meat. Repeat layers, ending with onion-tomato on top. Sprinkle remaining tablespoon of oil over top.

Cover tightly and bake in the oven at 325 degrees for 2½-3 hours. Serve with rice and refried beans. May be refrigerated and reheated. Also freezes well. Serves: 8-10

Hungarian Roast

6 pounds lean sirloin tip roast
1 teaspoon salt
¼ teaspoon pepper
1 tablespoon paprika
¾ pound Canadian bacon,
  thinly sliced
1 pound Swiss cheese, thinly
  sliced
¼ cup oil

Sauce:
2 tablespoons fat from
  roasting pan
1 teaspoon flour
1 cup sour cream
¼ cup white wine
¼ cup water
Salt and pepper, to taste
Water cress

Early in the day, cut roast crosswise to a depth of ¾-1 inch into 10 slices. Sprinkle roast top and slices with salt, pepper and paprika. In each cut, place three bacon slices, side by side, and 1 slice of Swiss cheese.

Tie roast lengthwise securely. Set on rack in shallow roasting pan. Refrigerate. Preheat oven to 375 degrees.

In a small saucepan, heat the oil and pour over top and sides of meat. Roast uncovered for thirty minutes, then reduce heat to 325 degrees. Cover with foil, basting occasionally. Use meat thermometer for desired degree of doneness. When done, remove roast to large serving platter. Remove strings.

Take 2 tablespoons of fat from the roasting pan and place in a clean saucepan. Add flour, sour cream, wine, water, salt and pepper to taste. Stir until smooth. Serve over meat or in a gravy dish. Garnish each slice with water cress. Serves: 10

Polynesian Chuck Steak

3 pound beef blade roast or
  round steak 2 inches thick
1 teaspoon pepper
1 cup water
¾ cup soy sauce
¼ cup brown sugar
¼ cup wine vinegar

¼ cup sherry
¼ teaspoon onion powder
¼ teaspoon garlic powder
½ teaspoon salt (optional)
1 teaspoon crystalized ginger
½ teaspoon dry mustard

Put meat in glass pan. Sprinkle ½ teaspoon pepper over one side of meat. Prick with fork. Mix remaining ingredients, except pepper. Pour marinade over meat and let set for one hour. Turn. Sprinkle with ½ teaspoon pepper and prick. Marinate 24 hours. Broil 15 minutes on each side adding marinade as needed. Serves: 6

Steak "Sandbar" Style

6 steaks, any cut suitable for grilling
½ pound soft butter
4 ounces well-aged blue cheese
1 tablespoon finely chopped green onions

1 tablespoon fresh rosemary or basil (dried may be substituted) use 1 teaspoon dried

Mix butter, cheese, onions and herbs. Shape into a roll. Take to picnic wrapped in plastic wrap. When steak is taken from grill top each with a generous portion of cheese roll.

Stuffed Sirloin Steak

2 pounds sirloin boneless steak cut 1½ inches thick
3 ounces blue cheese

1 tablespoon onions, minced
2 tablespoons fine dry bread crumbs

Have butcher cut a pocket in steak, being careful not to cut through the fatty part.

Mash blue cheese with fork. Stir in onions and bread crumbs. Spread mixture in pocket of steak.

Broil 3 inches from heat about 8 minutes on each side for rare. Turn carefully so stuffing doesn't fall out. An outdoor grill may also be used.

Allow to stand 2-3 minutes before slicing and serving. Serves: 3-4

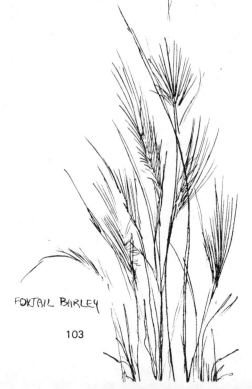

FOXTAIL BARLEY

Flank Steak Stuffed with Spinach

1 flank steak, 1½ pounds

Filling:

4 cups chopped spinach leaves	2 tablespoons oil and 1 tablespoon butter
3-5 chopped green onions	
2 tablespoons plain yogurt	½ cup dry white wine
¼ teaspoon dill weed	½ cup chicken broth
1 beaten egg	1 tablespoon mustard
½ cup finely grated Parmesan cheese	2 teaspoons flour
Salt and pepper, to taste	¼ cup cream

Sauté spinach and green onions in 1 tablespoon oil for 5 minutes. Add yogurt, dill weed, beaten egg, cheese, salt and pepper. Set aside.

Steak: Flatten flank steak between 2 pieces of waxed paper. Salt and pepper lightly. Spread cooled spinach mixture evenly over the meat. Roll steak, jellyroll fashion. Secure the roll with skewers along the seams and ends. Brown lightly in 2 tablespoons oil and 1 tablespoon butter in a roasting pan. Add ½ cup dry white wine and ½ cup chicken broth. Bring to boil. Remove from heat. Cover meat with foil and lid. Bake in 325 degree oven for 1 hour and 300 degrees for another 2 hours. Occasionally baste with meat juices.

Strain juice from the roasting pan. If liquid is less than 1 cup, add more chicken broth. Add the mustard and flour dissolved in a little water and the cream. Stir and bring sauce to boil. Correct seasoning, if necessary. Slice meat roll crosswise and serve with sauce. Serves: 4

Variation: Substitute 1½ pounds round steak.

London Broil

1½ pounds flank steak	½ teaspoon ginger
1 tablespoon unseasoned tenderizer	½ teaspoon garlic powder
	2 tablespoons dry onion flakes
¼-½ cup soy sauce	
2 tablespoons honey	

Pierce steak with fork on both sides and sprinkle with tenderizer. Make marinade with remaining ingredients and marinate steak 24 hours in refrigerator. Drain.

Broil 7 minutes on each side for medium well.

Slice on the diagonal and serve. Serves: 3

Barbecued Beef

5 pound sirloin or rump roast
2 cups onions, sliced
Salt and pepper

1 (16 ounce) jar barbecue sauce or your own homemade

Salt and pepper roast and cover with sliced onions. Bake covered at 350 degrees until done, about 2½-3 hours.

Remove from oven and let stand about 20 minutes. Slice roast and arrange in crock pot. Mix meat juices with barbecue sauce and pour over meat. Cook on low for about 8 hours. Serves: 8-10

Variation: Arrange meat in large casserole dish, cover and bake at 300 degrees for 4 hours. The meat gets very tender and moist.

Barbecue Sauce:
2 cloves minced garlic (optional)
1 teaspoon salt
1 teaspoon chili powder
1 teaspoon celery seed
¼ cup brown sugar

¼ cup vinegar
¼ cup Worcestershire sauce
1 cup ketchup
2 cups water
Few drops Tabasco
½ cup sherry

Mix in large saucepan and immer ½ hour.

Variation: Cook 1 grated onion and 1 minced clove of garlic 5 minutes in ¼ cup butter and add to the sauce.

McCormick Stew and Dumplings

3 pounds cubed beef or venison
3 tablespoons fat or oil
4 cups boiling water
2 teaspoons salt
2 cups dry white wine
2 teaspoons pepper
½ cup flour

3 small diced onions
8 carrots cut in 1" slices
1 cup diced celery
4 diced potatoes
1 teaspoon parsley
2 cups mushrooms, diced
1 (11 ounce) can biscuits

Melt fat in Dutch oven. Add meat and brown. Add water, wine, salt, pepper and parsley. Cover tightly and simmer 3½ hours.

Add vegetables last 30 minutes of cooking. Thicken with flour as desired. Use canned biscuits to cover top of stew.

Cook 12 minutes covered. Serves: 8-10

Beef Stroganoff

2 pounds fillet of beef
4 tablespoons butter
1 cup chopped onion
1 clove garlic, chopped
½ pound fresh mushrooms, sliced ¼ inch thick
3 tablespoons flour
2 teaspoons meat-extract paste
1 tablespoon ketchup
½ teaspoon salt
⅛ teaspoon pepper
1 (10½ ounce) can beef bouillon
¼ cup dry white wine
1 tablespoon snipped fresh dill or ¼ teaspoon dried dill weed
1½ cup sour cream
4 cups cooked wild or white rice or a mixture of both

Trim fat from beef and cut crosswise into ½ inch slices. Cut each slice across grain into ½ inch wide strips.

Slowly heat large, heavy skillet. Melt 1 tablespoon butter. Add beef strips. Sear quickly on all sides and remove from pan with tongs.

Heat 3 tablespoons butter in same skillet; sauté onion, garlic and mushrooms until onion is golden. Remove from heat. Add flour, meat-extract, ketchup, salt and pepper; stir until smooth. Gradually add bouillon. Bring to a boil, stirring. Reduce heat. Simmer 5 minutes. Over low heat add the wine, dill and sour cream stirring until well combined. Add beef. Simmer until hot.

Serve over rice with dill or parsley. Serves: 4-6

Beef Roulades

Top round steak or sirloin tip cut into six slices, ½ inch thick x 6 inches x 4 inches
¾ pound ground pork
1 teaspoon poultry seasoning
¾ teaspoon salt
½ clove garlic, crushed
2 tablespoons finely chopped onion
¼ cup soft white bread crumbs
6 slices bacon
3 tablespoons butter or margarine
1½ pounds small white onions, peeled
⅓ cup unsifted all-purpose flour
1 tablespoon meat-extract paste* (optional Kitchen Bouquet)
1 (10½ ounce) can condensed beef bouillon, undiluted
2½ cups red Burgundy or Bordeaux
1½ pound fresh mushrooms
1 bay leaf
1 tablespoon chopped parsley

Wipe beef with damp paper towels. Combine ground pork, poultry seasoning, salt, garlic, chopped onion and crumbs. Toss the mixture lightly to mix well. Place about ¼ cup pork mixture on each beef slice. Roll up from short side. Wrap each with a strip of bacon. Tie with string. In hot butter in Dutch oven brown beef roulades on all sides, removing them as they brown. Add onions. Brown on all sides. Remove Dutch oven from heat. Stir in flour and meat-extract paste. Gradually stir in bouillon and wine. Bring to boiling, stirring. Return roulades to Dutch oven with mushrooms and bay leaf. Meanwhile, preheat oven to 350 degrees. Bake roulades covered for two hours or until tender. If sauce seems too thick, thin with a little more wine. Discard bay leaf.

To serve: Remove string from roulades. Arrange roulades in center of a large, heated platter. Surround with onions and mushrooms. Spoon some of sauce over all. Sprinkle vegetables with chopped parsley. Pass rest of sauce. Serves: 6.

GOLDENROD

Sukiyaki

2 tablespoons lard, or other shortening
Sugar
2 pounds thinly sliced sirloin tip
2 bunches green onions, cut in 3 inch pieces
½ Chinese cabbage, cut in 3 inch pieces
1 package dried Japanese mushrooms soaked for one hour in warm water
1 (8 ounce) can sliced bamboo shoots, drained

1 medium potato, thinly sliced or 1 slightly cooked sliced carrot
1 (8 ounce) can or carton bean curd, drained and cubed

Sauce:
3 tablespoons soy sauce
1 tablespoon sugar
2 tablespoons sake (or dry sherry)
½ cup water

Combine sauce ingredients and set aside. Heat skillet and add two tablespoons lard. Sprinkle meat with a little sugar. Brown meat and add other vegetables and cook until done, adding sauce as you cook to keep sukiyaki from getting dry. Serves: 6-8

Indonesian Saté

½ cup soy sauce
¼ cup brown sugar
2 tablespoons olive oil
1 teaspoon ground ginger
¼ teaspoon cracked pepper

2 cloves garlic, minced
1½ pounds top sirloin steak, 1 inch thick, cut in strips ¼ inch wide

In a deep bowl, combine soy sauce, brown sugar, oil, ginger, pepper, and garlic. Mix well. Add meat and stir to coat. Let stand two hours at room temperature. Lace meat, accordian-style, on skewers. Broil over hot coals 10 to 12 minutes, or to rare or medium-rare stage, turning often and basting with marinade. Serves: 4

Huevos De Torritos or Prairie Oysters
(A prairie delicacy from a young male calf)

1 pint prairie oysters
1 cup cracker crumbs, finely crushed
1 egg, beaten
4 tablespoons butter and oil combination

¼ teaspoon salt
⅛ teaspoon pepper
1½ cups tomato base seafood sauce

Blanch oysters in boiling water for 2-3 minutes. When cool enough to handle peel outer membrane. Dip in egg and cracker crumbs. Sauté lightly in butter until no pink appears when slashed, about 5-7 minutes on medium heat. Serve with toothpicks and cocktail sauce.

Veal Smetana

12 veal scallops (veal round steak can be used — must be trimmed and pounded)
Flour and salt
6-8 tablespoons butter
1 large onion, finely slivered

1 pound sliced mushrooms
¼ cup brandy or more if needed
1 cup sour cream
¼-½ teaspoon salt

Sprinkle veal with salt, then flour. Heat two tablespoons butter in frying pan or chafing dish. Cook veal 3 minutes per side. Do not crowd. Remove to warm platter.

Cook rest of veal. Add onion to pan and sauté for 3 minutes. Add 2 tablespoons more butter and mushrooms and cook for 6-7 minutes, or until mushrooms are tender. You may need to stir the mixture occasionally. Add brandy to pan. Keeping your face away from it, light with a match. After the brandy has finished burning, add sour cream and salt. Heat just to boiling. Add veal to warm it. Do not let it boil. Serves: 6

Veal Chops with Sorrel Sauce

6 veal chops
Salt and pepper

6 tablespoons butter

Brown chops well in hot butter. Reduce heat to low and simmer until tender (about 15 minutes). Do not overcook. Season to taste.

Sauce:
3 tablespoons finely chopped carrots
3 tablespoons finely chopped onion
1½ cups dry white wine

3 tablespoons beef broth
1½ cups whipping cream
1½ cups chopped fresh sorrel leaves (easy to grow in garden or pot, do not substitute dried)
Chopped parsley

Add carrots, onion, wine and beef broth to pan drippings. Reduce liquid to half. Add cream and reduce to half again. Stir in sorrel and pour over chops. Sprinkle with parsley. Serves: 6

Note: If fresh sorrel is not available substitute 1½ cups fresh chopped spinach or watercress and 1 tablespoon fresh lemon juice.

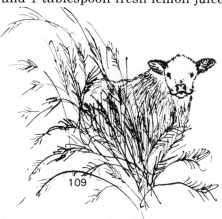

109

Korma (Indian Lamb Stew)

This is one of our favorites!

3 tablespoons chopped garlic cloves
3 tablespoons chopped ginger root
1 cup plain yogurt
¼ cup cashews
2 teaspoons poppy seed
½-¾ cup unsalted butter, approximately
2 large onions, chopped
2 pounds lean lamb, cut into 3-inch strips, 1¼ inches wide, ¼ inch thick

2 teaspoons ground coriander
1½ teaspoons curry powder
1 teaspoon ground cumin
1 teaspoon salt
¼ teaspoon cayenne pepper
½ teaspoon ground turmeric
¼ teaspoon ground cardamom
¼ teaspoon cinnamon
1 (16 ounce) can whole tomatoes, drained, seeded and chopped
2-3 tablespoons chopped fresh coriander or mint

Purée garlic and ginger root in a blender. Set aside in a small dish. Mix yogurt, nuts and poppy seed in blender until smooth. Set aside. Melt butter in a large skillet. Add onion. Sauté until soft and golden-colored. Stir in garlic-ginger root purée. Add lamb and sauté until browned, stirring and turning with a spatula to prevent sticking. Reduce heat to low. Add spices and cook lamb for about 5 minutes so that it is nicely glazed. Add yogurt mixture and tomato. Combine well. Increase heat to high, stirring constantly, until mixture bubbles. Place the lamb and sauce in a rectangular 2-quart pyrex baking dish. Cover loosely with foil and bake at 300 degrees for 45 minutes, or until lamb is tender. Stir occasionally. Garnish dish with coriander or mint. Serve with rice. Serves: 4-6

Netted Leg of Lamb with Apricot Sauce

1 boneless leg of lamb, rolled and netted
½ teaspoon salt
¼ teaspoon coarsely ground pepper
1 can (1 pound 14 ounces) apricot halves, drained with syrup reserved

¼ teaspoon ground ginger
1 teaspoon grated lemon peel
2 tablespoons lemon juice
½ teaspoon whole cloves
1 tablespoon cornstarch

Season lamb roast with salt and pepper. Place on rack in shallow roasting pan. Roast in 325 degree oven 35 minutes per pound or until meat thermometer registers 180 degrees.

Combine reserved syrup, lemon peel, juice and spices. Use ½ cup to baste lamb during last 45 minutes of cooking period. When roast is done let set 10 minutes before carving. Cut netting lengthwise on upper side and peel down carefully in one piece.

In saucepan gradually stir remaining syrup mixture into cornstarch and boil ½ minute, stirring constantly. Slice apricots and add to sauce Serve with roast.

Lamb Shish Kebabs

Marinade:

¼ cup lemon juice
¼ cup dry red wine
1 clove garlic, mashed
1 teaspoon salt

1 teaspoon dried oregano leaves
1 bay leaf
½ cup olive oil

5 to 6 pound leg of lamb, boned, all fat removed and cut into 1 to 1½ inch cubes.

Mix all marinade ingredients and the cubed lamb in a large non-aluminum bowl and refrigerate several hours or overnight.

Remove meat from marinade and skewer on large or individual skewers. Reserve marinade. Grill or broil the kebabs, basting several times with the marinade and turning the skewers as necessary, for about 15 minutes or until done. Serves 8.

Situ Kamas Yabrah
(Cabbage or Grape Leaf Rolls)

1 pound ground lamb
1 cup rice, cooked
2 cloves garlic, pureed
½ teaspoon salt
½ teaspoon cinnamon

1 (6 ounce) can tomato paste, diluted with equal part of water
1 large head of cabbage

Mix meat, rice and seasonings. Parboil cabbage until leaves are wilted. Remove cabbage from water and separate leaves on a cutting board. Cut each leaf so it can be rolled. Place about 1 tablespoon meat mixture in the center of each leaf (fold sides over filling) and roll like a cigar. Line large kettle with cabbage rolls and cover with diluted tomato paste. Simmer 1 hour covered.

Note: A (one pound) jar of grapevine leaves may be used in place of cabbage.

Marinated Lamb

1 butterflied leg of lamb
¼ cup lemon juice
1 clove garlic
1 teaspoon rosemary

½ teaspoon thyme
½ teaspoon marjoram
½ teaspoon prepared mustard
2 tablespoons oil

Mix all the above ingredients and pour over meat. Marinate and chill overnight. Use long skewers to hold meat together while cooking. Barbecue about 30 to 45 minutes depending on size of leg of lamb.

Roast Suckling Pig

Suckling pig should be reserved for the piece de resistance occasion. When inviting guests, tell them your menu. Some people may be squeamish about seeing a whole pig on a platter. The best size is from 14 to 18 pounds. This size will fit an oven. The meat has a rich paté -like taste.

Stuffing:
- 1 cup onion, sliced
- 1 cup apple, peeled and sliced
- 8-10 cups drained sauerkraut

- 1 (15 pound) suckling pig
- 1 teaspoon salt
- 1 teaspoon pepper
- ½ cup soft butter
- 1 lemon or red apple
- 1 pint fresh cranberries
- 15 ivy or laurel leaves

Combine stuffing ingredients.

Prepare the pig for roasting; rub the cavity with salt and pepper, stuff loosely and close with skewers laced with string. Put a rack in a large, shallow roasting pan. Cover with heavy foil allowing plenty of overhang. Place pig on foil, bending hind legs forward and front legs back, so the pig is in a crouched position. Turn foil edges up to catch dripping. Rub pig with butter. Cover ears and tail with foil and place a foil ball, the size of an apple, in the mouth. Roast uncovered for 15 minutes at 450 degrees. Reduce heat to 325 degrees and baste frequently with butter. Allow about 30 minutes per pound baking time.

To serve, place pig on serving platter. Remove skewers and foil. Place a lemon or apple in the pig's mouth, and a cranberry, secured with a toothpick, in each eye. String cranberries and leaves into 2 garlands and place around the neck. Decorate the ears with cranberry earrings. Serves: 12, allowing 1¼ pounds per person.

Picnic Pig

1 (40 to 50 pound) dressed pig   6 apples, quartered
  Salt and pepper   6 onions, quartered
1 gallon sauerkraut, drained

Dig a trench in the ground about two feet deep and at least as long and wide as the pig. Start a wood fire in the pit several hours in advance so that it becomes very hot and is reduced to flameless, white-hot coals before roasting begins. Wood should be added a little at a time during roasting to maintain the hot fire and keep the pit filled with coals. Set metal stanchions resting on large, saucer-shaped bases at each end of the fire pit. The stanchions must have metal spurs welded onto them at upward angles on several levels between two and four feet above the bases. The spit on which the pig is threaded will rest on these spurs and can be easily raised or lowered to control the cooking temperature.

Place the heavy, metal spit through the pig lengthwise. Secure the pig to the spit with wire so that it will not slip and can be rotated during roasting. Sprinkle the cavity with salt and pepper, stuff it with sauerkraut, apples, and onions, and close it with skewers and string. Wrap the whole pig with heavy-weight aluminum foil. Lift the prepared pig over the fire, resting the spit ends on the metal spurs two feet above the ground.

Begin roasting, keeping the fire hot, and rotating the pig every fifteen minutes to assure even cooking. When fat begins dripping from the wrapping, raise the spit to a higher spur to prevent the flames from burning the meat. Test the temperature of the pig at intervals during cooking by inserting a meat thermometer into the meaty part of the hind leg. Roast until the thermometer reads 180 degrees. Cooking time should be 4 to 5 hours. Plan on one pound of dressed pig per person.

Variation: This recipe may also be followed to roast a whole lamb. Rub the lamb cavity and skin generously with a butter and chopped garlic mixture before wrapping in foil. Omit stuffing.

Note: The metal spit and spurred stanchions can be designed and made by a tinsmith or a welding shop.

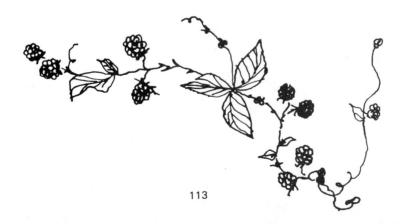

Adobo

2 pounds pork tenderloin, cut
  into 1 inch cubes
1 tablespoon butter
1 tablespoon oil
1 clove garlic, minced
1 tablespoon soy sauce
½ teaspoon black pepper

1 teaspoon salt
1 tablespoon paprika
4 tablespoons vinegar
2 cups chicken stock
3 tablespoons flour
¼ cup cold water

Sauté pork in hot butter and oil until browned. Add garlic, soy sauce, pepper, salt, paprika, vinegar and stock. Cover and simmer for one hour. Blend flour and cold water and stir slowly into meat mixture. Cook until thick, about 5 to 10 minutes. Serve with hot fluffy rice.
Serves: 6

Pork Chops Auvergne

2 small heads cabbage
2 cups heavy cream
  Salt
  Pepper

Shred cabbage and place in large saucepan; cover with water. Cook, covered, for 10 minutes, until tender. Drain cabbage. Return to saucepan. Stir in cream, salt and pepper. Cook over low heat for 20 minutes until cream is absorbed.

8 lean pork chops
6 tablespoons butter
1 teaspoon sage

1 cup dry white wine or water
  Grated parmesan cheese

Melt two tablespoons butter in skillet. Slowly brown pork chops. Remove from skillet and set aside.

Stir sage, wine or water into skillet and scrape down all brown solids. Mix in cabbage and correct seasoning.

Spoon ½ cabbage mixture into large, low baking dish. Place pork chops on top. Cover with remaining cabbage mixture. Sprinkle with Parmesan cheese and dot with 4 tablespoons butter. Bake 45 minutes at 350 degrees until surface is golden.

Baked Spareribs

4-5 pounds lean, meaty spareribs
¼ teaspoon salt
1-2 cups barbecue sauce

Place spareribs in a roasting pan. Salt lightly, cover and place in a slow oven of 275 degrees for 2 hours. Drain all fat. Spread with barbecue sauce, cover and bake an additional 30 minutes, uncovering the last 10 minues.

Barbecue Sauce:
1 cup tomato ketchup
1 cup hickory barbecue sauce
¾ cup maple syrup
¼ cup oil
¼ teaspoon Tabasco
Salt to taste

Mix all ingredients together.

Roast Loin of Pork in Ginger Marinade

2-3 pounds boneless pork loin, trimmed of all fat and tied into a cylindrical roll
1 clove of garlic, minced
1 1-inch piece of ginger root, peeled and minced
2 tablespoons soy sauce
4 tablespoons tomato sauce
1 tablespoon vinegar
4 tablespoons brown sugar
½ cup water

Place the meat into a non-aluminum bowl and cover with the marinade. Refrigerate several hours or overnight. Remove meat from marinade, place in a baking pan, and roast in a 350 degree oven for approximately 1½ to 2 hours or until the internal temperature reaches 180-185 degrees. Baste the roast with reserved marinade several times while it is baking. Serves 6 to 8.

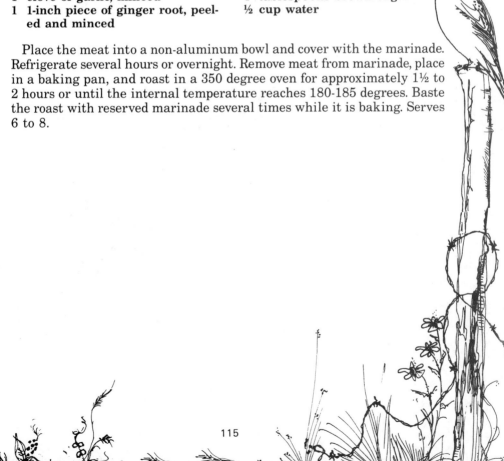

Pork Loin Roast with Sausage Stuffing

1 (5 pound) boneless pork
  loin roast, rolled
1 teaspoon seasoned salt
8 ounces bulk beef or pork
  sausage
6 slices bacon
2 tablespoons oil
1 tablespoon soy sauce

1 tablespoon vinegar
1 tablespoon molasses
¼ teaspoon pepper
1 (12 ounce) can apricot
  nectar
1 tablespoon cornstarch
Parsley

Cut string on rolled roast. Unroll and sprinkle with seasoned salt. Fill with sausage. Reroll and tie meat securely. Lay bacon strips over roast. Secure with toothpicks. Place on rack in shallow roasting pan. Roast at 325 degrees for 2½ hours or if using a barbecue unit, bake with indirect method 25-30 minutes per pound.

Combine oil, soy sauce, vinegar, molasses and pepper. Baste meat with mixture several times during latter part of roasting period.

In a sauce pan, blend apricot nectar and cornstarch. Cook and stir until mixture bubbles. Cook 1 minute more. During last 10 minutes, baste meat with some apricot sauce. Place meat on serving platter. Let stand 15 minutes. Spoon additional apricot sauce over roast. Garnish with parsley. Serves: 8-10

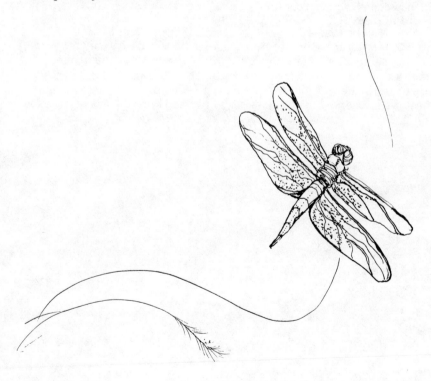

Layered Pork Tenderloin

Stuffing:

1 medium onion chopped, sautéed until soft
1 tablespoon butter
¾ pound ground veal
1 tablespoon chopped parsley
¼ teaspoon dried thyme
¼ teaspoon dried basil
¼ teaspoon dried sage
1 garlic clove, minced with 1 teaspoon salt
½ teaspoon black pepper
1 cup fresh bread crumbs
1 egg, slightly beaten

3 whole pork tenderloins
1 tablespoon oil
1 tablespoon butter
Salt and pepper, to taste
¼ cup dry sherry or white wine
1 cup chicken stock (or beef)
1 tablespoon cornstarch
¼ cup water
½ teaspoon prepared mustard
½ pound mushrooms (optional)

Mix all stuffing ingredients together.

Butterfly pork tenderloins. Open them and flatten slightly with a mallet. Layer stuffing between flattened pork tenderloins and tie in a roll with kitchen string. Tuck in ends and secure with toothpicks.

Heat oil and butter in an oblong roasting pan and brown the pork roll on all sides. Season with salt and pepper. Pour sherry and chicken stock over meat. Cover pan and bake at 350 degrees for 1½ to 2 hours. Baste meat a few times during baking. Remove pork from pan and keep warm. Remove excess fat from liquid in roasting pan. Mix cornstarch, water and mustard and stir into cooking liquid. Simmer until thickened. Remove string from roll and slice in thick slices. Serve with gravy. If desired, sautéed mushrooms may be added to gravy. Serves: 6-8

Beer Glazed Ham

1 (3 pound) ham, canned or pre-cooked
1 cup beer

Score ham and place on a rack fat side up in a baking pan. Pour 1 cup beer over ham and bake 45 minutes at 350 degrees, basting frequently with pan juices. Spread beer glaze on ham and bake 30 minutes.

Beer Glaze:
Combine: 4 tablespoons brown sugar
¼ teaspoon dry mustard
2 tablespoons tomato catsup
1 teaspoon finely grated onion
½ cup beer

Sweet and Sour Wild Etcetera

("A Very Versatile Recipe")

3 pounds wild game:
  pheasant, duck, rabbit,
  squirrel, venison, quail,
  partridge, grouse, goose
¾ cups flour
1½ tablespoons ginger
½ cup corn oil
2 (15 ounce) cans pineapple
  chunks, drained,
  juice reserved
½ cup vinegar
½ cup soy sauce

1 tablespoon salt
1 tablespoon Worcestershire
  sauce
¾ teaspoon pepper
¾ cup sugar
2 green peppers (or sweet
  red), chopped
1 can bean sprouts
2 (5 ounce) cans water
  chestnuts, sliced
2 tablespoons chili sauce

Cut in small bite size piece pieces (all game). Roll in a mixture of flour and ginger. Brown in oil. Mix the reserved pineapple juice with enough water to make 1¾ cups. Combine with the rest of the flour mixture, vinegar, soy sauce, salt, Worcestershire sauce, pepper and sugar. Pour over meat in skillet. Heat to boiling, stirring constantly. Simmer until meat is tender, about 1 hour covered.

Add pineapple chunks and cut up green peppers. Cook uncovered about 10 minutes.

Add bean sprouts, water chestnuts and chili sauce. Cook 5 minutes. Serve with rice or Chinese noodles.

Pheasant with Brandy and Cream

3 pheasants
1 medium onion, sliced
2 garlic cloves, minced
½ cup butter
½ cup brandy
2 cups chicken stock

6 strips bacon
  Salt and pepper, to taste
2 cups heavy cream
¼ cup creamed horseradish

Brown birds in butter with onions and garlic. Place in baking pan. Pour juices from skillet over breasts. Cover each breast with 2 bacon slices. Pour brandy over breasts and flame. Pour chicken stock over breasts and add salt and pepper, to taste. Roast uncovered at 375 degrees for 30-45 minutes, basting frequently. Add 1 pint heavy cream and ¼ cup horseradish. Continue roasting 15 minutes, basting frequently.

Serve with sauce from pan and wild rice. Serves: 6

Mallard Ducks

2 mallard ducks
1 large onion
1 tart apple

1 carrot
2-4 cups dry white wine, or
more if needed

Stuff each duck with ½ onion, ½ apple and ½ carrot. Place in a deep roasting pan crowding slightly. Pour white wine over the ducks until the breasts are submerged. Cover and bake at 350 degrees for 3 hours.

Glaze with:
⅓ cup honey

⅓ cup currant jelly
⅓ cup orange juice

Stir glaze over low heat until mixed. Turn ducks breast up and spoon glaze over the entire duck. Bake 30 minutes longer, basting frequently. Serves: 6

Wild Duck with Apricot Sauce

2 wild ducks
Lettuce and sliced onion
Garlic salt
Salt and pepper
Apricot sauce

In a heavy baking pan, such as a Dutch oven, make a bed of lettuce several inches thick; slice a medium onion over the lettuce. Place ducks on the lettuce bed. Sprinkle cavity of each duck with garlic salt; salt and pepper the outside of duck. Bake at 300 degrees for 3½ hours or until tender. Glaze the ducks with apricot sauce the last ½ hour of roasting. Serve the remaining apricot sauce (warmed) with the duck.

Apricot Sauce:
½ cup apricot preserves
¼ cup water

1 tablespoon mustard
1 tablespoon lemon juice
½ teaspoon savory salt

Heat the preserves until melted. Mix in other ingredients. If sauce thickens too much add a little more water. Serves: 6

Wild Game des Lacs

1 wild goose or 2 wild ducks,
skinned and cut up in pieces
Flour
¼ cup butter or oil
1½ cups chicken broth
¾ cup chopped onions

¾ cup chopped mushrooms
¾ cup chopped celery
1 tablespoon parsley
1 pinch thyme, salt and
pepper to taste
¼ cup sherry

Coat meat with flour. Place in hot skillet with melted butter or oil and brown. Add broth, onions, mushrooms, celery, parsley, seasonings and sherry. Cover and cook in 350 oven for about 2 hours, or until tender, basting occasionally. Serves: 4-6

Hasenpfeffer

2-3 cottontail or domestic rabbits
    cut into serving pieces
2 cups claret wine
½ cup cider vinegar
1 cup water
2 medium onions, sliced

1 tablespoon salt
2 tablespoons sugar
6 peppercorns
2 whole cloves
½ lemon, sliced
1 bay leaf

Place rabbits in a bowl and add remaining ingredients. Marinate, refrigerated, for 2 to 3 days, turning meat occasionally. Remove meat and pat dry with paper towels. Strain and reserve marinade.

1 cup flour
¼ cup butter
12 small onions, peeled
    Ginger snaps, crushed
    (optional)

1 teaspoon cornstarch
Salt and pepper

Dust meat lightly with flour and brown in butter. Add white onions, gingersnaps, and enough of the reserved marinade to barely cover the meat. Bake, covered, at 325 degrees for 1½ hours, or until fork-tender. Mix cornstarch with a bit of pan liquid, stir smooth, and use to thicken sauce. Season with salt and pepper to taste. Serves: 6-8

Venison Roast

1 (4-5 pound) venison roast,
    boned and tied
    Salt pork or bacon

Marinade:
1 cup red wine
½ cup oil
1 bay leaf

1 large clove garlic, cut in
    half
1-3 juniper berries
1 teaspoon rosemary or ½
    teaspoon thyme
¼ teaspoon freshly ground
    pepper
1 teaspoon salt

Stud venison with small pieces of pork fat or bacon. Put venison in large bowl or pan. Pour marinade over the roast. Let stand 1 to 3 days in refrigerator, turning several times. Drain meat, reserving marinade. Place meat in a roasting pan and cover with thin slices of salt pork or bacon. Cover and roast at 350 degrees for 2 hours basting frequently with a little marinade. Remove cover and roast for ½ hour. The roast should be well done. Remove meat to a warm platter.

To the roasting pan liquids add 1-2 tablespoons flour and scrape the pan well. Slowly add the remaining marinade and cook until it thickens. Strain the gravy. Serves: 8-10

Venison Stew

5 pounds boned venison
1 bottle dry red wine
2 tablespoons pickling spices
2 celery stalks with leaves
6 sprigs parsley
1 clove garlic, peeled
1 cup flour
⅛ teaspoon salt
1 slice salt pork (or 2 tablespoons bacon fat)

1 leek
1 large onion, quartered
1 (12 ounce) can chicken broth
1 teaspoon salt
1 pound fresh mushrooms, washed and unpeeled
2 tablespoons butter
⅓ cup red currant jelly

Marinate the venison in red wine to cover, with the mixed spices, 1 stalk celery, 2 sprigs of parsley and the garlic. Turn occasionally during the marinating (1-2 days). Remove and drain the venison, straining and saving the marinade. With a very sharp knife cut the venison in 1-inch cubes removing all fat and connective tissue. Shake the cubes in a sack with seasoned flour to coat evenly.

Render down the pork slice or melt the bacon fat. Brown the cubes well on all sides. Remove to a large pot. Add the remaining celery and parsley with the leek and onion to the pot.

Combine the broth with a like amount of the marinade and pour over the meat just to cover. Add 1 teaspoon salt. Cover, and let simmer 2 hours or more, adding more of the broth and marinade mixture if needed.

Quarter the mushrooms and sauté them in butter until tender. Add them with their butter and juices to the pot. Stir in the jelly. Adjust the seasoning. Serve piping hot over wild rice.

Venison Sausage

3 pounds ground venison or ground round steak
¼ teaspoon pepper
1¼ teaspoon garlic powder
1 tablespoon liquid smoke

4 tablespoons tender quick salt
1 cup water
1 teaspoon mustard seed

Mix all together. Arrange on foil and roll into logs, closing ends and long seam as tightly as possible. Chill 24 hours. Bake on jelly roll pan 1½ hours at 325 degrees. Liquid will leak out during baking process. Meat will still be red when done.

MALLARD

Beef Jerky

1¼-1½ pounds lean beef round
¼ cup soy sauce
1 tablespoon Worcestershire sauce
¼ teaspoon freshly ground pepper

⅛-¼ teaspoon garlic powder
½ teaspoon onion powder
⅛ teaspoon nutmeg
¼ teaspoon ground ginger

Remove all gristle and fat from meat. Cut across the grain in ⅛-¼ inch thick pieces. Mix remaining ingredients and pour over meat distributing marinade well. Refrigerate overnight. Drain meat. Arrange in single layer on dehydrator trays and dry about 5 hours or overnight. This can be done in a conventional oven using low temperature. Meats that can be used are: round steak, beef brisket or wild game meat.

Liver Pâté Stuffing

2 pounds chicken livers, chopped fine
1 medium onion, chopped fine
1 pound pork sausage (bulk)
2 egg yolks

4 cups soft bread crumbs
1 teaspoon sage
¼ teaspoon nutmeg
3 tablespoons brandy
Salt and pepper to taste

Mix all ingredients and stuff both cavities of a large turkey (18 pounds or more). Close cavities with trussing needles (pins) and kitchen thread.

Bake turkey until done. Remove stuffing while hot and serve with the turkey or pack the hot stuffing into a decorative mold. Unmold and serve paté in thinly cut slices with a crusty bread or crackers.

The turkey may also be served cold. Good for a cold buffet.

Note: Stuffing may also be used for ducks (4).

Wild Rice Stuffing

2 onions, chopped
2 tablespoons butter
½ pound pork sausage
1 pound mushrooms

1½ teaspoons salt
1 teaspoon thyme
6 cups wild rice

Sauté onion in butter until it is soft, but not brown. Add pork sausage. Sauté until it is cooked through, stirring frequently. Add mushrooms, seasonings and rice. Cook and stir 2 to 3 minutes. This is enough stuffing for a large turkey.

BREADS

Yogurt Crêpes

1 cup yogurt
½ cup water
3 eggs, slightly beaten
2 tablespoons oil

1 cup flour
1 tablespoon sugar
⅛ teaspoon salt

Stir yogurt until creamy. Add water and eggs, one at a time and mix. Add oil and mix. Stir in flour and salt. (This batter may be refrigerated for later use.)

Spoon 2-3 tablespoons of batter into a heated, lightly greased crêpe pan. Swirl pan until batter coats bottom. Lightly brown crêpe on both sides. Spread on wax paper to cool.

Hi-Rise Apple Pancake

1 red apple or 2 peaches
1 teaspoon lemon juice
2 tablespoons sugar
3 eggs

½ cup plus 2 tablespoons flour
½ cup plus 2 tablespoons milk
5 tablespoons butter

Preheat oven to 425 degrees. Slice fruit and toss with lemon juice and sugar. Combine eggs, flour and milk in a mixing bowl. Beat lightly. The batter should be slightly lumpy. Heat butter in a 12-inch skillet until hot and foamy. Remove from heat and quickly add the batter. (This is the key to making the pancake rise.) The apples, arranged in a pinwheel, may be added before or during baking. Place in upper one-third of the oven. Bake 25 minutes, or until the pancake is puffed and golden brown. Remove from oven and sprinkle with powdered sugar and lemon juice, or serve with a dollop of homemade jam. Serves: 2-4

Note: A mixture of cinnamon and sugar may be sprinkled on pancake before baking.

OATGRASS & JACKRABBIT

Blini a la Morton

Pancake Batter:

1 package dry yeast
¼ cup warm water
1¾ cups milk, scalded and cooled
2 tablespoons sugar

1 teaspoon salt
3 eggs
2 cups flour
⅓ cup butter, melted and cooled

Dissolve yeast in water. Add milk, sugar and salt. Beat in eggs, one at a time. Add flour and butter. Combine until smooth. Cover and refrigerate overnight. Let stand at room temperature one hour before making 4-inch pancakes.

Toppings:

1½ cups melted butter
1 cup sour cream
1 cup grated hard boiled egg
1 cup crumbled cooked bacon

1 (8 ounce) jar strawberry preserves
1 small jar black caviar
4-6 fresh strawberries (optional)

Arrange 3 4-inch pancakes in a clover pattern on each plate. Spoon some melted butter on each pancake. Spread some sour cream over buttered pancake. Sprinkle egg over sour cream. Sprinkle crumbled bacon over egg. Put a generous spoonful of strawberry preserves in the center of the pancakes. Put three half-teaspoons of caviar on pancakes where they overlap. Garnish with a fresh strawberry.

Swedish Pancakes

3 eggs
2 cups milk
1 cup flour

1 teaspoon baking powder
1 tablespoon sugar
1 teaspoon cinnamon

Beat eggs, add milk and then remaining ingredients. Lightly oil a large frying pan. Pour ½ cup of the thin batter into the hot frying pan lifting the pan so the batter covers the bottom. Turn pancake once.

Serve with syrup or lingonberries. Makes 12-14 pancakes.

Note: These can be made in a smaller frying pan and served cold. Place strawberries and whipped cream on ¼ of the pancake then fold it twice.

TORCH FLOWER

Cheese Blintzes

4 eggs
2 tablespoons sugar
1 teaspoon salt
2 cups flour
2 cups water

1 pound cottage cheese
2 egg yolks
2 tablespoons sugar
1 teaspoon vanilla
Butter for frying

Beat eggs, sugar and salt together in medium bowl. Beat in flour and water alternately. Refrigerate 2 hours.

Make a filling of all other ingredients. Refrigerate.

Heat 1 teaspoon butter in 10 inch skillet or crepe pan. Pour in ¼ cup batter, tipping pan from side to side to cover bottom. Cook pancake briefly. Turn out on waxed paper, browned side up. Place 1 tablespoon of filling in center. Fold over from both sides, then from top to bottom to form a small envelope.

In a small, buttered frying pan, brown each blintz lightly on both sides.

To warm, place blintzes in a casserole, side by side, in a slow 275 degree oven.

Serve with sour cream and strawberries or variety of jams. Makes 12 blintzes

German Pancakes

1 tablespoon corn oil
4 eggs
2 cups milk

2 cups flour
1 teaspoon salt
½ cup water

Mix above ingredients to form a batter. Heat 1 tablespoon oil in a 10-inch frying pan. (If using an electric skillet, preheat to 375 degrees). Oil must be very hot and well distributed. Pour in ½ cup batter, tipping pan to coat bottom. Cover and fry pancake until golden; turn and cook other side.

Pancakes may be served with savory or sweet fillings; Heat small pieces of cooked meat in thick gravy. Add sliced mushrooms, if desired. Spoon mixture on pancake and roll. Or, spread with applesauce, sprinkle with sugar and roll.

Beer Pancakes

2 cups packaged biscuit mix
2 tablespoons sugar
½ teaspoons ground cinnamon
  Dash ground nutmeg
5 eggs, beaten

½ cup beer
2 tablespoons oil
  Butter
  Maple syrup

In a large bowl combine biscuit mix, sugar, cinnamon and nutmeg. Set aside. Mix together the eggs, beer and cooking oil. Gradually add the dry ingredients, stirring just until moistened. Batter will still be lumpy. Add a little extra beer if thinner pancakes are desired.

Use ¼ cup batter to make each pancake. Cook on a hot, lightly greased griddle for about 2 minutes per side or until pancakes are golden. Serve with butter and maple syrup.

These pancakes can be made a few hours ahead of time and reheated by covering and placing in a 300 degree oven until hot. Yields: 10-12 4-inch pancakes

Yeast Waffles

1 package yeast
¼ cup lukewarm water
1 tablespoon sugar
2¼ cups milk
1 teaspoon salt

1 tablespoon butter
2½-2¾ cups flour
3 eggs, separated
1 teaspoon vanilla
1 orange rind, grated

Add sugar to lukewarm water; dissolve yeast in sugar water. Scald the milk; add salt and butter. Cool the milk to lukewarm. Mix in the yeast. Stir the flour into milk mixture. Beat well and let rise 1½ hours. Separate the eggs. Stir well-beaten egg yolks into waffle mixture. Fold in stiffly beaten egg whites. Add vanilla and orange rind. Bake in heated waffle iron. Serves: 6-8

Note: Club soda may be substituted for milk. The waffle will be crisper.

RUFFED GROUSE.

Freezer to Oven French Toast

4 eggs
1 cup milk
2 teaspoons vanilla
2 tablespoons sugar
¼ teaspoon nutmeg or
   cinnamon

8 slices day-old French bread,
   cut ¾ to 1 inch thick
¼ cup melted or soft butter or
   margarine

In a medium bowl, beat eggs, milk, sugar, vanilla and nutmeg or cinnamon.

Place bread slices on a rimmed, greased baking sheet. Pour egg mixture over bread. Let stand a few minutes. Turn slices and let stand until all of mixture is absorbed. Freeze uncovered until firm. Spread both sides of slices with soft butter. Package airtight and return to freezer. Bake frozen at 475 degrees for 8-10 minutes. Turn slices over for an additional 8-10 minutes until browned.

Note: Try adding 1 small can crushed pineapple (8 ounces) to egg mixture. Then sprinkle with powdered sugar and/or coconut after baking. This is a good make ahead recipe. Baking sheet may be lined with foil before greasing, to facilitate clean-up.

Dakota Muffins

4 cups wheat cereal
   (wheaties)
½ cup unprocessed bran
1¾ cups milk
2 eggs
⅔ cup sunflower oil
¾ cup sugar
1 cup white flour

2 cups whole wheat flour
2 tablespoons baking powder
1 teaspoon salt
2 teaspoons cinnamon
1 cup fruit (blueberries,
   apples, raisins or
   pineapple)

Mix cereal, bran and milk in bowl. Let sit. Mix eggs, oil and sugar. Add to cereal and milk mixture. Add dry ingredients and fruit to mixture. Stir only until dry ingredients are mixed in. Bake in greased muffin tins at 400 degrees for 20 minutes. Yield: 24 muffins

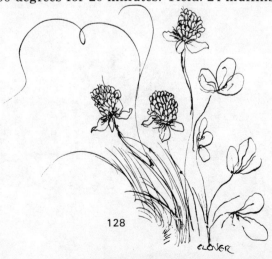
CLOVER

Whole Wheat Pecan Muffins

1 cup all-purpose flour
1 cup whole wheat flour
½ cup firmly packed brown sugar
2½ teaspoons baking powder
½ teaspoon salt

1 cup coarsely chopped pecans
¾ cup milk
½ cup vegetable oil
1 egg

Combine flours, brown sugar, baking powder and salt. Stir in pecans.

Combine milk, oil and egg. Add to dry ingredients and stir until just moistened. Fill 12 greased muffin cups. Bake in preheated oven at 350 degrees.

Serve warm with Cream Cheese Spread.

Cream Cheese Spread:

4 ounces cream cheese
¼ cup powdered sugar

2-3 tablespoons orange juice or lemon juice

Beat cream cheese with powdered sugar until light and fluffy. Cheese should be at room temperature. Beat in enough juice for spreading consistency. Makes about 1¼ cups.

Pumpkin Muffins

1 cup flour
½ cup brown sugar
2 teaspoons baking powder
1 teaspoon pumpkin pie spice
½ teaspoon salt (omit if using salted sunflower seeds)
¼ teaspoon baking soda

¾ cup canned pumpkin
1 egg, slightly beaten
¼ cup milk
¼ cup sunflower oil
1 cup oats
½ cup sunflower seeds

Sift dry ingredients. Combine pumpkin, egg, milk and oil. Add to dry ingredients. Add oats and sunflower seeds. Fill greased muffin tins ¾ full. Sprinkle with topping. Bake about 18-20 minutes at 400 degrees. Yield: 12-14 muffins

Topping:

Heat 1 tablespoon sunflower oil
Add: ⅓ cup brown sugar
1 tablespoon flour

¼ teaspoon pumpkin pie spice
3 tablespoons sunflower seeds

Mix until crumbly.

Zucchini-Cheddar Bread

¼ cup margarine
1 cup chopped onion
2½ cups Bisquick
1 tablespoon parsley
¼ cup milk

3 eggs
1½ cups grated Cheddar cheese
1-2 cups zucchini, shredded
¾ cup toasted chopped
  almonds (optional)

Cook onion in margarine until tender. Cool slightly. Mix together onion, Bisquick, parsley, milk and eggs. Stir in remaining ingredients. Pour into a greased and floured 9x1½ round pan. Bake in 400 degree oven for about 40 minutes, or until toothpick inserted in center comes out clean. Serves: 8

Mexican Corn Bread

1 cup corn meal
½ teaspoon soda
½ teaspoon salt
1 cup cream style or
  whole kernel corn, drained
¼ cup melted margarine or oil
⅔ cup buttermilk

2 eggs, beaten
1½ cup grated cheddar cheese
1 (4 ounce) can green chilies,
  chopped and drained
1 medium onion, chopped
  finely

Preheat oven to 350 degrees. Grease an 8 or 9 inch square baking pan. Mix all ingredients together, reserving ½ cup cheese. Sprinkle cheese on top. Bake 1 hour, or until center is set. Cut into squares and serve while warm. Serves: 6

Blueberry Coffee Cake

2 cups sugar
1 cup shortening
3 eggs
3 teaspoons baking powder
5 cups cake flour

1 cup milk
3 cups fresh, washed
  blueberries
½ teaspoon cinnamon
⅓ cup sugar

Cream sugar and shortening. Add eggs. Mix baking powder and cake flour. Add to mixture, alternating milk and flour. Fold in blueberries. Bake on ungreased, jellyroll pan with high sides. Sprinkle with cinnamon and sugar mixture. Bake for 35 minutes at 350 degrees.

Swedish Kringler Coffee Cake

1 cups flour
½ cup butter
1 tablespoon water
1 cup water

½ cup butter
1 cup flour
3 eggs
½ teaspoon almond flavoring

Mix like pie crust: 1 cup flour, ½ cup butter, 1 tablespoon water. Pat on cookie sheet in 2 long strips, 12x3 inches.

In a saucepan, stir 1 cup water and ½ cup butter to boiling. Remove from heat. Stir in 1 cup flour and beat until smooth. Beat in eggs, one at a time; Add flavoring. Spread on first mixture. Bake for 55-60 minutes at 350 degrees. Cool. Spread with frosting. Top with slivered almonds. Serves: 6

Frosting:
1 cup powdered sugar

1 tablespoon butter
½ teaspoon almond flavoring

Cream, enough for spreading consistency.

Rhubarb Coffee Cake

½ cup butter
1 cup brown sugar
1 egg, beaten
1 cup sour cream
2 cups raw rhubarb, chopped

1 teaspoon vanilla
½ teaspoon salt
1 teaspoon soda
2 cups flour

Cream butter and brown sugar. Add beaten egg and mix well. Add sour cream, rhubarb (if using frozen do not thaw) and vanilla. Mix salt and soda into flour and add to batter. Mix well. Put into greased pan, 9x13 inches. Sprinkle topping on cake. Bake 30 to 40 minutes at 350 degrees.

Topping:
½ cup brown sugar
2 tablespoons butter

1 teaspoon cinnamon
¾-1 cup chopped walnuts or
pecans

Mix all ingredients.

131

Orange Bread

2 cups sifted all-purpose flour	½ cup finely shredded thin
1 cup sugar	candied orange peel (recipe
2½ teaspoons baking powder	follows)
½ teaspoon salt	1 egg, beaten
¼ cup butter or margarine	⅓ cup orange juice or ⅓ cup milk

Sift dry ingredients into mixing bowl. Cut in butter or margarine until mixture is slightly coarser than corn meal. Mix in orange peel. Combine egg and orange juice or milk. Add egg mixture to dry ingredients. Stir just enough to moisten ingredients. Spread evenly in well-greased 8½x4½x2½ inch loaf pan. Let stand 30 minutes at room temperature. Bake at 350 degrees for 50 to 60 minutes or until firm and lightly browned. Turn loaf out of pan onto cake rack. Cool thoroughly before storing or freezing. Loaf may be wrapped in aluminum foil and frozen and sliced as needed.

Note: Recipe may be doubled.

Candied Orange or Grapefruit Peel:

Peel 6 oranges, keeping the peel in pieces as large as possible. Cover peel with cold water and boil 5 minutes. Drain. Repeat 4 times or until peel is tender. Save 1 cup of the last cooking water. Scrape out part of the white membrane. Weigh drained and scraped peel. Combine an equal amount of a mixture of honey and sugar, using approximately half of each. Add to the sugar and honey ⅓ cup of the reserved cooking water for each cup of honey-sugar mixture. Blend thoroughly in a saucepan and bring to simmer. Cut peel into ¼ inch strips. Add peel to syrup; simmer until honey-sugar mixture is transparent, about 20 minutes. Drain thoroughly in colander or sieve, then roll in granulated sugar. If necessary, spread candied peel on foil or wax paper and dry until stickiness is gone.

Note: All sugar may be used. Proceed as above, using 1 cup of sugar with ½ cup cooking water.

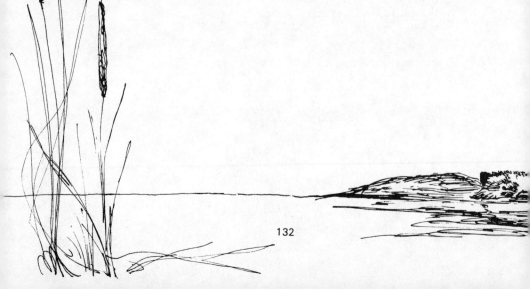

Lemon Pecan Bread

3 cups cake flour
2 teaspoons baking powder
⅛ teaspoon salt
1 cup finely chopped pecans
2-3 tablespoons grated lemon
   zest
4 eggs separated and at room
   temperature

¼ teaspoon cream of tartar
1 cup unsalted butter at room
   temperature
1½ cups sugar
1 cup milk

Sift flour, baking powder and salt. Reserve 1 tablespoon of the mixture to combine with the pecans and lemon zest. In a medium bowl, beat egg whites and cream of tartar just until stiff peaks form. Set aside. In a large mixer bowl, cream butter and gradually add sugar. Beat until fluffy. Add egg yolks, one at a time, beating well after each. Add flour mixture alternately with milk, folding in carefully with mixer or by hand. Toss walnuts and lemon zest with the reserved 1 tablespoon of flour and fold into batter. Stir ¼ of the egg whites into batter and gently fold in the rest. Bake in 2 greased and floured 9 by 5 inch loaf pans at 350 degrees for 50 to 60 minutes, or until done. Cool in pans on a wire rack for 10 minutes. Remove from pans and brush on lemon syrup glaze.

Glaze:
½ cup sugar
¼ cup fresh lemon juice,
   strained
¼ cup water

Combine and cook in a small pan, stirring constantly, over medium heat until mixture boils.

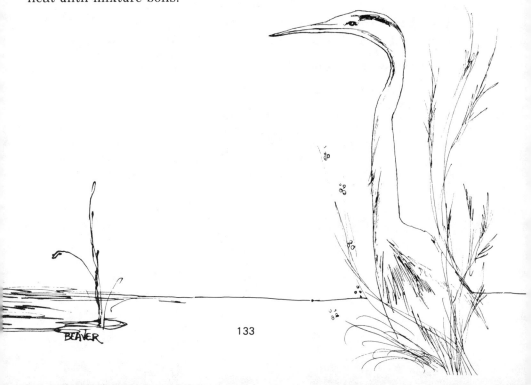

Sour Cream Nut Bread

3 eggs, separated
¼ teaspoon cream of tartar
   Pinch of salt
1 cup butter or margarine,
   room temperature
1 cup sugar
¾ cup sour cream
1 tablespoon lemon rind,
   finely grated

1 tablespoon orange rind,
   finely grated
2 cups flour, sifted
1 teaspoon baking powder,
   sifted with flour
½ teaspoon baking soda, sifted
   with flour
1 cup walnuts, finely chopped

In a small bowl, beat egg whites with cream of tartar and salt until stiff but not dry. Set aside.

In a large bowl, cream the butter and sugar until fluffy. Add egg yolks, one at a time. Stir in sour cream and grated rinds. Stir in flour mixture and nuts. Mix well. Fold in stiffly beaten egg whites.

Pour into buttered and floured 9-inch tube pan. Bake in a preheated 350 degree oven for 50 minutes. Cool for 5 minutes in pan then turn the cake out onto a rack. Brush with lemon-orange glaze.

Glaze:
   Juice of 1 lemon
   Juice of 1 orange
½ cup sugar

Combine in a small saucepan and bring to a boil. Cool slightly before glazing cake.

Walnut Bread

3 cups sifted flour
1 cup sugar (less if you prefer
   it less sweet)
4 teaspoons baking powder
1½ teaspoons salt
1½ cups coarsely chopped
   walnuts

1 egg, beaten
¼ cup soft shortening
1½ cups milk
1 teaspoon vanilla

Resift flour with sugar, baking powder, and salt. Stir in 1½ cups walnuts. Blend in remaining ingredients. Grease and flour loaf (9x5x3) or small tube pan. (May sprinkle ¼ cup walnuts on top.) Bake in 350 degree oven for 60 to 70 minutes. Turn onto wire rack to cool. Makes 1 loaf.

Apricot Bread

1 cup coarsely cut, dried
  apricots (6-8 ounce bag)
2 cups boiling water
¾ cup sugar
2 tablespoons shortening
1 egg, well beaten

½ teaspoon vanilla
½ cup chopped walnuts
1¾ cups flour
2 teaspoons baking powder
½ teaspoon baking soda
½ teaspoon salt

Place apricots in bowl. Cover with 2 cups boiling water. Let stand 1 hour. Drain and dry. Reserve ½ cup of liquid.

Add sugar and shortening to apricots. Heat the ½ cup of reserved liquid to boiling point and add to apricot mix, stirring until shortening is melted. Blend in egg and vanilla. Add walnuts. Mix together flour, baking powder, baking soda and salt. Gently add to apricot mixture, mixing only lightly. Turn into loaf pan. Bake at 375 degrees for 1 hour. Store overnight before cutting. Yields: 1 loaf

Zucchini Bread

2 cups sugar
1 cup oil
2 cups zucchini, shredded
3 eggs
1 cup raisins, chopped
1 cup walnuts, chopped
1 can (4 ounce) crushed
  pineapple, drained

1 teaspoon vanilla
2 teaspoons cinnamon
1 teaspoon soda
1 teaspoon salt
1 teaspoon baking powder
2 cups flour

Mix sugar and oil. Add eggs. Beat well. Add zucchini, raisins, walnuts, pineapple, vanilla and cinnamon. Mix soda, salt and baking powder into flour. Add to first mixture, stirring until blended. Put into 2 greased and floured loaf pans, 9x5 inches. Bake 50 minutes at 350 degrees.

Sunflower Wheat Bread

1½ cups whole wheat flour
1 cup all-purpose flour
½ cup quick cooking rolled oats
½ cup brown sugar, packed
1 tablespoon finely shredded orange peel
½ teaspoon baking powder
½ teaspoon baking soda
½ teaspoon salt
1¾ cups buttermilk
1 egg, slightly beaten
½ cup sunflower seeds
Honey and sunflower seeds

In a large bowl combine whole wheat flour, all-purpose flour, oats, sugar, orange peel, baking powder, baking soda and salt until well blended. Add milk and egg. Stir just until ingredients are moistened. Stir in sunflower seeds. Pour into greased 9x5 bread pan. Bake in 350 degree oven for 50-60 minutes or until bread tests done. If necessary, cover loaf during last 15 minutes of baking to prevent over-browning. Cool in pan for 10 minutes. Turn onto wire racks to allow thorough cooling.

Brush top of loaf with honey and sprinkle with additional sunflower seeds. Yields: 1 loaf.

Scottish Scones

⅔ cup butter
⅓ cup cream
2 eggs, beaten well
1½ cups flour
1¼ cups quick cooking or regular oats
¼ cup sugar
1 tablespoon baking powder
1 teaspoon cream of tartar
½ teaspoon salt
½ cup raisins

Add softened butter, cream and beaten eggs to combined dry ingredients. Stir until dry ingredients are moistened. Add raisins. Shape dough into ball. Pat out on lightly floured board to form 8 inch circle. Cut into wedges or roll out to a rectangular shape, ¾-inch thick, and cut into squares. Bake on greased cookie sheet at 425 degrees for 12-15 minutes or until lightly browned.

Serve warm with butter, honey or preserves. Serves: 12

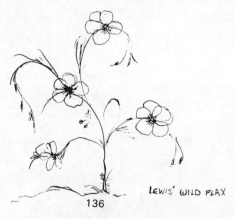

LEWIS' WILD FLAX

Kuchen
(German)

Basic Dough: (10 kuchen)
    Soak 2 cakes of yeast (or packages) in ½ cup lukewarm water. Set aside.

    In a large bowl, pour 1 cup boiling water over ½ cup shortening. Stir until melted.
Add:
    1 cup cold water
    2 teaspoons salt

½ cup sugar
2 eggs, beaten

    Beat 1 minute. When lukewarm add yeast and 2 cups flour. Beat well.
Add:
    5 cups flour (1 cup at a time). Knead well. Place in greased bowl, cover with greased, waxed paper and let rise until double in size.

Divide dough into 10 equal parts. Grease 8 inch or 9 inch cake pans. Roll out dough to fit tins and stretch dough up the sides. Let rise 20 minutes. Top 5 kuchen with cream topping (add thinly sliced fruit, if desired) and top 5 kuchen with streusel topping. Bake in a preheated 350 degree oven for 30 minutes. Sprinkle warm kuchen with a little sugar and cinnamon. Yield: 10 Kuchen

Cream Topping: (5 kuchen)
5 eggs
2 cups sugar

4 tablespoons flour
4 cups sour cream
1 tablespoon vanilla

Beat eggs, sugar and flour. Add sour cream and vanilla. Cook in double boiler until thickened.

Streusel Topping: (5 kuchen)
    1½ cups flour
    ½ cup white sugar

½ cup brown sugar
1 teaspoon cinnamon
½ cup margarine

Mix well until crumbly.

Note: If one topping recipe is preferred over the other, double the recipe. Kuchen may have both cream and streusel toppings. Double both topping recipes.

Danish Pastry

½ cup water (115 to 120 degrees)
2 envelopes yeast
½ teaspoon sugar
⅓ cup (minus ½ teaspoon sugar)

¾ cup cold milk
2 eggs
3 cups flour (may use unbleached)
1 teaspoon salt
4 sticks (1 pound) butter

Dissolve yeast in water in small bowl. Stir in sugar. Set aside for 10 minutes. Mixture should bubble and double in volume.

Combine sugar, milk, eggs, flour, salt and the yeast mix. Beat with electric mixer at medium speed for 3 minutes. Scrape beaters off, add 1¼ cups flour and mix in thoroughly. Cover the dough (should be soft dough) with plastic wrap and refrigerate 30 minutes.

Place the butter on a sheet of wax paper, 1 inch apart. Cover with another sheet of wax paper. Roll the butter into a 12 inch square by alternating direction of rolling pin. Chill about 30 minutes.

Combine the dough and butter as follows: Flour pastry cloth heavily (about 1/3 cup flour). Turn dough out, sprinkle some flour on top of dough and roll into 18x13 inch rectangle. Peel wax paper off butter and invert butter on 2/3 of dough. Peel off other sheet of wax paper. Score the butter down the center. Fold dough over butter (covering middle 1/3). Fold the exposed butter-dough 1/3 to middle. Turn dough so open side is away from you. Roll dough into 24x12 inch rectangle. Fold ends to middle, then fold in half. Refrigerate 30 minutes. (It keeps the butter from oozing into dough and also gives dough a chance to relax making it easier to roll out). Roll dough out to 24x12 inch rectangle, fold as before and refrigerate 30 minutes. Repeat above process 2 more times (4 times in all). Refrigerate at least 1 hour or more (even over night). Use this dough with almond filling in Danish pastry variations.

Almond Filling: (Will fill ½ dough)
4 ounces almond paste

4 tablespoons butter
½ cup sugar

Mix in small bowl until smooth and well blended.

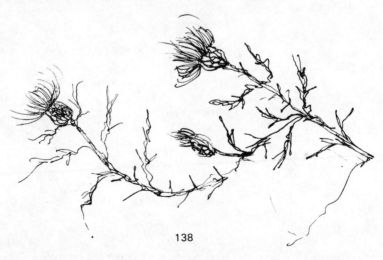

(Danish Pastry Variations)
Borgmester Krans (Mayor's Braid)

½ recipe dough
1 recipe almond filling

1 slightly beaten egg
Sugar
Sliced almonds

Roll dough to 30x9 inch rectangle. Divide dough in thirds, length-wise. Divide filling into 3 parts and place down middle of each strip and seal to form 3 long tubes. Seal ends of tubes. Braid the 3 tubes loosely. Ease braid onto ungreased cookie sheet and form into a ring (about 9 inch diameter). Join ends securely. Let rise until double (about 45 minutes). (Don't force by heating). Brush with egg. Sprinkle with sliced almonds and sugar. Place in 400 degree oven. Turn down imme-diately to 350 degrees. Bake 40 minutes, or until golden. Remove to wire rack and cool. (Bread spreads when baked. To keep more compact, place foil collar around braid just prior to baking.)

Mandelhorn (Almond Crescent)

½ recipe dough
½ recipe almond filling

1 slightly beaten egg
Sugar
Sliced almonds

Roll dough into 20x15 inch rectangle. Cut into 5 inch squares. Place 1 large teaspoon almond filling on corner of 5 inch square. Roll towards diagonal corner to form roll. Bend into crescent and place on ungreased cookie sheet 2 inches apart. Let rise until double (about 30 minutes). Brush with egg. Sprinkle with sugar and sliced almonds. Place in 400 degree oven. Turn down immediately to 350 degrees. Bake for 20 to 25 minutes. Cool on wire rack.

Abrikos Slojfe (Apricot Bow Ties)

½ recipe dough
1 cup apricot preserves
1 slightly beaten egg

2 tablespoons chopped walnuts
2 tablespoons sugar

Roll dough as for Mandelhorn and cut same way. Place one tables-teaspoon apricot preserve along one edge of 5 inch square ½ inch from edge. Fold in half. Press edges to seal. With sharp knife cut slit to within 1 inch of each end. Slip one end under and up through slit. Place on ungreased cookie sheet 2 inches apart. Let rise until double in size (about 30 minutes). Brush with egg and sprinkle with mixture of: 2 tablespoons chopped walnuts and 2 tablespoons sugar. Place in 400 degree oven. Turn down immediately to 350 degrees and bake for 20 minutes until golden brown. Cool on wire rack.

139

Almond Horns

¼ pound butter or margarine, softened
½ cup sugar
5 eggs, slightly beaten
2 packages dry yeast
⅓ cup warm water

⅔ cup milk, scalded
5½-6 cups flour
1 teaspoon salt
¼ pound cold butter or margarine

Thoroughly mix butter, sugar and eggs. Soften yeast in water according to package directions. Stir into butter mixture. Add milk, salt and enough flour to make a soft dough. Cover and chill 3 hours or longer. On lightly floured board or pastry cloth, roll out the dough to a 14 inch square. Dot half of the square with 2 tablespoons of the cold butter. Fold dough over it and roll to a 12x20 inch oblong. Dot 1/3 of the dough with 2 tablespoons of the cold butter and fold dough into thirds. Roll into 12x20 inch oblong and repeat two more times or until all cold butter is used. Cover dough with plastic wrap and chill until ready to use. (Keeps in refrigerator up to 3 days). Divide dough into fourths. Roll each piece into a 9 inch circle, cut into 8 wedges. Place a teaspoon of filling on each piece and roll up into crescents. Place on greased baking sheets. Let dough rise (about 45 minutes). Brush with beaten egg and bake at 350 degrees for 20 to 25 minutes.

Almond Filling:
1 cup (½ pound) almond paste
⅔ cup sugar
1 egg
  Mix together.

Nut Filling: (Alternate)
¼ cup butter, soft
½ cup brown sugar
½ cup chopped nuts (almonds, walnuts or pecans)

Kulich (Ukranian Easter Bread)

1 cup warm water
3 packages dry yeast
1 teaspoon sugar
1 pound butter or margarine, melted and cooled
1 quart milk, scalded and cooled
5 whole eggs
10 egg yolks
3 cups sugar

1 tablespoon vanilla extract
1 tablespoon rum extract
3 teaspoons salt
Dusted in a little flour:
  Grated rind from 2 lemons and 2 oranges
12 ounces golden raisins

21 cups flour (bread flour is best)

In a large bowl, dissolve yeast in warm water and sugar according to package directions. Add half of the melted butter. Add milk, eggs, egg yolks, sugar, extracts and salt. Mix well. Gradually begin to add flour; mixing with a wooden spoon as long as possible, then use hands. When dough begins to form a mass, transfer it to a large greased bowl (2-3 gallon capacity) and pour a little melted butter over it. Knead and alternately add more flour and more melted butter until the dough becomes a well-formed mass and leaves the sides of the bowl. Work in raisins and grated peels. (The dough is slightly sticky and would use too much flour if kneaded on a floured board in the conventional manner).

Place the bowl, covered with a piece of buttered waxed paper, in a warm, draft-free place. Let dough rise about 2 hours, or until doubled in bulk. Punch down and let rise a second time (about 1½ hours). On a lightly floured board, divide dough into 10 portions; roll each into a ball.

Easter bread is traditionally baked in cylindrical forms but can be baked braided or in bread pans. Large 3 pound size Crisco cans work well. Grease 10 cans and put a dough ball in each. Let dough rise, loosely covered, in a warm, draft-free place (approximately 1 hour).

Bake in preheated 325 degree oven (in lower third of oven) 50 to 60 minutes or until done. When bread is cool, it may be frosted with a powdered sugar glaze. Kulich freezes well. Yield: 10 Kulich

Glaze: Melt ½ cup butter or margarine and mix with powdered sugar (approximately 4 to 6 cups) and a little hot milk or water until it has a spreading consistency.

Christmas Morning Loaf

1 cup sugar
½ cup shortening
2 teaspoons salt
2 cups scalded milk
½ cup warm water
2 packages dry yeast

2 eggs, beaten
7¾ cups sifted all-purpose flour
1 cup seedless raisins
2 cups mixed candied fruit
1½ teaspoons ground
    cardamom seeds

Put sugar, shortening, salt and scalded milk in a large mixing bowl. Stir until shortening melts. Cool to lukewarm. In a small bowl, pour warm water and sprinkle with yeast. Stir until dissolved. Add eggs and yeast to lukewarm milk mixture. Blend. Add 2/3 of flour. Beat until smooth. Add remaining flour gradually, mixing well after each addition. Stir in fruits and cardamom. Knead until smooth and elastic. Place in a greased bowl. Brush with melted shortening. Cover and let rise until double in bulk, about 1½ hours. Punch down. Divide in 3 equal portions and shape into 3 loaves. Place in greased loaf pans. Let rise again until double in bulk. Bake about 50 minutes at 350 degrees. Loaves may be frosted and decorated.

Dakota Rolls

1 package dry yeast
¼ cup water (110-115 degrees)
1 cup scalded milk
3 tablespoons shortening

3 tablespoons sugar
1 teaspoon salt
1 egg, well beaten
3½ cups enriched flour

Soften yeast in warm water; let stand for 5 minutes. Combine milk, shortening, sugar and salt. Cool to lukewarm. Add softened yeast and egg. Gradually stir in flour to form soft dough. Beat vigorously. Cover with greased wax paper and towel. Let rise until double in bulk, about 2 hours. Turn out on flour dusted canvas or board and roll ¼ inch thick in oblong shape, 8x16 inches. Brush with warm butter and sprinkle with ¼ cup brown sugar. Roll as for cinnamon rolls. Cut in 1 inch slices. Heat slowly in a greased shallow pan or muffin pans the following:

Caramel Sauce:
1 cup brown sugar
2 tablespoons light corn syrup

1 tablespoon butter
¼ cup cream

Set aside to cool. When cool, place rolls cutside down over the mixture. Cover and let rise until double in bulk. Bake for 25 minutes at 375 degrees. Remove from pan while hot, and cool, bottom side up. Yield: 2 dozen or one 9x13 pan

Raisin Buns

1 cup raisins
1 package dry yeast
½ cup warm water
3-3½ cups all-purpose flour
¼ cup nonfat dry milk
1 teaspoon salt
1 pinch ginger
½ cup sugar

1 stick butter, room
   temperature
1 egg

Glaze:
1 tablespoon milk
1 egg

Plump raisins in warm water for ½ hour. Dry.

In large bowl sprinkle yeast over warm water; stir and let stand until creamy, about 5 minutes. Add 1 cup flour, dry milk, salt, ginger and sugar. Stir briskly. Beat in soft butter then the egg. The batter will be thick. Sprinkle in raisins and continue to add all flour until dough is soft and velvety.

Flour your work surface and knead dough for 3-4 minutes. Put in greased bowl. Cover with plastic wrap. Put in warm place for 1 hour. The dough may not rise very much. Turn dough out and knead briefly. Divide into 8 equal portions. Roll each into tight ball and place on greased baking sheet. Press down top of each bun slightly. Cover and let rise about 50 minutes. Again they will not rise very much but will in oven. Pre-heat oven to 375 degrees. Baking time is 30 minutes. Brush buns with glaze. Brush again halfway through baking and, 5 minutes before removing from oven, glaze again. Buns are done when they are a rich golden brown on top and have a deep brown crust on bottom. Buns are large. Try them sliced and served with cream cheese.

Butterhorns

1 package dry yeast
1 cup warm water
½ cup sugar
¼ teaspoon salt

¾ cup butter, melted and
   cooled
3 eggs, slightly beaten
4 cups flour

Dissolve yeast in warm water according to package directions. Add remaining ingredients in order and mix well. Refrigerate 8 to 12 hours. Divide dough into 4 parts and roll each portion on a lightly floured board into a 9 to 10 inch round shape. Cut into 8 wedges. Brush with melted butter and roll up into a crescent shape. Place onto a greased baking sheet. Cover lightly and let rise in a warm, draft-free area until doubled in size (5 hours or less). Bake in a preheated 350 degree oven for 12 minutes or until done. Yield: 32 butterhorns

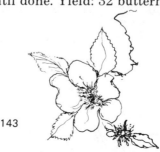

Sesame Bagels

¾ cup scalded milk
¼ cup butter
1 tablespoon sugar
1 teaspoon salt
1 package dry yeast
(dissolved in ¼ cup warm
water and ½ teaspoon
sugar)

3 medium eggs
3¾ cups sifted all-purpose flour

Combine milk, butter, sugar and salt. Cool. When mixture is lukewarm add yeast mixture. Blend in 3 eggs and flour. Knead this soft dough for about 10 minutes, adding more flour to make it firm enough to handle. Let rise in greased bowl, covered, until double in bulk. Punch down. Divide dough into 12 to 18 equal pieces. Roll each piece into a flattened ball and poke a hole in the center with the end of a wooden spoon.

Drop each bagel into a
solution of:
2 quarts, almost boiling water
1 tablespoon sugar

As the bagels surface, turn them over and cook about 3 minutes longer. Skim out and place on a greased baking sheet. Brush each with egg white and sprinkle with sesame seeds. Bake in preheated oven at 375 degrees for 20 minutes or until bagel turns a golden brown. Serve split and toasted with cream cheese and jelly.

Note: To make cinnamon-raisin bagels, decrease eggs to 2, add 1 teaspoon cinnamon and 1½ cups raisins to dough before letting it rise.

Cheese and Wine Bread

3 cups flour
1 package yeast
½ cup dry white wine
½ cup butter
2 teaspoons sugar

1 teaspoon salt
3 eggs
1 cup cubed Monterey Jack
cheese

Heat wine, butter, sugar and salt in sauce pan until warm, stirring until butter melts. Add to dry mix of flour and yeast which should be in a mixer bowl. Add eggs. Beat at low speed for ½ minute. Scrape bowl sides. Beat 3 minutes at high speed. Stir in cheese by hand with enough additional flour to make a soft dough. Knead. Place in a lightly oiled bowl, turning once. Cover and let rise for 2 hours. Punch down, cover, let rise 10 minutes. Shape a round loaf. Place in an oiled 9 inch pie pan. Cover and let rise 45 minutes. Bake 45 minutes at 375 degrees. Yield: 1 loaf

Dill Cottage Cheese Bread

1 package dry yeast
¼ cup water
1 teaspoon sugar
1 cup creamed cottage cheese
  (heated to lukewarm)
2 tablespoons sugar
1 tablespoon minced onion
2 tablespoons butter,
  softened

2 teaspoons dill seed
1 teaspoon salt
¼ teaspoon baking soda
1 egg
2¼-2½ cups flour
Soft butter
Coarse salt

In a small bowl, soften yeast in the water and mix with the sugar.

In a mixing bowl, combine yeast mixture, cottage cheese, sugar, onion, butter, dill seed, salt, soda and egg. Mix well. Gradually add the flour to form a stiff dough, beating well after each addition.

Cover and let rise in a warm place until double. Stir down and place in a well greased and floured 8-inch casserole dish. Let rise until doubled.

Bake in preheated oven at 350 for 40-45 minutes.

While the bread is still warm, brush with soft butter and sprinkle with coarse salt. Yield: 1 loaf

Potato Loaf

5½ cups flour (about)
2 packages yeast
2 teaspoons salt
2 tablespoons sugar
1 cup plus 2 tablespoons
  potato flakes

1⅓ cups milk
1 cup plus 2 tablespoons
  water
½ cup margarine

Blend the flour (2 cups), yeast, salt, sugar and potato flakes in mixing bowl. Heat milk, water and margarine in a saucepan until very warm, but not hot. Add to dry ingredients. Mix at medium speed for 2 minutes. Add remaining flour gradually, mixing with a spoon. Knead by hand about 10 minutes until dough is smooth and elastic. Cover and let rise until doubled. Shape into 2 long loaves. Place on cookie sheets. Let rise until doubled. Bake at 375 degrees for 30 to 40 minutes, or until loaf sounds hollow when tapped.

Upland Plover

Oatmeal Bran Bread

1 cup oatmeal	2 tablespoons molasses
½ cup Kellogg's All Bran	3 cups boiling water
⅓ cup brown sugar	1 package dry yeast
2 teaspoons salt	7-8 cups flour
½ cup shortening	

Mix oatmeal, bran, brown sugar, salt, shortening and molasses. Pour boiling water over mixture in a large bowl. Cool to lukewarm. Dissolve yeast in lukewarm mixture. Add flour gradually, kneading until dough is stiff. Put into greased bowl. Cover and let rise until double in bulk. Make into 3 loaves. Put into greased bread pans. Let rise until rounded above pans sides. Bake for 1 hour at 375 degrees.

Braided Bread

4-4½ cups unbleached white flour	¼ cup oil
2 packages dry yeast	2 tablespoons sugar
2 cups warm water	1 tablespoon salt

In large bowl, combine 2 cups of the flour and the yeast. Add warm water, oil, sugar and salt to dry mixture. Beat at low speed, with electric mixer, for ½ minute, scraping sides of bowl. Beat 3 minutes at high speed.

By hand, stir in enough of the remaining flour to make moderately stiff dough. Turn out onto lightly floured surface and knead until smooth and elastic (8-10 minutes). Shape into a ball and place in a greased bowl, turning once to grease surface. Cover and let rise until double in bulk.

Punch down and divide dough in half. Divide each half into thirds. Shape into 6 balls. Cover; let rest 10 minutes. Roll each ball to a 16-inch rope. Line up 3 ropes, 1-inch apart on greased baking sheet. Braid very loosely, beginning in the middle. Pinch ends together; tuck under. Repeat with remaining ropes. Cover; let rise until double in bulk.

Bake at 375 degrees for 30 minutes. Yield: 2 loaves

Italian Parmesan Bread

1 package active dry yeast
¾ cup warm water
2 tablespoons sugar
1 teaspoon salt
3 cups flour
4 eggs

½ cup soft butter
1 cup Parmesan cheese
1 cup shredded Monterey Jack cheese
1 teaspoon dried oregano

Sprinkle yeast into warm water in a large bowl. Let stand until dissolved. Add sugar, salt and 1 cup flour. Beat well. Add 3 eggs, one at a time. Beat until smooth. Beat in butter. Gradually add enough remaining flour to make a soft dough. Turn onto a floured board and knead until smooth and satiny. Place in a greased bowl. Butter top of dough lightly. Cover with kitchen towel and let rise in warm place until doubled. Turn out on floured board. Knead lightly. Roll into a rectangle about 10x16 inches. Beat remaining egg. Blend in cheese and oregano. Spread cheese filling over dough. Roll up firmly from narrow end. Shape into a round by folding ends underneath. Place in greased 2 quart soufflé or round baking dish. Cover. Let rise in warm place until doubled. Bake in 350 degree oven for 40 minutes or until golden brown and loaf sounds hollow when thumped. Cool 10 minutes. Remove from pan. Yield: 1 loaf

French Bread

1 package dry yeast
1 tablespoon sugar
2 teaspoons salt
2 cups warm water

4 cups flour
1 egg white sprinkled with ½ teaspoon salt, well beaten

In large bowl dissolve the yeast and sugar in water. Let stand 10 minutes. Stir in flour and salt and turn out onto a floured surface. Using a pastry scraper, lift and turn the dough which will be very soft until it coheres enough to knead. Add more flour, if necessary, and knead for 10 minutes until smooth. Place in a greased bowl and cover with plastic wrap. Let rise for 45 minutes. Punch down, and let rise for another 30 minutes. Turn dough out on a lightly floured surface, pat flat and fold in half. Cut into 4 equal pieces, form into balls and let rest 5 minutes. Flatten each ball into an oval with the palms of your hands; roll up, like a jelly roll, into a loaf almost the length of a French bread pan, by gently rolling back and forth. Let loaves rise another 30 minutes in the bread pans.

Brush loaves with a beaten, salted egg white and slash each loaf diagonally 3 times with a sharp knife. Bake at 425 degrees for 20-25 minutes. Yield: 4 loaves

Sourdough French Bread

1 cup milk	1 package dry yeast
2 tablespoons butter	1½ cups starter
3 tablespoons sugar	5-6 cups all-purpose or bread
1 teaspoon salt	flour

Combine milk and butter over low heat until butter melts. Pour into large mixer bowl. Add sugar, salt and yeast. Blend 2-3 minutes until yeast is dissolved. Yeast may be dissolved in ¼ cup warm water, with a sprinkle of sugar, if desired. Add starter and 1 cup flour. Beat 2 minutes. Stir in additional flour to form a firm dough. Knead until smooth and elastic.

Cover and let rise until doubled in bulk in a large, greased bowl. Punch down, pat into a circle, fold in half then fold in quarters. Return to bowl for another ½ hour. Punch down, fold in half, cut into 4 pieces. Roll each piece like a jellyroll, about 16 inches long.

Put clean cloth in French bread pans. Let bread rise on it. When bread has risen, pull cloths out of pan and flip dough into pans. Slash 3 times with a very sharp knife or cut with a sharp scissors. Brush with a mixture of 1 egg white and ½ teaspoon salt.

Bake 20 minutes at 350 to 375 degrees. Remove from pans and cool on a rack.

Note: The entire process takes about 2½ hours.

Sourdough Starter:

1¾ cups flour	1 tablespoon salt
1 tablespoon sugar	1 package dry yeast
	2½ cups water

Mix all ingredients together and let stand 2-3 days in a warm place until it bubbles and develops a sour fragrance. Can be stored in refrigerator for 2 weeks. For best results, use when fresh. Each time starter is used, replenish with ½ cup flour and ½ cup milk. Let stand for a day, stirring occasionally, then refrigerate.

"Best Ever" Brown Bread

1 package yeast	⅓ cup molasses
½ cup warm water	¾ cup brown sugar
2 cups milk	1 egg
2 cups whole wheat flour	1 tablespoon salt
6 tablespoons shortening	4 cups white flour

At night, soften 1 package dry yeast in ½ cup warm water. Scald 2 cups milk and while hot, stir in 2 cups whole wheat flour, 6 tablespoons shortening, 1/3 cup molasses and ¾ cup brown sugar. Cool. Add 1 beaten egg, 1 tablespoon salt, 4 cups white flour and softened yeast. Mix well.

Knead down about 5 minutes. Set in a cool place overnight. Punch down in the morning. Shape in 2 loaves. Let rise. Bake 45 minutes at 350 degrees.

Icelandic Brown Bread

5 cups hot water
2 tablespoons salt
4 tablespoons shortening
2 tablespoons honey
3 tablespoons brown sugar
3 packages dry yeast
¾ cup warm water with 2
　　teaspoons sugar

1½ cups blackstrap molasses
2 cups cracked wheat flour
3 cups stoneground wheat
　　flour
Unbleached white flour

In a large bowl mix hot water, salt, shortening, honey and brown sugar. In a small bowl mix dry yeast and warm water with sugar. When it bubbles add it to the large bowl. Add molasses and enough white flour to make mixture like pancake batter. Add 2 cups cracked wheat flour and 3 cups stoneground wheat flour. Knead and let rise. Repeat. Knead and let rise. Divide into 4 loaves and put into greased pans. Let rise. Bake at 365 degrees for 40-45 minutes.

Dakota Bread

This recipe was developed by the North Dakota and South Dakota Wheat Commissions as a special Centennial project.

1 package active dry yeast
½ cup warm water, (105-115 degrees)
2 tablespoons sunflower oil
1 egg
½ cup cottage cheese
¼ cup honey

1 teaspoon salt
2-2½ cups bread flour
½ cup whole wheat flour
¼ cup wheat germ
¼ cup rye flour
¼ cup rolled oats
Cornmeal

Sprinkle yeast in warm water; stir to dissolve. In a large bowl, mix sunflower oil, egg, cottage cheese, honey and salt. Add dissolved yeast and 2 cups bread flour, beating until flour is moistened. Gradually stir in whole wheat flour, wheat germ, rye flour and oats, plus enough bread flour to make a soft dough.

On a floured surface, knead dough about 10 minutes or until dough is smooth and elastic. Place dough in greased bowl; cover loosely with oiled plastic wrap. Let rise in warm place until doubled in size, about one hour. Punch down dough. Shape into one round loaf. Place in a greased glass pie pan sprinkled with cornmeal. Cover with oiled plastic wrap and let rise until doubled in size, about 1 hour. Brush with egg white and sprinkle with wheat germ, sunflower kernels or oatmeal. Bake at 350 degrees for 35-40 minutes. If too dark, cover loosely with foil the last 10-15 minutes of baking. Remove from pie pan and cool on a wire rack. Optional: Add 1 cup cooked barley with the whole wheat flour. (Cook ½ cup 'Quick' pearl barley for 10 minutes to make 1 cup of cooked barley.)

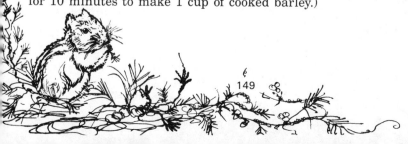

Seeded Rye Bread

½ cup warm water
1 teaspoon sugar
¼ teaspoon ground ginger
3 packages dry yeast
1½ cups lukewarm water
½ cup dark molasses
2 tablespoons caraway seeds
2 tablespoons dill seed

2½ cups rye flour
3 teaspoons salt
4 tablespoons shortening
4-5 cups white flour
1 teaspoon instant coffee
2 tablespoons water
Corn meal

In a small bowl, combine ½ cup warm water, sugar, ginger and yeast. Let the yeast mixture stand in a warm place until it bubbles.

In a large bowl, mix 1½ cups warm water, molasses, caraway, dill seeds and rye flour. Add the yeast mixture. Beat well. Add salt, shortening and 3 cups white flour. Stir well.

Spread 1 cup of flour on pastry board. Turn dough on board and knead vigorously for several minutes. Shape the dough into a ball and turn the bowl upside down over the dough on the board. Let dough rest for 15 minutes. Knead again for several minutes, working in all flour possible. Return to bowl, grease top of dough and cover with a towel. Let rise until doubled.

Turn the dough out on the board. Knead well and divide into 2 parts. Form each half into a long tapered loaf. Cover with a damp towel and allow to rise until doubled and light. Make slashes across top of loaves. Before baking, brush with instant coffee and water. Sprinkle with corn meal. Bake 350 degrees in preheated oven for 45 minutes.

Cracked Wheat Bread

2 cups boiling water
1 cup cracked wheat
½ cup brown sugar
1 tablespoon salt
3 tablespoons butter or
    shortening of choice

1 cup whole wheat flour
2 tablespoons yeast
½ cup warm water and ½
    teaspoon sugar
2 eggs, beaten slightly
5½ cups bread flour

Pour 2 cups boiling water over cracked wheat, salt, brown sugar and butter. Cool to lukewarm. Add 1 cup whole wheat flour and 1 cup white bread flour. Beat well. Proof yeast in ½ cup warm water and ½ teaspoon sugar. Add slightly beaten eggs to flour mixture. Add yeast mixture when it has bubbled. Add about 4½ cups more of white bread flour. Knead 8-10 minutes. Place in greased bowl in warm place until double in bulk. Punch down and let rise again. Divide into 4 large loaves. Put in large, greased, loaf pans. Let rise. Bake at 350 degrees for 30-40 minutes.

Grandma Larson's Lefse

8 cups, white russet potatoes
⅔ cup water
1 teaspoon salt
1 teaspoon sugar

⅓ cup vegetable vegetable shortening
2¾ cups flour, sifted

Peel potatoes and cut into chunks. Boil in water until tender. Drain. Mash potatoes with water, salt, sugar and shortening. Cover with damp cloth and chill 12 hours or overnight. Add flour, in small amounts, mixing well after each addition. Scoop balls of dough onto a tray with ice cream scoop. Keep dough chilled while working with it.

Roll one ball into a thin round on a floured board, using a stockinette covered rolling pin.

On a preheated electric griddle, 450 degrees, bake lefse until brown spots appear; turn over and cook other side. Cool and store in an airtight container. Freezes well.

Bismarcks

3 to 3½ cups flour
2 packages dry yeast
¾ cup milk
⅓ cup sugar
¼ cup shortening
1 teaspoon salt

2 eggs
Oil for deep-fat frying
Any favorite jelly or jam for filling
Sifted powdered sugar

In large mixer bowl combine 1½ cups of the flour and the yeast. In a saucepan heat milk, sugar, shortening and salt just until warm (115 degrees) stirring constantly until shortening almost melts. Add to dry mixture in mixer bowl; add eggs. Beat at low speed with electric mixer for ½ minute, scraping sides of bowl. Beat 3 minutes at high speed. Stir in enough remaining flour to make a moderately soft dough. Turn dough out onto a lightly floured surface. Knead 5 to 8 minutes until dough is smooth and elastic. Shape into a ball. Place in a lightly greased bowl, cover and let rise until dough has doubled in size, about one hour. Punch dough down; turn out onto a floured surface. Divide dough in half. Let rest 10 minutes. Roll each half ⅜ inch thick. Cut with a floured 2½ inch cookie cutter, rerolling trimmings. Cover; let rounds of dough rise 30 minutes or until dough is very light. Fry in hot deep oil (375 degrees) about 1 minute per side. Drain on paper toweling. With a knife, cut a wide slit in the side of each Bismarck. Place 2 teaspoons jelly or jam into each one and roll it in powdered sugar.

Piragi (Latvian)

Filling:
2 pounds bacon, diced
2 finely chopped onions
   Salt and pepper, to taste

2 cups milk
2 sticks margarine
   (1 cup)
1 teaspoon salt
2 tablespoons sugar
2 packages dry yeast
8 cups flour

Cook filling over moderate heat 15 to 20 minutes, stirring frequently. Drain off fat.

Heat milk. Add margarine, salt and sugar. Stir to dissolve. In separate, small bowl soften yeast in a small amount of warm water and ½ teaspoon sugar.

Sift flour. Add ½ of the flour to milk, beating with a wooden spoon. Add yeast and the rest of the flour. Knead until dough is pliable and is not sticky to touch. Cover and let rise in warm place until double in bulk. Take small amount of dough; roll it to a long, log shaped form. Cut in pieces the size of a large walnut. Flatten each piece and roll it into a 3 inch circle. Put 1 teaspoon of filling in the middle of each round. Bring edges together to form crescent. Seal edges. Put in jellyroll pans. Brush with beaten egg.

Bake in 375 or 400 degree oven for 20 minutes. Makes 60 to 80 pirogis.

Spiedini

1 loaf French bread
1 cup unsalted butter, melted
3 garlic cloves, minced

1 tablespoon dried basil
1 pound mozzarella cheese

Trim the top and side crusts from bread. Slice bread almost through in one-half inch intervals. Cut a cheese slice for each bread slice. Mix butter, garlic and basil. Dip cheese slices into butter mixture and put between bread slices. Put bread loaf in a foil package and pour remaining butter over top of loaf before sealing package. Refrigerate overnight. Preheat oven to 375 degrees; bake for 30 minutes; open foil and bake 15 minutes more. To serve, slice at an angle, or pull apart.

Lemon Pepper Sandwich Loaf

1 loaf French bread
½ cup softened butter
  Lemon-pepper seasoning
1 tablespoon prepared
  mustard

2 teaspoons poppy seeds
8 slices Swiss cheese
8 slices bacon, crisp-cooked,
  drained, crumbled

Slice bread, cutting to but not through bottom crust. Combine butter and lemon-pepper seasoning, to taste. Add the mustard and poppy seeds. Mix well. Set aside 3 tablespoons mixture. Spread remaining mixture on all surfaces of bread. Place ½ slice cheese (cut diagonally) in each cut; sprinkle bacon over cheese. Spread reserved butter mixture on top of loaf. Bake on ungreased baking sheet in 350 degree oven for 15-20 minutes, or wrap in foil to heat through.

French Loaf

1 loaf French bread
½ cup mayonnaise
½ cup butter, softened

½ teaspoon garlic salt
  Grated Parmesan cheese
  Parsley flakes
  Paprika

Cut French bread loaf in half horizontally, separating top and bottom. Combine mayonnaise, butter and garlic salt. Spread mixture on the cut-side of each half. Garnish with cheese, parsley flakes and paprika on top. Bake at 350 degrees for 10 minutes. Serve warm.

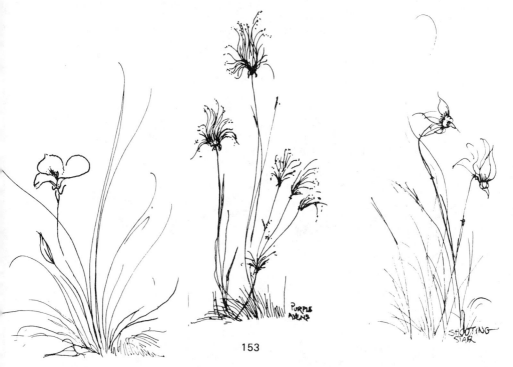

PURPLE AVENS

SHOOTING STAR

MARIPOSA LILY

Lavosch

2 packages dry yeast
2½ cups warm water (105°-115°F.)
3 tablespoons sugar
1 teaspoon salt
⅔ cup oil

3 cups whole wheat flour
¼ cup wheat germ
3 cups bread flour
1 egg beaten with ¼ cup water
Sesame Seeds

Dissolve yeast in water. Blend in sugar, salt, and oil. Beat in whole wheat flour and wheat germ until smooth. Stir in sufficient bread flour to make a soft dough that pulls away from the side of the bowl. Knead for 8-10 minutes. Place dough in a greased bowl, turning to coat top. Let double, 1½ hours. Punch down, knead lightly, shape into 12 equal, smooth balls. Cover and let rest 35 minutes.

Arrange oven racks with one at the top and one at the bottom. Preheat oven to 400 degrees. Roll out 1 piece of dough at a time on a lightly floured board to a round of 10 to 12 inches in diameter. It will be paper thin. Pick up carefully and transfer to ungreased baking sheet. Brush with the egg glaze and sprinkle with sesame seeds. Prick surface several times with a fork and place on lowest rack of oven. Bake 4-5 minutes on lowest rack and quickly transfer to upper rack for 4 minutes. Bread will puff a bit and become golden brown.

Pile on a rack to cool and store in a plastic bag or tin box.

Serve as a cracker-type bread or melt your favorite cheese on it in a 350 degree oven for 5 minutes.

DESSERTS

Cranberry Sherbet

2 (12 ounce) packages fresh
  cranberries
1 quart water

3 cups sugar
Juice of 3 lemons

Boil cranberries in water until tender; Force cranberries and liquid through colander or sieve. Add 3 cups sugar and juice of 3 lemons.

Put in freezer. When partially frozen, beat with mixer until fluffy.

This is a nice palate refresher with a holiday dinner. May also be used as a dessert. Pour a tablespoon of orange liqueur over each individual serving. Serves: 12

Frozen Lemon Frost Soufflé

Crème Pâtissière:
  (makes one cup)
2 egg yolks
½ cup sugar
1 tablespoon plus 1 teaspoon
  flour

1 cup milk, scalded
¼ teaspoon vanilla

Place yolks in small, deep saucepan. Beat with a whisk until light and frothy. Gradually add sugar, beating constantly, until mixture is thick and lemony. Add flour and beat until smooth. Add hot milk, a little at a time, beating constantly until well blended. Place saucepan over medium heat. Cook, stirring constantly, until mixture is thick and coats a spoon. Pour into a bowl; stir in vanilla. Cool, cover and chill.

2 cups whipping cream
  Crème pâtissière, cooled

1 cup strained, fresh lemon
  juice

Whip cream in large bowl until soft peaks form. Fold in crème pâtissière and lemon juice. Set aside.

7 egg whites, room
  temperature
¼ teaspoon cream of tartar

¼ teaspoon salt
1 cup plus 1 tablespoon sugar

Whip egg whites in a large, separate bowl until foamy. Add cream of tartar, salt and continue beating until soft peaks form. Gradually add sugar, beating until mixture is stiff and glossy. Fold whites into lemon-créme.

Generously butter bundt pan. Sprinkle with sugar. Spoon soufflé into prepared pan; cover top with foil. Freeze at least 6 hours. To unmold, dip bundt pan in hot water for approximately 2 minutes. Garnish with orange colored coconut or candied lemon peel. Serves: 8-10

Pavlova

4 egg whites, room
  temperature
⅛ teaspoon salt
1 teaspoon white vinegar
1 teaspoon vanilla
1 cup sugar
1 tablespoon cornstarch
1 cup whipping cream
1 tablespoon powdered sugar
½ teaspoon vanilla

2-3 cups sliced fruit:
  Kiwi fruit, strawberries,
  peaches, bananas

Raspberry sauce:
1 (10 ounce) package frozen,
  sweetened raspberries,
  thawed and sieved

Preheat oven to 400 degrees. Cover cookie sheet with brown paper. Draw a 9-inch circle on it.

Beat egg whites in a large bowl until frothy. Sprinkle with salt and vinegar. Beat on high speed until soft mounds form. Add vanilla. Add sugar gradually and beat in the last tablespoon of sugar mixed with cornstarch. Beat until stiff peaks form, but do not beat dry.

Spoon the meringue in a circular shape on the prepared brown paper. Place in oven. Reduce heat to 250 degrees. Bake 1½ hours. Do not open oven door during baking time.

Place on wire rack to cool slightly, 5-10 minutes. With a spatula, loosen meringue around edges. Remove from paper. Cool completely on rack. Put meringue in airtight container (large plastic sack works well). May be kept for 24 hours at room temperature. May be frozen until ready to serve. Do not defrost. Cut with a sharp serrated knife.

To serve, whip cream with powdered sugar and vanilla; spread on meringue. Decorate with fruit. Drizzle each serving with raspberry sauce.

THISTLE

Hazelnut Torte

6 eggs, separated	⅓ cup fine bread crumbs
1 whole egg	1 teaspoon flour
¾ cup sugar	Hazelnuts, ground and
1 cup hazelnuts, ground	whole for decoration

Preheat oven to 300 degrees.

In small mixer bowl, beat egg yolks and whole egg until thick and lemony. Gradually add ½ cup sugar, then ground hazelnuts and then bread crumbs. Beat until thick. Set aside.

Beat egg whites in a large bowl with clean beaters until foamy. Add remaining sugar slowly while beating until stiff peaks form. Fold ¼ of the beaten egg whites into mixture in small bowl. Sprinkle with flour and fold. Transfer to large bowl and fold in remaining egg whites, gently, until there is no trace of white showing.

Butter and flour a 10-inch springform pan. Remove excess flour by tapping pan on bottom. Pour batter into pan and smooth top.

Bake, centered on middle rack, for 1 hour or until cake shrinks slightly from sides. Remove from oven and cool on rack, about 45 minutes. Remove from pan when completely cool.

Divide in 2 layers with a sharp knife. Fill and decorate with ground and whole hazelnuts.

Filling:

1¾ cups whipping cream	1 teaspoon sugar
	⅛ teaspoon vanilla

Combine and beat until very stiff.

RED FOX KIT

158

Zabaglione Cake

Cake:
- 6 eggs, separated
- 1 cup sugar
- 2 tablespoons water
- 1 lemon rind, grated
- ⅛ teaspoon salt
- 1 cup cake flour

Glaze:
- 1 cup sugar
- ¾ cup water
- 3-5 cloves
- 1 lemon rind, cut in pieces
- 1 orange rind, cut in pieces
- 2 teaspoons rum extract or
- ¼ cup rum

Filling:
- 1 egg
- ¾ cup sugar
- ¼ cup flour
- Grated rind and juice of 1 orange
- 1 cup heavy cream, whipped
- Toasted almond slices
- Fruit for decoration

For the cake, beat egg yolks, sugar, water, lemon rind and salt until light and fluffy (about 15 minutes at high speed). Carefully mix in the flour, a little at a time. In a separate bowl, with clean beaters, beat egg whites until soft peaks form (don't overbeat). Gently but thoroughly fold the whites into yolk mix. Place equal quantities of batter in three greased 8-inch round cake pans, bottoms lined with greased wax paper. Bake in moderately slow oven, 325 degrees, for 30 to 40 minutes until golden. Invert layers on wire racks. When still warm to the touch, loosen edges with spatula and remove from pans. Peel off paper. Cool. Meanwhile make glaze and filling.

Place all glaze ingredients except rum in sauce pan. Simmer gently for about 20 minutes, or until consistency of thin syrup. Remove from heat and add rum or extract. Remove cloves, orange and lemon peel.

Place all filling ingredients, except cream, in top of double boiler and heat, stirring until thick and smooth. Cool. Fold in whipped cream. Brush all cake layers liberally with glaze and spread with filling. Leave enough filling to thinly frost top and sides. Decorate with toasted almond slices and/or fruit. Serves: 10

Griesstorte or Eingebrockeltes (German)

6 eggs, separated
2 cups powdered sugar
¾ cup white bread crumbs,
   finely crushed

¾ cup farina or cream of wheat
1 teaspoon vanilla
1 cup walnuts, finely chopped
¼ teaspoon cream of tartar
   Maraschino cherries

Beat egg yolks until lemony. Gradually add the sugar and beat until thick and creamy. Stir in bread crumbs, farina, vanilla and walnuts. Beat egg whites and cream of tartar with clean beaters, in a large bowl, until stiff peaks form. Fold into batter.

Pour into two round 8-inch cake pans, greased and floured. Bake at 350 degrees for 25-30 minutes. Cool in pans for 10 minutes. Gently loosen cakes around edges and remove from pans. Cool.

When cakes are cool, split and fill with whipped cream filling. Stack layers together with cream filling. Frost top and sides. Decorate top with maraschino cherries. Serves: 8-10

Filling:
1 pint whipping cream
3 tablespoons powdered
   sugar

1 teaspoon vanilla

Whip cream until stiff. Add powdered sugar and vanilla. Beat well.

Note: 5-6 ripe peaches, peeled and sliced, or sliced sweetened strawberries may be added to the filling.

German Ladyfinger Torte

4 eggs, separated
1 cup whipping cream
5 ounces unsalted butter
5 ounces sugar

1½ ounces cognac
3½ ounces blanched almonds,
   chopped
48 ladyfingers

Beat egg whites until stiff peaks form. Set aside. Whip cream until stiff. Set aside.

Cream butter and sugar. Add egg yolks, one at a time. Add cognac and almonds.

Fold egg whites, whipping cream and butter cream together.

Line large bread pan with foil, leaving enough overlap to cover top. Spread some of the cream mixture in bottom of pan. Cover, lengthwise, with ladyfingers. Sprinkle ladyfingers with a little cognac, to slightly moisten. Continue to layer until all cream mixture is used; end with a cream layer. Fold foil over cake in pan. Refrigerate for 3-6 hours to allow ladyfingers to absorb some of the moisture from the creamy mixture. Freeze at least 1 day before serving.

To serve, cut in thin slices while frozen.

Mocha Torte

3 eggs, separated
¼ teaspoon cream of tartar
1 cup sugar

¼ cup hot, strong coffee
1 cup flour
1 teaspoon baking powder

In a small mixer bowl beat the egg whites with cream of tartar until stiff. Set aside.

In a medium-sized bowl beat egg yolks until thick. Gradually add sugar and beat until lemony and mixture forms a ribbon when beaters are lifted. Add hot coffee. Sift flour with baking powder; add to mixture and beat well. Fold egg whites into batter and pour into two 8½x1½-inch round cake pans which have been buttered and floured.

Bake at 350 degrees for 25 minutes. Cool on racks for 10 minutes. Turn out of pans and cool completely. To assemble, split each cake layer horizontally. Spread frosting between each layer and frost top and sides. Chill before serving. Serves: 12

Mocha Frosting:

1 teaspoon instant coffee
1½ teaspoons boiling water
2 ounces sweet chocolate, cut
   in small pieces

1 tablespoon whipping cream
1½ cups whipping cream
1 tablespoon sugar

Dissolve coffee in boiling water. Pour over chocolate and stir until chocolate is melted. Cool. Thin with 1 tablespoon whipping cream. Set aside. Whip 1½ cups whipping cream with 1 tablespoon sugar until stiff. Add cooled mocha-chocolate mixture. Mix well.

SNIPE

Bûche de Noel
(Christmas Log)

4 egg yolks
1 cup sugar
½ teaspoon vanilla
4 egg whites

1 cup sifted cake flour
½ teaspoon baking powder
¼ teaspoon salt
2 tablespoons rum

In small bowl, beat egg yolks until thick and lemon-colored. Gradually add ½ cup of sugar, beating constantly. Stir in vanilla. In large bowl, beat egg whites until soft peaks form. Gradually add remaining sugar, beating to form stiff peaks. Gently fold in yolk mixture. Sift together flour, baking powder and salt. Fold into egg mixture. Spread evenly in greased and floured jellyroll pan (15½x10½x1 inch). Bake at 375 degrees for 10-12 minutes. Immediately after removing from oven, loosen edges and turn out onto kitchen towel sprinkled with powdered sugar. Sprinkle cake evenly with rum. Roll the cake and towel together, starting at the long end of cake. Cool thoroughly.

Chocolate Filling:
⅔ cup sugar
⅓ cup water
2 egg yolks
½ cup softened butter or
    margarine

1½ squares unsweetened
    chocolate, melted
1 tablespoon rum
1 teaspoon instant coffee
    powder

In small pan, heat sugar and water to boiling. Cook to soft ball stage. In small bowl, beat egg yolks until thick and lemon-colored. Gradually add the hot syrup, beating constantly. Continue beating until mixture is cool. Beat in butter or margarine, 1 tablespoon at a time. Add melted chocolate and instant coffee. Continue beating until mixture is thick. Unroll cake. Spread ½ filling evenly over cake. Roll cake, starting with the long end. Wrap in plastic wrap and chill until filling is firm.

To assemble, make a diagonal cut 4 inches from end of roll. This forms a "branch". Frost log with filling. Press "branch" into log and frost. With tines of fork, mark to resemble tree bark. Decorate with frosting designs, if desired.

MARIPOSA LILY

Caramel Custard Flan with Brandy

¾ cup sugar
2 cups Carnation evaporated milk
2 cups light cream
6 eggs, room temperature

½ cup sugar
½ teaspoon salt
3 teaspoons vanilla
⅓ cup brandy

Place ¾ cup sugar in a heavy skillet. Over medium heat melt sugar until it becomes a light brown syrup. Immediately pour syrup into a heated 8-inch, extra deep, round cake pan. Holding pan with potholders, rotate pan to cover bottom and sides with syrup. Set aside.

In medium saucepan, heat milk and cream just until bubbles form around edge of pan.

In a large bowl, beat eggs slightly with mixer. Add sugar, sal and vanilla. Gradually stir in hot milk mixture. Add brandy. Pour into prepared baking pan.

Set in a shallow pan filled with ½ inch hot water. Bake at 325 degrees for 45-50 minutes or until a knife inserted in center comes out clean. Let custard cool, then refrigerate.

To serve, run a small spatula around edge of baking pan. Invert on shallow serving dish or plate. Warm 1 tablespoon brandy, ignite and quickly pour over flan. May also be served with whipped cream and berries in season. Serves: 10-12

Rum Pudding Dessert

6 egg yolks
1 cup powdered sugar
2 tablespoons gelatin
½ cup cold water

1 pint whipping cream
18 macaroons or ladyfingers
1 cup rum or fruit juice

Beat egg yolks with powdered sugar. Soften the gelatin in cold water in a small container. Place container in a small pan of hot water and stir gelatin until dissolved. Cool. Beat into egg mixture. Whip cream and fold in the egg-gelatin mixture. Dip macaroons into rum briefly.

Put half of egg mixture into a 9x13-inch pan or an 8½-inch spring-form pan, lined with plastic wrap. Layer with rum-dipped macaroons. Cover with remaining egg mixture. Refrigerate until ready to serve.

Note: Recipe for macaroons on page 186.

English Trifle

1 cup sugar
1 tablespoon cornstarch
½ teaspoon salt
4 cups milk
8 egg yolks
2 teaspoons vanilla
1 tablespoon cream sherry
2 (8 inch) sponge cake layers
¾ cup cream sherry

6 tablespoons raspberry
preserves (or fresh/frozen
blackberries, raspberries)
6 tablespoons toasted,
slivered almonds
½ cup heavy cream, whipped
½ cup candied cherries or
fresh berries

In a heavy saucepan, combine sugar, cornstarch and salt. Gradually add milk, stirring until smooth. Cook over medium heat, stirring constantly until mixture thickens and comes to boiling point. Boil 1 minute. Remove from heat.

In a small bowl, beat egg yolks slightly. Gradually add a few tablespoons of hot mixture; stir back into hot mixture in pan. Cook over medium heat, stirring constantly, to boiling point. Remove from heat. Stir in vanilla and 1 tablespoon cream sherry. Strain custard immediately into bowl. Cool and refrigerate several hours or overnight.

Split sponge cake layers in half, crosswise, to make 4 layers. Sprinkle with cream sherry. Spread each of 3 layers with 2 tablespoons preserves or berries and 2 tablespoons almonds.

In a deep, glass bowl, stack prepared layers, jam/berry-almond side up, spreading each with about 1 cup of custard. Top with plain layer and remaining custard. Refrigerate until served.

May be decorated with whipped cream, candied cherries or fresh berries. Serves: 8-10

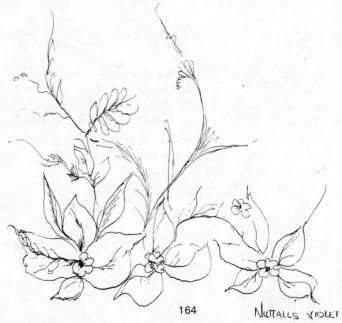

NUTTALLS VIOLET

Chocolate Almond Cheesecake

Crust:

1½ cups chocolate wafer
  crumbs
1 cup blanched almonds,
  lightly toasted and chopped
⅓ cup sugar
6 tablespoons butter, softened

Combine all ingredients and pat onto bottom and sides of a buttered 9½-inch springform pan.

Cheesecake:

1½ pounds cream cheese,
  softened
1 cup sugar
4 eggs
⅓ cup heavy cream
¼ cup almond flavored
  liqueur, such as Amaretto
1 teaspoon vanilla

In a large bowl cream cheese and sugar. Beat in eggs, one at a time, beating well. Add cream, Amaretto and vanilla, beating until mixture is light and creamy. Pour batter into springform pan and bake in the middle of a preheated 375 degree oven for 30 minutes. Remove from oven and transfer the cake to a rack. Let stand for 5 minutes. The cake will not be set.

Topping:

2 cups sour cream
1 tablespoon sugar
1 teaspoon vanilla

Combine sour cream, sugar, vanilla and spread mixture evenly on cake. Bake for 5-8 minutes. Let cake cool completely and chill overnight, lightly covered. Remove sides of pan; transfer to a cake stand. Press slivered almonds around the top edge, if desired. Serves: 12

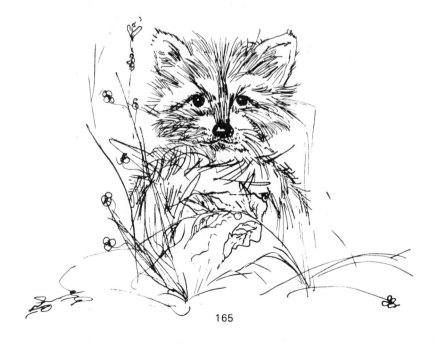

Cheese Cake

Crust:
1 cup zwieback or graham
  cracker crumbs

¼ cup sugar
¼ teaspoon cinnamon
¼ cup margarine, melted

Mix all ingredients and pat over the bottom and 1 inch up the sides of a 9 inch springform pan.

Filling:
4 eggs, separated
¼ teaspoon cream of tartar
1 cup sugar
2 tablespoons flour
¼ teaspoon salt

1 teaspoon vanilla or
1 tablespoon lemon juice and
  grated rind from half a
  lemon
1 pound cream cheese,
  softened
1 cup sour cream

Beat the egg whites until frothy. Add cream of tartar and continue to beat until soft peaks form. Gradually add ¼ cup sugar and beat until stiff peaks form. Set aside.

In a separate bowl beat the egg yolks until thick and gradually beat in ¾ cup sugar. Beat in all remaining ingredients. Fold in the egg whites. Pour mixture into prepared pan. Bake in a preheated 325 degree oven for 1 hour. Turn off oven. Open oven door and leave the cheesecake in turned-off oven for 20 to 30 minutes. Remove from oven and cool. Chill before using. Serves: 12

Note:
1 cup of sour cream
2 tablespoons of sugar

1 teaspoon of vanilla or lemon
  extract

May be mixed together and spread over the top of the baked cheese cake. Bake for 5 minutes in a 400 degree oven. Cool and chill before serving.

Hint: Cut cheese cake (and light textured cakes) with dental floss in a sawing motion.

wood lily

Purple Coneflower

Harebell

New York Cheese Cake

Crust:
1 cup flour
½ cup sugar
1 teaspoon lemon rind, grated

1¾ cups sugar
3 tablespoons flour
1 egg yolk, beaten
¼ teaspoon vanilla

Combine first 3 ingredients and cut in butter until mixture crumbles. Add egg yolk and vanilla. Pat 1/3 of dough in bottom of 9-inch spring-form pan, removing sides first. Bake at 400 degrees for 8 minutes or until golden brown. Cool. Attach sides of pan and pat remaining dough on sides of pan.

Filling:
5 (8 ounce) packages cream cheese
¼ teaspoon vanilla
¾ teaspoon lemon peel, grated
1¾ cups sugar

3 tablespoons flour
¼ teaspoon salt
1 cup eggs (4-6)
2 egg yolks
¼ cup whipping cream

Have cream cheese at room temperature. Beat until creamy. Add vanilla and lemon peel. Add next 3 ingredients gradually, blending into mixture. Add eggs and egg yolks, one at a time. Gently stir in whipping cream. Pour into crust. Bake at 450 degrees for 12 minutes. Reduce heat to 300 degrees and continue baking 55 minutes. Remove from oven. Loosen sides with a spatula after ½ hour. Remove sides after 1 hour. Can be glazed with a fruit glaze. Chill before serving.
Serves: 12-16

Strawberry Cream Puffs

Shells:
¼ pound butter
1 cup cold water

1 cup all-purpose flour
4 eggs, room temperature

Bring butter and water to a boil. Stir flour into boiling water all at once. Stir until mixture forms a mass. Remove from heat and add 4 eggs, one at a time, beating briskly. Drop batter onto cookie sheet in 12 well-shaped mounds.

Bake at 400 degrees for 40 minutes.

Filling:
¾ cup whipping cream
¼ cup powdered sugar

1 tablespoon Grand Marnier
1½ cups strawberries, sliced

Whip cream with sugar until very stiff. Stir in Grand Marnier. Fold in sliced strawberries.

To fill shells, cut off tops 1/3 of the way down. Scoop out any doughy pieces. Fill and replace tops and dust with powdered sugar.
Serves: 12

French Custard

⅓ cup sugar
1 tablespoon flour
1 tablespoon cornstarch
¼ teaspoon salt
1½ cups milk

1 egg yolk, beaten
1 teaspoon vanilla
1 cup whipping cream, whipped

Mix sugar, flour, cornstarch and salt in a saucepan. Gradually stir in milk. Cook and stir mixture until it boils and thickens. Cook and stir 2-3 minutes longer.

Stir a little hot mixture into egg yolk. Return to hot mixture, stirring constantly. Bring just to boiling point. Add vanilla. Cool completely.

Beat the custard to smooth consistency. Fold in stiffly beaten cream.

Note: Good filling for cream puffs.

Eggs à la Neige

Meringue:
6 egg whites
¾ cup sugar

¼ teaspoon salt
3 cups milk, heated

Beat egg whites until foamy. Gradually add sugar and salt, beating until stiff.

Heat milk in a large pan. (Milk should be about 2 inches deep). Drop egg-shaped mounds of meringue into the milk and poach for 2½ minutes on one side. Turn and poach other side for 2½ minutes, being careful to keep a small space between meringues. Remove with slotted spoon and drain on paper towels. Repeat process until meringue is used. Should make about 8 meringues. Cover with waxed paper and refrigerate.

Custard Sauce:
1½ cups heavy cream, scalded
1½ cups milk from poached
  meringue, strained

6 egg yolks, beaten
½ cup sugar
Pinch of salt
1½ tablespoons flour

Add a little cream-milk mixture to egg yolks. Mix well and stir into remaining cream mixture. Heat until it coats a spoon. Cool thoroughly.

2 pints fresh strawberries,
  cleaned and dried

1 square semi-sweet
  chocolate, shaved

Serve by placing a meringue in a dessert bowl. Top with strawberries and custard. Garnish with shaved chocolate curls. Serves: 8

Pots de Créme

6 (1 ounce) squares semi-sweet chocolate
½ cup whipping cream
2 tablespoons sugar
3 egg yolks

1½ teaspoons grated orange peel
1 tablespoon orange liqueur
½ cup whipping cream
6 orange peel strips (optional)

Stir chocolate, ½ cup whipping cream and sugar in double boiler over simmering water until smooth. Remove from heat.

Beat egg yolks until thick. Beat chocolate mixture into egg yolks gradually. Stir in orange peel and liqueur. Refrigerate, covered, for 1 hour.

Whip cream until stiff. Fold in chocolate mixture. Spoon into pot de creme cups or sherbet cups. Garnish with an orange peel strip. Refrigerate, covered. Serves: 6

Romme Grot

1 pint thick cream
1 cup flour
1½ pints milk, heated to boil
2 tablespoons sugar

1 teaspoon salt
½ cup sugar
1 teaspoon cinnamon

Simmer cream until it has an oily look on top. Sprinkle ½ of flour on cream, stirring constantly. Cook until thickened and butter appears on top. Skim butter and reserve. Sprinkle rest of flour on porridge, stirring constantly, continuing to cook for 2-3 minutes. Gradually add hot milk. Stir to keep smooth consistency. Add salt and sugar.

Pour into serving dish. Serve with reserved butter, sugar and cinnamon. Serves: 6-8

Scandinavian Sotsuppe
(Fruit Soup)

½ cup pearl tapioca
1 cup raisins
1 cup prunes
2 quarts water
1 cup sugar

2 sticks cinnamon
1 lemon, sliced
1 tablespoon vinegar
8 ounces grape jelly
or grape juice

Soak tapioca, raisins and prunes overnight in water. Over low heat, cook for 1 hour.

Add sugar, cinnamon, sliced lemon and vinegar. Simmer for 15 minutes. Add jelly or juice. Simmer for 15 minutes. Serve hot or cold. (If served cold, remove lemon and cinnamon sticks before storing in refrigerator). Serves: 12-14

Sweet Soup

2 pounds of prunes
2 cups raisins
1 cup sugar
½ cup minute tapioca

5 cups cold water
Juice of 1 lemon (2 tablespoons)
2 packages frozen raspberries (10 ounce)

Place prunes and raisins in a 5 quart kettle with water to cover; soak for about 1 hour. Cook slowly until tender; stir in 1 cup sugar.

In a large saucepan, cover tapioca with cold water. Cook on medium heat, stirring frequently, until thick. Pour into prunes and raisins. Remove from stove and add juice of lemon. Cool.

Add 2 packages frozen raspberries. Fold in gently. Soup will thicken after it is thoroughly chilled.

Serves: 16

Custard Angel Food Cake

1¼ cup sugar
½ cup water
8 eggs, separated
1 cup cake flour, sifted

½ teaspoon salt
1 teaspoon cream of tartar
1 teaspoon vanilla

Combine water and sugar. Cook until it reaches 230 degrees. Beat egg yolks until very light and lemony. Continue to beat while adding hot syrup in a thin stream. The mixture will definitely thicken. Cool.

Sift flour and salt to mix well. Fold into the yolk mixture which has cooled to lukewarm.

In large, clean bowl with clean beaters, beat egg whites. When foamy add cream of tartar, beating until stiff, but not dry. Fold in yolk-flour mixture very carefully. Add vanilla.

Bake in an ungreased tube pan at 300 degrees for 1½ to 1¾ hours.

Note: This cake is firmer than a regular angel food. It is especially good filled with fresh strawberry mousse or topped with fresh fruits and whipped cream.

Mrs. Harris' Pound Cake

½ pound butter or margarine
½ cup vegetable shortening
3 cups sugar
1 teaspoon vanilla extract
1 teaspoon lemon extract

6 eggs
3 cups flour
½ teaspoon baking powder
Pinch of salt
1 cup milk

Cream butter, shortening and sugar until light and fluffy. Add vanilla and lemon extract. Blend well. Add eggs, one at a time, and continue beating after each addition.

Sift flour, baking powder and salt together; add, alternately with milk, to creamed mixture.

Pour into a greased, floured tube or bundt pan. Bake at 325 degrees for 1 hour and 30 minutes or until cake tests done.

Apple Cake with Rum Sauce

2 cups sugar
½ cup butter
2 eggs
2 cups flour
2 teaspoons soda

1 teaspoon nutmeg
½ teaspoon salt
½ teaspoon cinnamon
7-8 apples, pared and finely chopped

Cream sugar and butter in a large bowl. Add eggs.

Add flour, soda, nutmeg, salt and cinnamon. Mix well. Add apples, mixing after each addition. The batter will be very thick.

Bake in 9x13-inch pan, greased and floured, at 350 degrees for 30-45 minutes.

Rum Sauce:
1 cup butter
1 cup cream

2 cups sugar
1 teaspoon vanilla
1 teaspoon rum flavor

Bring butter, cream and sugar to a rolling boil. Add vanilla and rum flavoring. Serve hot over warm cake.

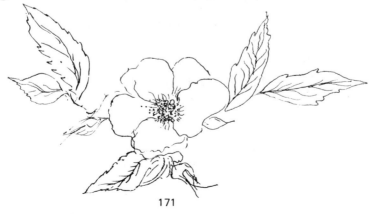

Chocolate Sheet Cake

2 cups sugar
2 cups flour
3½ tablespoons cocoa
½ cup margarine
1 cup water

½ cup oil
2 eggs
½ cup buttermilk
1 teaspoon soda
1 teaspoon vanilla

Do not use mixer. Combine sugar, flour and cocoa in large bowl.

In saucepan combine margarine, water and oil. Bring to a boil. Pour over flour and sugar mixture.

Combine eggs, buttermilk, soda and vanilla. Add to batter and blend thoroughly.

Pour into greased 12x18-inch jellyroll pan. Bake at 400 degrees for 18-20 minutes. Remove from oven. Immediately spread frosting over hot cake. Yield: 40 squares

Frosting:
½ cup margarine
⅓ cup milk
1 pound powdered sugar

3½ tablespoons cocoa
1 teaspoon vanilla
1 cup nuts, chopped
1 cup coconut

Bring margarine and milk to a boil in saucepan. Add powdered sugar, cocoa and vanilla. Mix well. Add nuts and coconut.

Carrot Cake

4 eggs
1½ cups oil
2 cups sugar
2¼ cups flour
2 teaspoons cinnamon
2 teaspoons soda
2 teaspoons vanilla

1 teaspoon salt
2 cups coconut
2 cups carrots, shredded
1 cup walnuts, chopped
1 (8 ounce) can crushed
  pineapple, drained

Combine all ingredients, as listed. Mix with wooden spoon. Place in 9x13 pan, greased and floured.

Bake 1 hour at 350 degrees. Cool. Spread with cream cheese frosting.

Frosting:
½ cup butter
1 (8 ounce) package cream
  cheese

2 teaspoons vanilla
1 pound powdered sugar

Cream butter, cream cheese and vanilla. Add sugar and blend to a smooth spreading consistency.

Lemon Sponge Pie

1 unbaked 9-inch pie shell
3 eggs, separated
1 cup sugar
¼ cup butter or margarine, melted and cooled
3 tablespoons flour

1½ cups milk
¼ cup fresh lemon juice (the juice of 1 lemon)
Grated lemon rind from one lemon

Line the pie shell with wax paper. fill with a single layer of dried beans and bake in a preheated 375 degrees oven for 10 minutes. Remove beans and paper and continue baking 3 to 5 minutes longer. Cool crust.

Beat the egg whites in a small bowl until stiff. Set aside. In a large bowl, beat the egg yolks. Gradually add the sugar and all remaining ingredients. Gently fold in the stiffly beaten egg whites and spoon filling into pie shell. Bake in a preheated 350 degree oven for 40 minutes. Serve warm or chill.

Sour Cream Apple Dessert

2 cups flour
2 cups brown sugar, firmly packed
¾ cup soft butter
1 cup nuts, chopped
1½ teaspoons cinnamon
1 teaspoon soda

½ teaspoon salt
1 cup sour cream
1 teaspoon vanilla
1 egg
2 cups apples, pared, finely chopped

Preheat oven to 350 degrees.

In large bowl combine flour, brown sugar and butter. Blend until crumbly. Stir in nuts. Press 2¼ cups crumb mixture into ungreased 13x9-inch pan.

To remaining mixture add cinnamon, soda, salt, sour cream, vanilla and egg. Blend well. Stir in apples. Spoon evenly over crumb mixture in pan.

Bake 25-35 minutes or until toothpick, inserted in center, comes out clean.

Serve with whipped cream or ice cream. Serves: 12-15

Plum Kuchen with Streusel (German)

Dough:
- ½ cup butter or margarine, soft
- ½ cup sugar
- 1 teaspoon vanilla extract
- 2 eggs
- 1½ cups all-purpose flour (or 1 cup plus 2 tablespoons all-purpose flour and ⅓ cup cornstarch gives a finer texture)
- 2 teaspoons baking powder
- ¼ teaspoon salt
- 2-4 tablespoons milk

Topping:
- 20-21 Italian plums, halved and pitted or
- 1 pound pared and thinly sliced tart baking apples

Streusel:
- ½-⅔ cups flour
- ½-¾ cups sugar
- 1 teaspoon cinnamon
- ⅓ cup butter or margarine, cold

Combine streusel ingredients. Set aside. Cream butter and gradually add sugar. Beat until mixture is fluffy. Add eggs and beat well. Add dry ingredients, which have been sifted together, alternately with milk. Spread dough into greased and floured 9x13x2 inch pan; top with plums, skin side down. Sprinkle with streusel.

Bake in 350 to 375 degree oven for 40 to 45 minutes. Sprinkle warm cake with powdered sugar. Serve cake, warm or cold, with slightly sweetened whipped cream.

Crumb Cake
(German Kruemelkuchen)

Dough:
- 1 cup butter or margarine
- 1 cup sugar
- 1 egg
- 1 teaspoon vanilla
- ½ teaspoon salt
- 3¾ cups flour
- 2 teaspoons baking powder

Filling:
- 3 tablespoons fine dry bread crumbs or zwieback crumbs
- 1½ pounds tart apples, thinly sliced and dusted with ½ cup sugar and 1 tablespoon flour

Cream butter and sugar until light and fluffy. Add egg and vanilla and mix. Add half of the flour (mixed with salt and baking powder) and mix. Work remaining flour in with fingers to make a stiff mixture. Crumble (or grate with a coarse grater) half of dough into a greased 9x13 inch pan. Sprinkle bread crumbs over it. Spread fruit evenly over mixture in pan and crumble remaining dough over top. Bake at 350-375 degrees for 40 minutes or until done. If desired, sprinkle warm cake with powdered sugar. Cut into squares and serve warm or cold with slightly sweetened whipped cream.

Note: 2 cups of cranberry jelly or any jam may also be used as filling.

Grandma's Boiled Raisin Cake

1 cup raisins
2 cups water
2 teaspoons baking soda
½ cup butter
1 cup brown sugar

1 egg
2 cups flour
½ teaspoon cinnamon
½ teaspoon nutmeg
1 teaspoon vanilla

Boil raisins with water for 10 minutes. Let cool. Add 2 teaspoons baking soda. Set aside.

Cream butter and brown sugar. Add egg and beat well. Add raisins and water mixture alternately with the dry ingredients. Add vanilla. Turn into greased and floured 9x13 inch pan. Bake at 350 degrees for 40 minutes. Frost cooled cake with icing.

Penuche Icing:
½ cup butter
1 cup brown sugar

¼ cup milk
1¾-2 cups powdered sugar

Melt butter in saucepan. Add brown sugar. Boil and stir over low heat for 2 minutes. Add milk and bring to a boil, stirring constantly. Cool to lukewarm. Gradually beat in 1¾ to 2 cups powdered sugar. Beat until thick enough to spread.

Springtime Rhubarb Crumble

1 cup flour
¼ teaspoon salt
1 cup quick cooking oats
½ cup sugar
6 tablespoons butter, melted

4 cups rhubarb, diced
1¼ cups sugar
¼ teaspoon cinnamon
2 tablespoons flour
1 egg, beaten

Sift flour and salt. Add oats, sugar and butter. Blend with pastry fork until crumbly. Press ½ of mixture on bottom and sides of a 9-inch pie plate.

Mix rhubarb, sugar, cinnamon, flour and egg. Pour into crust. Top with rest of crumbs.

Bake 45 minutes at 350 degrees.

Serve warm or cold with whipped cream or ice cream.

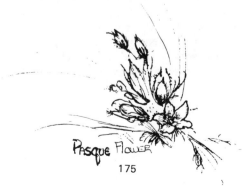

Pasque Flower

Chocolate Truffle Cake

24 ounces semi-sweet chocolate
   chips
¾ cup unsalted butter
1 tablespoon flour

1 tablespoon sugar
1 tablespoon hot water
6 eggs, separated
2 teaspoons vanilla

Preheat oven to 400 degrees. Grease an 8-inch springform pan. Line the bottom with a circle of wax paper. Grease the paper and lightly flour lining and sides of pan. Melt chocolate and butter in the top of a double boiler. Add flour, sugar and water. Blend well. Remove from heat and add egg yolks one at a time, beating well after each addition. Add vanilla. Beat egg whites until soft peaks form. Fold into chocolate mixture. Turn into pan and bake for 20 minutes. Cake will look uncooked in the center. Cool completely, then chill or freeze. As cake cools, it will sink a bit. To serve, remove from pan, trim edges, turn upside down and peel off wax paper. Cut into at least 12 portions and serve with sweetened whipped cream.

Indian Pudding

2 heaping tablespoons
   cornmeal
2 tablespoons tapioca
½ cup brown sugar
   Dash of ground ginger
   Dash of salt

1 quart whole milk
½ cup molasses
½ cup raisins
1 cup sour milk
1 tablespoon butter

Mix cornmeal, tapioca, brown sugar, ginger, salt, 1 quart milk, molasses and raisins in 2 quart casserole. Bake uncovered at 325 degrees for 2 hours, stirring occasionally.

Add 1 cup sour milk and butter. Bake 1 hour longer.

Serve warm with vanilla ice cream. Serves: 6-8

Steamed Plum Pudding
(Christmas Pudding)

1 cup flour
1 pound chopped suet: 2 cups
½ pound dark raisins
½ pound light raisins
1 pound currants, washed
  and dried
¼ pound chopped citron
¼ pound glace red cherries
1 whole nutmeg, grated
1 tablespoon cinnamon
½ tablespoon mace
½ teaspoon allspice

½ teaspoon ground cloves
1 teaspoon salt
¼ cup sugar
¼ cup brown sugar
7 egg yolks, slightly beaten
¼ cup heavy cream
½ cup brandy, sherry or rum
3 cups grated fresh white
  bread crumbs (crusts
  removed)
7 egg whites, stiffly beaten

Sift the flour into a large bowl. Mix the suet, raisins, currants, citron and cherries in another bowl and spoon some of the flour over the fruit. Toss well and set aside. Resift the remaining flour with the nutmeg, cinnamon, mace, allspice, cloves, salt, sugar and brown sugar. Return all ingredients to the large bowl. Add egg yolks, cream, brandy and bread crumbs and mix well by hand. Fold in egg whites. Pour batter into a greased and sugared 1 gallon mold, or several smaller molds. Use decorative tin molds, or any tin can. Fill the containers no more than 2/3 full. Cover them very securely with waxed paper and foil, and tie in place with string.

Place molds on a trivet in a large kettle over 1 inch of boiling water. Cover the kettle tightly. Cook on high heat until steam begins to escape, then decrease temperature. Steam for about 6 hours. This long slow cooking period is necessary so that all the suet melts before the flour particles burst. If the pudding cooks too fast and the flour grain bursts before the fat melts, the pudding will be tough and hard. Cool pudding before using. Serve with hard sauce. Pudding freezes well.

Note: Be sure to check water level from time to time during the steaming period, and add more water as needed.

Hard Sauce for Plum Pudding:

1 cup powdered sugar
5 tablespoons butter,
  softened

2 tablespoons brandy, sherry
  or rum

Combine sugar and butter. Beat in brandy, sherry or rum.

Makes 1 cup. Recipe may be doubled, if desired. This is an uncooked sauce. It keeps well if tightly covered and refrigerated.

Louise Burke's Holiday Fruitcake

1½ cups figs, chopped
½ cup candied orange peel
½ cup pitted prunes, cooked
1½ cups dates

1⅔ cups apricots, cooked
1½ cups raisins
1½ cups currants
2 cups honey

Mix well and let stand one week.

¼ cup candied pineapple
½ cup citron
½ cup candied cherries, cut in half
¾ cup pecans, coarsely chopped

¾ cup walnuts, coarsely chopped
¾ cup almonds, coarsely chopped

Add to the honey-fruit mixture.

Cake mixture:
1 cup butter
3 eggs, beaten
½ cup brandy or strong coffee
3½ cups flour

¼ teaspoon cloves
¼ teaspoon nutmeg
¼ teaspoon allspice
¾ teaspoon cinnamon

Cream shortening, add honey mixture. Add well-beaten eggs and brandy. Sift together flour and spices; add to mixture. Mix well. Place in 8 pans (7½x3½x2½), greased and lined with 2 layers of brown paper. Bake at 250 degrees for 2 hours. Cool. Wrap cooled cakes in cheese cloth, moistened with brandy, then in aluminum foil. Yield: 8 cakes, 1-1¼ pounds

CRESTED
WHEAT GRASS

Icelandic Vinarterta

1 cup butter	4 cups sifted flour
1 cup sugar	2 teaspoons baking powder
2 eggs	½ teaspoon salt
1 teaspoon vanilla	4 tablespoons milk

Cream butter and sugar. Mix until light and fluffy. Add eggs, one at a time. Add vanilla.

Sift together flour, baking powder and salt. Add to butter mixture, alternately, with milk. Dough should be smooth and medium heavy. Chill.

Filling:

2 pounds prunes, pitted	1½ cups sugar
2 cups water, enough to cover prunes	1 teaspoon vanilla
	¼ teaspoon salt
	½ teaspoon ground cardamom

Cover prunes with water; simmer until tender. Cool. Drain, reserving liquid. Coarsely chop prunes in food processor or grinder. Return pulp to reserved liquid. Add sugar. Cook until thick. Cool. Add vanilla, salt and cardamom. Chill.

To assemble, divide dough in 7 portions. Roll each, on a lightly floured surface, in a 9-inch circle. Lift onto the outside bottom of a 9-inch, layer cake pan. Trim circle to fit pan bottom. Bake at 350 degrees for 10 minutes or until light brown. Repeat baking until all 7 layers are baked and cooled.

Spread prune filling between each layer. Wrap cake in waxed paper; enclose in a plastic bag and store in a cool place for 48 hours before serving.

To serve, cut cake in quarters and then in thin slices.

Note: Cake will keep for several weeks tightly wrapped and stored in a cool place.

Charlie's Pirouette Pie

1 baked 9-inch pie shell,
  sprinkled with ¼cup
  pecans
¾ cup sugar
½ cup butter
1½ teaspoons vanilla
2 (1 ounce) squares
  unsweetened baking
  chocolate, melted

2 eggs
1 (3¼ ounce) package Jello
  Instant Vanilla Pudding
½-¾ cup whipping cream
⅓ cup chocolate curls

Cream sugar and butter until fluffy. Add vanilla. Add melted chocolate. Gradually add eggs, one at a time. Beat each egg 1½ minutes.

Pour into pie shell and chill.

Prepare pudding as directed on package. Pour over chocolate layer. Chill for 2 hours.

Garnish with whipped cream; add chocolate curls. Chill.

Lemon Meringue Pie

1 cup sugar
3 level tablespoons
  cornstarch
1 tablespoon butter
  Pinch of salt
2 egg yolks

Grated rind of 1 lemon
Juice of 1 lemon
Grated rind of ½ orange
Juice of ½ orange
1 cup water

Cook in double boiler until thick. Put in 8-inch unbaked pie shell.

Meringue:
3 egg whites
¼ teaspoon salt
¼ teaspoon extract or 1
  teaspoon lemon juice

6 tablespoons fine granulated
  sugar

Have egg whites at room temperature. If eggs are cold, put into a pan of warm water to bring to room temperature before separating. Add salt and extract or lemon juice to egg whites; beat to a coarse foam. Add sugar, 1 tablespoon at a time, beating constantly. Beat meringue until it forms definite peaks. It should be stiff and glossy. Spread meringue on lukewarm filling. It should touch pastry at all points, completely sealing in the filling. Bake in a moderate oven at 350 degrees for 12 to 15 minutes, or until golden brown.

180

BLUE BUNCH WHEAT

Sour Cream Blueberry Pie

1 (9 inch) pie shell, unbaked	1 cup sugar
½ tablespoon butter, melted	1½ cups sour cream
1 (16 ounce) package frozen	2 tablespoons sugar
blueberries or 4 cups fresh	¼ teaspoon vanilla
¼ cup flour	⅛ teaspoon cinnamon

Spread melted butter over bottom of crust. The butter will seal the crust and help keep it crisp.

Mix blueberries, flour and 1 cup sugar. If using frozen blueberries, let stand at room temperature for 15-20 minutes. Put blueberry mixture into pie shell.

Bake at 400 degrees for 12 minutes. Turn oven to 350 degrees and bake until mixture bubbles and thickens, about 25-30 minutes. Cool slightly.

Mix sour cream, 2 tablespoons sugar and vanilla. Spread over the slightly cooled pie. Sprinkle with cinnamon. Bake at 250 degrees for 10 minutes. Cool before serving. Serves: 6-8

Chocolate Angel Strata

1 (9 inch) pie shell, baked	¼ cup water
2 egg whites	2 egg yolks, slightly beaten
¼ teaspoon vinegar	2 cups whipping cream
¼ teaspoon salt	½ teaspoon cinnamon
¼ teaspoon cinnamon	½ cup sugar
½ cup sugar	
6 ounces semi-sweet	
chocolate chips	

Beat egg whites until soft peaks form. Add vinegar, salt and cinnamon. Gradually add sugar. Beat until stiff peaks form. Spread on bottom and sides of baked shell.

Bake at 325 degrees for 12-18 minutes until meringue is lightly brown. Cool.

In a double boiler melt chocolate chips in water. Add egg yolks. Stir until mixture thickens.

Spread 3 tablespoons of this mixture on the meringue.

Whip cream and cinnamon until soft mounds form. Gradually beat in sugar until the cream is stiff.

Spread half of this mixture over chocolate layer.

Fold remaining whipped cream-cinnamon mixture and remaining chocolate mixture together. Spread on top of pie. Chill 6 hours. Serves: 8-10

Chocolate Pecan Pie

2 (1 ounce) squares
  unsweetened chocolate
3 tablespoons butter
1 cup light corn syrup
¾ cup sugar
3 eggs, slightly beaten

1 teaspoon vanilla
1 cup pecans, chopped
1 (9 inch) pie shell, unbaked,
  brushed with melted butter
1 cup whipped cream

Melt chocolate and butter over hot water. Boil syrup and sugar together 2 minutes. Add chocolate and butter. Pour slowly over eggs, stirring constantly. Add vanilla and nuts. Pour into pie shell. Bake at 375 degrees for 50 minutes. Cool. Top with whipped cream. Serves: 8

Poppy Seed Pie

1 (9 inch) pie shell, unbaked
½ tablespoon butter, melted
1 (12½ ounce) can poppy seed
  filling
½ cup walnuts, finely chopped

½ cup raisins, chopped
½ cup sour cream
1 egg
1 ounce brandy
2 tablespoons sugar

Prepare pie shell by spreading melted butter over bottom of crust. The butter will seal the crust, helping to keep it crisp.

Mix all ingredients together. Pour into pie shell. Top with lattice strips of pie dough, if desired.

Bake at 350 degrees about 45 minutes or until crust is golden.

Make a powdered sugar glaze: 2-3 tablespoons hot water
  1 cup powdered sugar

Combine and drizzle over top of pie. Serves: 8-10

KILLDEER

Nut Meringue Pie

3 egg whites
1 cup sugar
1 teaspoon vanilla
1 teaspoon baking powder

¾ cup Ritz, graham, or soda
   crackers, crushed
1 cup pecans or walnuts,
   chopped
   Fresh berries
   Whipped cream

Preheat oven to 350 degrees.

Beat egg whites until stiff and gradually add sugar, beating until the mixture is glossy and holds stiff peaks. Add vanilla and baking powder. Fold in crushed cracker crumbs and nuts.

Spread mixture into well-greased pie plate, pushing mixture high on the sides.

Bake 25-35 minutes. Cool.

Fill with fresh strawberries, or berries of choice, and slightly sweetened whipped cream. Serves: 6-8

Note: Pie freezes well without filling. Remove from freezer, add fruit and whipped cream. Serve immediately.

Apple Crumb Pie

1 (9 inch) pie shell,
   unbaked
4-5 large tart cooking apples
½ cup sugar

1 teaspoon cinnamon
½ cup sugar
¾ cup flour
⅓ cup butter

Pare apples. Cut in eighths and arrange in pie shell. Mix sugar and cinnamon. Sprinkle over the apples.

Mix sugar, flour and butter until crumbly. Sprinkle as a topping over the pie.

Bake at 450 degrees for 10 minutes, and at 350 degrees for 40 minutes. Serves: 6-8

Never Fail Pie Crust

3 cups flour
½ teaspoon baking powder
½ teaspoon salt
1 teaspoon sugar

1¼ cups shortening
1 egg
5 tablespoons water
1 tablespoon vinegar

Blend dry ingredients together with shortening. Add liquid. Form into 4 balls and roll out on pastry canvas, lightly floured. Yield: Dough for 2 double crust pies

Partially Baked Pie Crust

Fit dough into pie plate and trim away excess pastry. Flute the rim of pie crust. Prick bottom and sides, at intervals, to prevent puffing.

Line the crust with waxed paper and fill with 2 cups dried beans.

Bake at 400 degrees for 12 minutes. Remove beans and fill with desired filling. Finish baking.

Note: Beans are used to keep the crust flat and are not harmed by heat.

Chocolate Truffles

¼ cup heavy cream
2 tablespoons orange liqueur
6 ounces sweet or semi-sweet chocolate chips

4 tablespoons unsalted butter, softened
Finely chopped nuts
Chocolate sprinkles

Boil cream in a small, heavy saucepan until it is reduced to 2 tablespoons. Remove from heat, stir in orange liqueur and chocolate chips. Return to low heat and stir until chocolate melts. Beat in the softened butter until mixture is smooth. Pour into a shallow bowl and refrigerate for 40 minutes, or until firm. Spoon out into rough one-inch balls. Roll half the balls in finely chopped nuts, and the other half in chocolate sprinkles. Cover truffles and store in the refrigerator. Let them stand at room temperature for 30 minutes before serving. Yield: 24 truffles

Note: Any favorite liqueur may be substituted for the orange liqueur.

Orange Balls

1 (12 ounce) package vanilla wafers, crushed
1 cup powdered sugar
1 cup coconut
1 cup walnuts or pecans, chopped

1 (6 ounce) can frozen orange juice, thawed
1½ cups powdered sugar, for dipping

Mix crushed wafers, 1 cup powdered sugar, coconut, nuts and orange juice. Chill. Roll into small balls. Roll in powdered sugar.

Store in tight container. Yield: 3 dozen

Rum or Bourbon Balls

3 cups vanilla wafers, crushed
3 tablespoons light corn syrup
1½ tablespoons cocoa
1 cup walnuts, finely chopped

4 ounces white rum or bourbon
½ cup powdered sugar

With wooden spoon mix all ingredients, except powdered sugar. Add drops of hot water, as needed, to retain stickiness. Roll into small balls. Roll in powdered sugar. Store in tight container.

Finsk Bröd

½ cup butter
¼ cup sugar
1¼ cups flour

1 egg, beaten
½ cup almonds, finely chopped

Cream butter and sugar together. Gradually add flour, mixing well until blended.

Shape dough into 2½x½-inch sticks. Brush tops with beaten egg. Sprinkle with almonds.

Bake on ungreased baking sheet at 325 degrees for 20-25 minutes. Yield: 3 dozen

Pecan Crisps

½ cup butter
1 cup sugar
1 egg yolk
2 tablespoons milk

2 cups all-purpose flour
1 egg white, unbeaten
1⅓ cup pecans, finely chopped

Cream butter. Add sugar gradually and cream thoroughly. Blend in egg yolk and milk. Add flour.

Roll dough out to ¹⁄₁₆ -inch thickness. Dough needs to be very thin to be crisp. Brush egg white over dough surface. Sprinkle with chopped nuts. Carefully roll a rolling pin over the nuts to press them into dough.

Cut into 1½-inch squares with a very sharp knife.

Place on greased cookie sheet. Bake at 375 degrees for 15 minutes.

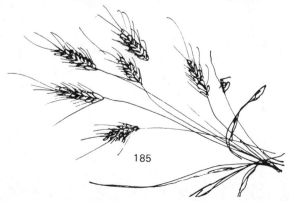

Danish Bonbons

1 cup butter
⅓ cup powdered sugar
¾ cup cornstarch

1 cup flour
1 cup pecans, finely chopped

Cream butter and sugar until fluffy. Add cornstarch and flour. Chill.

Shape dough into 1-inch balls. Scatter nuts on wax paper. Flatten each ball on top of nuts.

Place bonbons on ungreased cookie sheet, nut side up. Bake at 350 degrees for 15 minutes.

When cool, frost with frosting on bottom side.

Frosting:
1 cup powdered sugar
1½ tablespoons butter

1 tablespoon lemon juice
1 tablespoon lemon rind, optional

Combine all ingredients and mix well.

Meringue Drops

4 egg whites, stiffly beaten
1 cup sugar
¾ cup dates, chopped
1 cup graham cracker crumbs

½ cup chopped nuts
1 cup coconut
Dash of salt

Mix together in order given. Drop by teaspoon on a greased cookie sheet. Bake at 300 degrees for 10-12 minutes or until lightly browned

German Makronen
(Macaroons)

3 egg whites
5 ounces sugar
½ teaspoon vanilla
5 ounces blanched almonds, ground

1 tablespoon flour
¼ teaspoon almond extract

Beat egg whites until stiff. Beat in sugar a little at a time. Add vanilla. Mix ground almonds with the flour and fold into egg whites. Add almond extract.

Drop by teaspoon, making 12 makronen, on a well-greased cookie sheet. Bake at 350 degrees for 10-12 minutes or until lightly browned.

Mexican Wedding Cakes

½ cup butter
½ cup shortening
½ cup powdered sugar
1¾ cups flour

1 teaspoon vanilla
⅔ cup nuts, chopped
1½ cups powdered sugar, for dipping

Cream butter and shortening. Add ½ cup sugar and mix well. Sift flour and add to cream mixture. Add vanilla and nuts. Chill in refrigerator. Make into small balls. Bake 10 minutes at 350 degrees. Remove, cool slightly and roll in powdered sugar. When completely cool, roll in powdered sugar again.

Store in tight container in a cool place. May be frozen.

Fattigmann
(Norwegian cookie)

6 egg yolks
4 tablespoons sugar
1 tablespoon butter, melted
⅛ teaspoon salt

2 cups flour
6 tablespoons cream
⅛ teaspoon ground cardamom

Beat egg yolks until creamy. Add sugar; beat until thick and ivory colored. Add rest of ingredients.

Roll dough thin and cut in diamond shapes. Fry in deep fat, at 370 degrees, for 2-3 minutes, or until golden. Drain on paper toweling. Sprinkle with powdered sugar.

Rosettes
(Norwegian)

1 cup flour
½ teaspoon salt
1 tablespoon sugar

2 eggs, slightly beaten
1 cup milk
1 tablespoon salad oil
Oil for deep fat frying

Sift flour, salt and sugar together. Add to beaten eggs, milk and oil. Beat only until smooth.

Heat oil to 370 degrees in a saucepan or deep fat fryer. Heat rosette iron in hot oil; tap excess from iron. Dip iron into batter until 2/3 covered. Fry until golden brown. Drain on paper towel. Sprinkle with powdered sugar.

187

Krumkaka

3 large eggs
¾ cup sugar
1 teaspoon cardamom or
   vanilla

½ cup butter, melted
1 cup plus 2 tablespoons flour,
   sifted

Beat eggs until thick. Gradually add sugar. Add either cardamom or vanilla. Alternately, add butter while folding in flour.

Bake in preheated krumkaka iron. Place 1 teaspoon of batter on iron and turn immediately. Bake until light brown. Roll, while warm, on the handle of a wooden spoon or a krumkaka cone. Yield: 4 dozen

Spritz

½ teaspoon baking powder
3 cups flour
1 cup cornstarch
1 cup sugar

2 cups butter
1 egg
1 teaspoon vanilla

Sift dry ingredients together. Blend in butter until mixture resembles coarse crumbs. Stir in egg and vanilla. Beat well. Chill.

Put dough through a cookie press onto an ungreased baking sheet. Bake at 375 degrees for 8-12 minutes or until cookies are golden.

Note: If dough becomes soft, return to refrigerator.

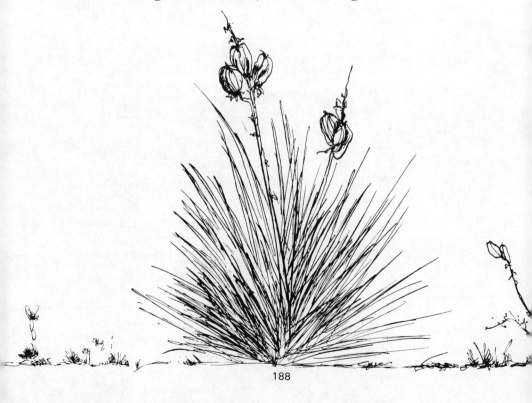

Pfeffernusse I

4 eggs
2 cups sugar
4 cups flour
1 teaspoon baking powder
½ teaspoon cloves, ground
½ teaspoon nutmeg
½ teaspoon allspice
2 teaspoons cinnamon

¼ teaspoon pepper
1 tablespoon rum
Rind of 1 lemon, grated
3 ounces candied citron, chopped
3 ounces almonds, finely chopped

Beat eggs and sugar in a large mixer bowl until fluffy.

Sift flour, baking powder, cloves, nutmeg, allspice, cinnamon and pepper together. Add to egg mixture.

Mix in rum, lemon rind, citron and almonds. Knead dough until smooth.

Roll out to about ½-inch thickness. Cut with 1-inch round cookie cutter. Place on greased baking sheet.

Bake at 350 degrees for 15-20 minutes. Remove from oven. Glaze while hot. Yield: 10 dozen.

Glaze:

8 ounces powdered sugar
2 egg whites

1 teaspoon rum

Sift powdered sugar and beat with egg whites until foamy. Add rum.

Peppernuts II

½ cup and 6 tablespoons dark karo syrup
½ cup and 6 tablespoons honey
½ cup sugar
½ cup shortening
1 egg

1 teaspoon ground cloves
½ teaspoon baking powder
½ teaspoon soda
½ teaspoon anise extract
5 cups flour, enough to make a stiff dough

Mix all ingredients together in order given. Refrigerate in covered bowl for 1-3 days. When ready to bake, preheat oven to 375 degrees. On lightly floured board, roll 1 cup dough into a long rope. Cut into pieces about ½-inch wide. Place each piece on greased cookie sheet, leaving a space between pieces to allow for spreading. Bake 12-15 minutes. Store in tightly covered container. Yield: 10 dozen

Cream Wafers

1 cup butter	2 cups flour
⅓ cup whipping cream or	1½ cups granulated sugar, for
⅓ cup evaporated milk	dipping

Mix butter, cream or milk, and flour together. Chill.

Roll dough to ⅛ to ¼-inch thickness. Cut with a small, round cookie cutter. Coat with sugar on both sides. Place on an ungreased cookie sheet. Prick with a fork. Bake at 375 degrees for 7-9 minutes. Cool and put together with filling.

Filling:

¼ cup butter	1 egg yolk
¾ cup powdered sugar	1 teaspoon vanilla

Mix all ingredients together and fill cookies.

Bonket
(A Dutch Pastry)

Filling:	Crust:
8 ounces almond paste,	1 cup butter or margarine
softened	2 cups flour, sifted
3 eggs, beaten	4-6 tablespoons ice water
¼ teaspoon lemon extract	

For the filling, combine almond paste, beaten eggs and lemon extract. Mix into a smooth paste. Refrigerate.

For the crust, cut butter into the flour until crumbly. Add water, 1 tablespoon at a time. Do not overmix. Press into 3 balls. Chill in refrigerator for 1 hour.

On lightly floured board roll out each ball to ⅛-inch in thickness, 10-inches long and 4-inches wide.

Reserving 2 tablespoons of the filling, spread each length, down the center, with ⅓ of the remaining filling. Moisten edges with water and fold dough over filling, sealing side seam and ends.

Place on heavy cookie sheet, side by side. Brush with melted butter and reserved filling. Slash diagonally every 2 inches. Bake at 400 degrees for 20 minutes. Remove from oven. Cool on rack.

Almond Lace Wafers

½ cup butter
½ cup sugar
¾ unblanched almonds,
   finely ground

1 tablespoon flour
1 tablespoon cream
1 tablespoon milk

Combine all ingredients in a small, heavy saucepan over low heat, stirring until butter melts. Drop by teaspoons on a non-stick cookie sheet. Place only 4 or 5 cookies at a time. Bake at 350 degrees about 7 minutes or until slightly brown and still bubbling in the center.

Let cool only until the edge is firm enough to lift with a spatula. Quickly lift cookies onto waxed paper, turning topside down. Roll around the handle of a wooden spoon. Wafers must be warm to roll easily. Yield: 3 dozen

Jellyroll Cookies

¾ cup dates
1 cup boiling water
1 tablespoon flour
⅔ cup flour
½ teaspoon baking powder
½ teaspoon salt
3 eggs, beaten

¾ cup sugar
½ teaspoon vanilla
½ cup pecans, chopped
20 maraschino cherries
1 cup powdered sugar
1 cup pecans, chopped

Place dates in sieve and pour boiling water over them. Finely cut dates with scissors and coat with 1 tablespoon flour. Set aside.

Sift flour, baking powder and salt. Beat eggs until foamy. Add sugar. Beat until thick and ivory colored. Add vanilla. Fold in chopped pecans and dates. Spread in 15x11-inch jellyroll pan, lined with waxed paper, greased and floured lightly.

Drain 20 maraschino cherries. Arrange cherries across each end of the batter about ½ inch from the edge. Bake in 325 degree oven for 30-35 minutes.

Turn out onto waxed paper which has been sprinkled with powdered sugar. Remove paper from bottom. Cut off hard edges and cut in half. Roll each rectangle beginning with cherries. Wrap in waxed paper and chill.

Frost with butter frosting, roll in 1 cup chopped pecans and slice.

Frosting:
2 tablespoons butter
1¼ cups powdered sugar

¾ teaspoon cream
1 teaspoon vanilla

Combine all ingredients and beat until smooth.

Pecan Tarts

Crust:

2 (3 ounce) packages cream
  cheese

2 sticks butter or margarine
2 cups flour

Mix cream cheese, butter and flour together. Divide into 48 small balls. Flatten and press each into bottom and sides of small-size cupcake pans to form little pie shells.

Filling:

1 cup brown sugar
1 tablespoon butter
¼ cup water

1 egg
½ cup pecans, chopped

Mix in small saucepan over medium heat but do not boil. Add 1 rounded teaspoon nut mixture to each shell. Bake at 350 degrees for 20 minutes. Remove from pans while warm. May be frozen until ready to serve.

Kourabiedes
(Greek Butter Cookies)

1 cup soft butter
¼ cup granulated sugar
2 egg yolks
1 teaspoon vanilla extract
¼ teaspoon almond extract

2½ cups all-purpose flour
½ cup walnuts, finely chopped
32 whole cloves
1 cup powdered sugar

Preheat oven to 350 degrees. In large bowl with electric beater at medium speed, beat butter, granulated sugar, egg yolks, vanilla and almond extracts until light and fluffy. Add flour and nuts; mix well with hands. Turn dough onto lightly floured surface. Divide in half. With hands shape each half in a roll 16-inches long. Cut each roll in 16 pieces (1-inch size) and shape in balls. Press a whole clove into center of each ball.

On ungreased cookie sheets, place balls 1-inch apart. Bake 20 minutes or until brown. Remove to wire rack. Sprinkle lightly with powdered sugar while still warm. Cool. Before serving, sprinkle with powdered sugar again. Yield: 32 cookies

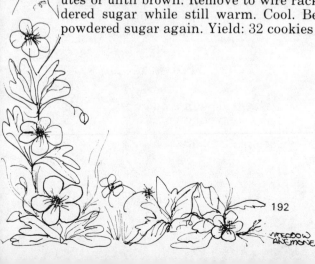

MEADOW
ANEMONE

Super Sugar Cookies

1 cup powdered sugar	1 teaspoon baking soda
1 cup granulated sugar	1 teaspoon cream of tartar
1 cup butter or margarine	4 cups flour plus 4 rounded
1 cup oil	tablespoons, sifted
2 eggs	1½ cups sugar
1 teaspoon vanilla	½ teaspoon nutmeg
½ teaspoon salt	

Cream together the sugars, butter and oil until light and fluffy. Beat in eggs. Add vanilla. Sift dry ingredients together and add to creamed mixture. Chill 2 hours.

Mix sugar and nutmeg in a shallow bowl. Coat small, walnut-size pieces of dough with mixture. Place on ungreased cookie sheet. Press down with glass dipped in sugar-nutmeg mixture. Bake at 375 degrees for about 10 minutes. Yield: 7 dozen

Peanut Butter Cookies

1 cup butter	1 teaspoon vanilla
1 cup peanut butter	1 cup pared, grated apple
1 cup sugar	3 cups flour
1 cup brown sugar, firmly	1 teaspoon soda
packed	1 teaspoon salt
2 eggs	1 teaspoon cinnamon

Cream butter, peanut butter, sugar and brown sugar. Add eggs, one at a time, beating well. Add vanilla and apple. Sift flour, soda, salt and cinnamon together. Add to creamed mixture. Drop rounded teaspoonfuls of dough onto cookie sheet. Flatten each one with a fork. Bake at 350 degrees for 12-15 minutes. Yield: 6 dozen

Pecan Crispies

1 cup butter or margarine	½ cup potato chips, crushed
½ cup sugar	½ cup pecans, chopped
1 teaspoon vanilla	2 cups flour

Cream butter, sugar and vanilla. Add potato chips and nuts. Stir in flour. Form into small balls and place on ungreased cookie sheet. Press flat with bottom of glass dipped in sugar. Bake at 350 degrees for 15-18 minutes or until lightly browned.

Crunchy Cookies

1 cup butter or margarine
1 cup sugar
1 cup brown sugar
1 egg
1 cup oil
1 cup regular oats
1 cup cornflakes, crushed
½ cup coconut, shredded
½ cup walnuts, chopped
3-4 cups flour
1 teaspoon baking soda
1 teaspoon salt
1 teaspoon vanilla extract

Cream butter and gradually add remaining ingredients in order given. Roll into walnut-size balls. Place them on ungreased baking sheet and press down with a fork. Bake at 325 degrees for 12 minutes. Cool slightly before removing from baking sheet.

Carrot Oatmeal Cookies

1 cup brown sugar
½ cup shortening
2 eggs
½ cup milk
1 cup carrots, shredded
1½ cups flour
1 teaspoon baking powder
½ teaspoon soda
½ teaspoon salt
½ teaspoon cinnamon
½ teaspoon nutmeg
2 cups quick-cooking oatmeal
2 cups raisins

Cream sugar, shortening and eggs until light and creamy. Add milk and carrots. Stir until well blended.

Sift flour, baking powder, soda, salt, cinnamon and nutmeg together. Add remaining ingredients to flour mixture, stirring to coat raisins with flour. Blend into creamed mixture.

Drop by heaping teaspoons on a greased cookie sheet. Bake at 375 degrees for 12 minutes or until golden. Yield: 6 dozen

Oatmeal Cookies

½ cup raisins
1 cup boiling water
½ cup butter
1 cup sugar
1 cup quick cooking oatmeal
1 egg, slightly beaten
1 cup flour
½ teaspoon soda
½ teaspoon cinnamon
Dash of salt
1 teaspoon vanilla
½ cup nut meats, chopped

Plump raisins in boiling water. Set aside. Melt shortening. Add sugar and oatmeal. Add egg. Sift flour with soda, cinnamon and salt and add to creamed mixture. Add vanilla, nut meats and drained raisins. Mix well.

Roll into small balls. Dip top of ball in sugar. Place on greased cookie sheet and press down on top with fork dipped in milk. Bake at 350 degrees for 10-12 minutes. Yield: 3 dozen

Old Fashioned Gingersnaps

1 cup sugar	3¼ cups flour
1 cup shortening	1 teaspoon ginger
¾ cup molasses	1 teaspoon soda
1 egg	½ teaspoon salt

Cream sugar and shortening. Add molasses. Mix well. Add egg, continue to stir. Sift dry ingredients together and add to first mixture. Mix well. Roll in balls and dip in granulated sugar. Flatten slightly. Place on greased baking sheet. Bake at 370 degrees until cookies spread out and crack on top, about 10-12 minutes. Yield: 5½ dozen

Anise Nut Rusks
(Twice-Baked Italian Cookies)

1 cup butter or margarine, softened	¼ cup anise seed, finely crushed
2 cups sugar	6 eggs
¼ cup anise flavored liqueur (or 3½ tablespoons water with 1 teaspoon anise extract)	5½ cups flour
	1 tablespoon baking powder
	1 teaspoon salt
3 tablespoons bourbon or brandy	2 cups almonds, pecans or walnuts, finely chopped

In large bowl mix butter, sugar, anise liqueur, bourbon and anise seed. Add eggs, one at a time and mix well. Sift flour, baking powder and salt. Add to creamed mixture. Add nuts. Chill dough, covered with plastic wrap, for several hours or overnight.

Divide the sticky dough into 4 parts. On lightly floured board, shape each piece with hands into a 24-inch long log. Cut in half and place the 2 logs, lengthwise, 4 inches apart on a well-greased baking sheet. Pat and press the logs into flat loaves about 2-inches wide and ½-inch thick. Proceed with the remaining dough in the same manner but keep dough chilled until ready to use.

Bake in preheated oven at 375 degrees for 20 minutes or until loaves are lightly browned. Cool loaves on the baking sheets.

Cut baked loaves diagonally into ½ to ¾-inch slices. Arrange slices with cut side down and close together in one layer on baking sheets. Toast them in 375 degree oven for 15-20 minutes or until lightly toasted. Cool on wire racks. Store in airtight containers.

Note: The rusks are a perfect complement to a glass of wine, a cup of tea or to a crisp green salad.

Orange-Lemon Bars

⅓ cup brown sugar, firmly
   packed
¾ cup flour
⅓ cup butter or margarine
2 eggs, beaten
½ cup brown sugar, firmly
   packed
¾ cups flaked coconut
½ cup chopped walnuts
⅛ teaspoon baking powder

¼ teaspoon salt
½ teaspoon vanilla
1½ tablespoons fresh orange
   juice
1½ tablespoons fresh lemon
   juice
½ teaspoon grated orange rind
½ teaspoon grated lemon rind
1½ cups powdered sugar

Mix ⅓ cup brown sugar and flour. Cut in butter until mixture resembles coarse meal. Press mixture into a 9x9 inch pan. Bake at 350 degrees for 15 to 20 minutes until set, but not brown. Combine eggs, brown sugar, coconut, nuts, baking powder, salt and vanilla. Spread over partially baked dough. Bake at 350 degrees for 20 minutes. Mix juices, grated rind and powdered sugar until smooth. Remove bars from oven and immediately spread with frosting. Cool to room temperature before cutting in squares.

Custard Bars

First layer:

1 cup margarine
½ cup sugar
2 eggs, beaten

4 cups graham cracker
   crumbs
2 cups flaked coconut

In a large saucepan mix margarine and sugar. Add eggs. Cook over medium heat for 5 minutes, stirring constantly. Remove from heat and add graham cracker crumbs and coconut. Press firmly into 9x13-inch pan. Chill.

Second layer:

½ cup margarine
1 (3¾ ounce) package instant
   vanilla pudding

6 tablespoons milk
3 cups powdered sugar

Beat all ingredients together and spread over first layer. Chill thoroughly.

Third layer:

1 (6 ounce) package chocolate
   chips
2 tablespoons margarine

2 tablespoons white karo
   syrup
1 tablespoon water
1 teaspoon vanilla

Melt chocolate chips in double boiler. Add margarine. Cool. Add karo syrup, water and vanilla. Mix well and spread on second layer. Chill. May be frozen.

Creme de Menthe Squares

First layer:
½ cup butter or margarine
½ cup unsweetened cocoa
½ cup powdered sugar

1 egg, beaten
1 teaspoon vanilla
2 cups graham cracker
  crumbs

In saucepan combine butter and cocoa. Heat and stir until well blended. Remove from heat and add powdered sugar, egg and vanilla. Stir in graham cracker crumbs. Mix well. Press firmly into ungreased 9x13-inch pan. Chill.

Second layer:
½ cup butter or margarine
⅓ cup green creme de menthe
  liqueur

3 cups powdered sugar

Melt butter. In small mixer bowl combine melted butter and creme de menthe. At low speed beat in the powdered sugar. Beat until smooth. Spread over first layer and chill at least 1 hour.

Third layer:
¼ cup butter or margarine

1½ cups semi-sweet chocolate
  pieces

In small saucepan combine butter and chocolate pieces. When melted, spread over second layer. Cut in small squares. May be frozen until ready to use.

Cheesebake Dreams

⅓ cup brown sugar
1 cup unsifted flour
½ cup walnuts, chopped
⅓ cup butter
1 (8 ounce) package cream
  cheese

¼ cup sugar
1 egg
2 tablespoons milk
1 tablespoon lemon juice
1 teaspoon vanilla

Preheat oven to 350 degrees. Mix sugar, flour and walnuts together. Blend in butter. Reserve ⅓ cup of the mixture. Pat remaining mixture in an 8-inch pan. Bake for 12-15 minutes. In small mixer bowl, beat cream cheese and sugar until smooth. Add egg, milk, lemon juice and vanilla. Continue to beat until creamy. Pour over baked crust. Sprinkle with reserved crumbs. Bake 25 minutes more, or until set. Cool. Cut into 2-inch squares, then diagonally in half. Yield: 32 bars

Brownies

½ cup butter or margarine
2 ounces unsweetened chocolate
2 eggs, room temperature
1 cup sugar

1 teaspoon vanilla
½ cup flour
⅛ teaspoon salt
½ cup walnuts, chopped (optional)

In a saucepan melt butter and chocolate together. Cool. Set aside. In small mixer bowl beat eggs until pale, about 2 minutes. Gradually add sugar. Beat until thick, about 10 minutes. Add cooled butter-chocolate mixture and vanilla. Fold in flour and nuts. Pour into a greased and floured 8x8x2-inch pan. Bake in a preheated oven at 350 degrees for 25 minutes. Brownies will be underbaked.

While still warm, spread with filling:

1½ cups powdered sugar
⅓ cup butter
½ cup whipping cream

4-6 (1 ounce) Hershey bars

Cook sugar, butter and cream in saucepan over medium heat to soft ball stage. Remove from heat and beat to spreading consistency. Spread over brownies. While still warm place Hershey bars over filling. When soft, spread over all. Yield: 25 brownies

Lattice Jams

3 cups all-purpose flour
½ cup sugar
3 teaspoons baking powder
1 cup butter or margarine
2 eggs, slightly beaten
¼ cup milk
1 teaspoon vanilla

1 (8 ounce) jar grape jam, using 5¼ ounces
1 (8 ounce) jar strawberry jam, using 5¼ ounces
1 (8 ounce) jar peach or apricot preserves, using 5¼ ounces
Powdered sugar

In a large bowl stir flour, sugar, baking powder and salt together. Cut in butter until mixture resembles coarse crumbs. Combine eggs, milk and vanilla. Add to dry ingredients. Mix well and knead gently on floured surface until smooth. Set aside ⅓ of the dough. Roll remaining dough into a 15x10-inch rectangle. Place in baking pan. Spread each jam crosswise over ⅓ of the dough, using peach or apricot for middle strip. Roll the reserved ⅓ of dough into a 12x10-inch rectangle. Cut into ½-inch strips. Carefully form strips into a lattice top, diagonally, over jam-topped dough.

Bake at 400 degrees for 20-25 minutes. Cool. Dust with powdered sugar. Cut into bars. Yield: 28-32 bars

Cream Cheese Puffs

2¼ cups unsifted all-purpose
    flour
¼ teaspoon salt
1 cup butter or margarine,
    chilled

½ cup sour cream or yogurt
1 egg yolk

Combine flour and salt. Cut in chilled butter until size of peas. In a separate bowl, combine sour cream and egg yolk. Stir into flour mixture. Using hands, shape into a ball. Divide dough in half and shape each into flat 8-inch rounds. Cover with plastic wrap and refrigerate. May be chilled overnight, if desired.

Sweet Cheese Filling:
1 (8 ounce) package cream
    cheese, room temperature
1 egg

½ cup sugar
1 teaspoon vanilla
1 teaspoon lemon rind, grated

Blend all ingredients. Mix until smooth.

Roll one of the discs on lightly floured surface until it is about 1/16-inch thick. Trim edges and cut into 3-inch squares.

Place a teaspoon of filling in the middle of each square and ease it into an ungreased, miniature muffin pan. Press opposite corners to the center, squeezing lightly. Chill in refrigerator while preparing second disc. Bake at 375 degrees, or until lightly browned, for 25-30 minutes.

Almond Bars

¾ cup butter or margarine
1½ cups flour

3 tablespoons sugar

Cut butter into flour and sugar mixture until it is cornmeal consistency. Press into an ungreased 9x13-inch pan. Bake at 350 degrees for 20 minutes.

Filling:
6 eggs, beaten
2 cups sugar

2 cups flaked coconut
3 tablespoons almond extract

In medium bowl beat eggs until creamy. Add sugar. Beat well. Add coconut and almond extract. Stir well. Pour batter over the partially baked crust. Bake at 350 degrees for 30 minutes. Cool. May be frozen.

Hip Loader Bars

Filling:
1 (14 ounce) can
sweetened, condensed milk

6 ounces chocolate chips
2 tablespoons butter
1 teaspoon vanilla

In a saucepan mix condensed milk, chocolate chips, butter and vanilla. Heat to melt butter and chocolate chips. Stir well. Set aside.

Crust:
½ cup butter
1 cup brown sugar
1 egg, unbeaten
1¼ cups flour

1½ cups quick cooking oatmeal
¼ teaspoon salt
½ teaspoon soda
1 teaspoon vanilla

Cut softened butter into sugar. Add egg, flour, oatmeal, salt, soda and vanilla. Press ⅔ of mixture into a greased 9x9 pan. Pour reserved chocolate mixture over top. Crumble remaining crust mixture over filling. Bake at 350 degrees for 25 minutes.

Pumpkin Bars

4 eggs
1⅔ cups sugar
1 cup oil
1 (16 ounce) can pumpkin
2 cups flour

2 teaspoons baking powder
2 teaspoons cinnamon
½ teaspoon salt
1 teaspoon baking soda

In a large mixer bowl beat eggs, sugar, oil and pumpkin together until light and fluffy. Add dry ingredients and mix thoroughly.

Spread batter in ungreased 15x10x1-inch pan. Bake at 350 degrees for 25-30 minutes. Cool and frost with cream cheese frosting.

Frosting:
1 (3 ounce) package cream cheese

½ cup butter
1 teaspoon vanilla
2 cups powdered sugar

Beat cream cheese and butter in small mixer bowl. Stir in vanilla. Add powdered sugar, a little at a time, beating well until smooth. Spread on bars and cut into squares.

Matrimonial Squares
(Date Bars)

½ cup shortening
¼ cup margarine
1 cup brown sugar
1¼ cups quick-cooking oatmeal

1½ cups flour
½ teaspoon soda
½ teaspoon baking powder
Dash of salt

Combine ingredients and mix well. Press ½ of mixture in a 9x13-inch ungreased pan. Set remaining mixture aside.

Filling:
1 pound dates

½ cup sugar
1 cup water

Combine the ingredients. Cook over medium heat until mixture is of spreading consistency. Cool slightly. Spread the date mixture over the crumb crust. Sprinkle the remaining crumbs over the top and press down slightly. Bake at 350 degrees for 20-25 minutes or until lightly browned.

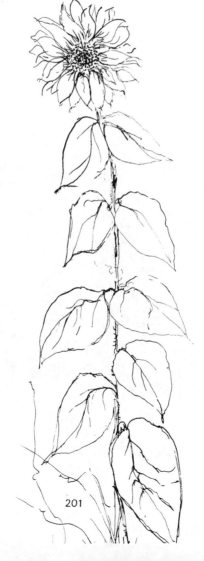

Sour Cream Raisin Bars

2 cups raisins   ¾ cup water

Place raisins in a small saucepan with water and bring to a slow boil; simmer for 10 minutes. Drain water. Cool. Set aside.

Crust: 1⅓ cups quick cooking oatmeal
  1 cup butter   1¾ cups flour
  1 cup brown sugar   1 teaspoon soda

Cream butter and brown sugar. Add oatmeal, flour and soda. Pat ½ of mixture in greased 9x13-inch pan. Bake at 350 degrees for 7 minutes.

Filling: 1½ cups sour cream
  3 egg yolks   2½ tablespoons cornstarch
  1 cup sugar   ¼ teaspoon ground cloves
  ¼ teaspoon salt   1 teaspoon cinnamon
  ½ teaspoon nutmeg   1 teaspoon vanilla

Mix all ingredients and bring to a boil. Reduce heat, stirring constantly until mixture thickens. Add raisins and vanilla. Pour over baked crust. Sprinkle remaining crumb mixture over top. Bake for an additional 30 minutes.

"NICE EXTRAS"

Chocolate Topping

½ cup light corn syrup
1 cup sugar
1 cup water
3 (1 ounce) squares
   unsweetened chocolate,
   melted

1 teaspoon vanilla
1 cup evaporated milk

Cook syrup, sugar and water to the soft ball stage. Add melted chocolate and vanilla. Slowly add evaporated milk. Store in refrigerator.

Note: This is not a pouring sauce; it is a spooning one.

Creamy Pralines

1 (14 ounce) can sweetened
   condensed milk
1 can water
2½ cups sugar

2 tablespoons butter
1 teaspoon vanilla
4 cups pecans

Combine milk, water, sugar and butter in a heavy saucepan. Bring to a rolling boil over high heat, stirring constantly. Reduce to medium heat; continue to stir until mixture becomes glossy and will form a soft ball when tested in cold water. Cooking process will take 45 to 60 minutes. Remove from heat. Add vanilla and pecans. Beat with a wooden spoon until mixture cools slightly. Drop by tablespoons on waxed paper. Cool and store in airtight container.

Million Dollar Fudge

1 (14 ounce) can evaporated
   milk
2 tablespoons butter
4½ cups sugar
⅛ teaspoon salt
2 cups nuts, chopped
1 (pint) jar marshmallow
   cream

12 ounces semi-sweet
   chocolate pieces
12 ounces German sweet
   chocolate or 4 (1 ounce)
   squares unsweetened
   chocolate

Combine evaporated milk, butter, sugar and salt in large saucepan. Bring to a boil for 6 minutes, stirring constantly. Pour over remaining ingredients in a large bowl and beat until chocolate is melted. Turn into 2 greased 8-inch square pans. Cool and cut into squares. Yield: 4 pounds

Caramels

2 cups sugar
1 cup butter
2 cups cream

1½ cups corn syrup
2 teaspoons vanilla
1 cup nuts, chopped

Combine sugar, butter, 1 cup of cream and corn syrup. Bring to a boil. Add second cup of cream and continue to cook until a firm ball forms in cold water (250 degrees on candy thermometer). Remove from heat and stir in vanilla and nuts. (For chocolate caramels, add 2 tablespoons chocolate.) Pour into buttered 8-inch pan. Cool. Cut and wrap candy pieces in waxed paper.

Almond Roca

1 pound butter
2½ cups granulated sugar
5-6 ounces slivered almonds
1 (8 ounce) giant milk chocolate
   candy bar

½-¾ cups walnuts, finely
   chopped

Melt butter over medium heat in a large, cast iron or aluminum skillet. When partially melted, add sugar and almonds. Stir constantly, very slowly and gently, for about ½ hour. Do not be alarmed if butter seems to separate. Gentle stirring will combine butter and sugar as it cooks. Cook until mixture becomes smooth and a dark brown, toffee color appears.

Remove from heat; pour on a greased jellyroll pan. While still hot, break ½ of candy bar into pieces and place on top of roca. Spread over the surface. Sprinkle with ½ of walnuts. When chocolate hardens put another jellyroll pan on top of candy and turn it over. Candy will now be in second pan but roca side up.

Melt remaining half of candy bar. Spread on roca side. Sprinkle chocolate with remaining walnuts. After candy is thoroughly cooled, break into pieces with knife handle. Store in airtight container.

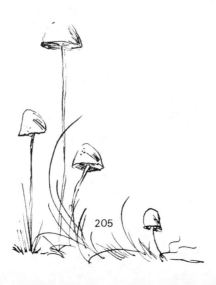

Strawberry Jam

2½ cups sugar
½ cup water

1 quart fresh strawberries,
washed and hulled

Mix 2 cups sugar and the water in large kettle. Boil until soft crack stage (290 degrees). Add all strawberries at once. Gently fold into hot syrup. Return to boiling and slowly simmer for 10 minutes, stirring gently. Stir in remaining ½ cup sugar and boil 5 minutes longer. Pour into shallow pan and let stand in cool place overnight. In the morning bring to a boil and ladle into hot sterilized jars. Cover with melted parafin to seal. Yield: 4 half pints

Alternate method of sealing jars: Place hot preserves in warm, sterilized jars. Put a little gin or vodka on top of hot preserves and light with a match. While burning, screw lid very tightly on top to seal. (This serves the same purpose as putting hot wax on top.)

Jezabel

1 cup ground bell peppers
¾ cup ground hot peppers
6½ cups sugar
1½ cups cider vinegar

1 bottle Certo
¼ teaspoon green food
coloring

Remove seeds from peppers, grind and save juice. Measure ground peppers with juice. Bring sugar, vinegar and peppers to a rolling boil. Boil for 10 minutes. Remove from heat, add Certo and food coloring. Pour into sterilized jars. (Wear rubber gloves when handling the hot peppers.) This is great with fowl and meats. It is good with Munster cheese and cream cheese and may be served with crackers for hors d'oeuvres. Yield: 6 to 7 half-pints

Hot Curried Fruit

1 (1 pound 14 ounce) can sliced
peaches
1 (15½ ounce) can pineapple
chunks
1 (16 ounce) can apricot
halves

1 (16 ounce) can pears, sliced
½ cup butter, melted
½ cup brown sugar
1 teaspoon to 1 tablespoon
curry powder, as desired

Drain all fruit. Combine butter, brown sugar and curry powder. Toss fruit in mixture. Bake uncovered for 30 minutes at 350 degrees. Serve warm. Makes 8 servings.

Serving suggestions: Use as an accompaniment for brunch dishes, roast pork, baked ham, baked leg of lamb, meat balls, or as a dessert served with slightly sweetened whipped cream.

Butternut Squash Chutney

2 lemons
1 orange
1 to 1¼ pounds butternut squash
2 cups sugar

2 tablespoons chopped ginger root
½ teaspoon grated nutmeg

Remove the outer skin (zest only) from the lemons and orange and reserve it. Squeeze the fruit and reserve the strained juice. Quarter the unpeeled squash and remove the seeds. Cut squash into paper thin slices. Combine fruit zest and juice, squash slices and all other ingredients in a shallow saucepan. Bring to a boil, stirring frequently. Reduce heat, cover and cook 20 minutes. Uncover and cook on low heat for 30 to 45 minutes, stirring frequently. The chutney will keep several weeks in the refrigerator. It may also be processed in a water bath and preserved.

Yogurt

1 quart milk
½ cup instant nonfat dry milk

3 tablespoons plain yogurt at room temperature

In a bowl, mix dry milk with 1 cup milk; stir in remaining milk. Rinse a 2 quart pan with cold water, and pour milk mixture into it. Heat to 190-210 degrees. Do not boil! Remove from heat and cool milk to 110 degrees. In a small bowl, stir yogurt until creamy. Mix ⅓ cup warm milk into the yogurt, then stir mixture into remaining warm milk. Mix well. Pour into a 1½ quart Pyrex casserole. Cover, and wrap casserole in a towel. Heat oven to its lowest temperature and turn off. Place wrapped casserole in the turned-off oven. Let yogurt stand, undisturbed, for 4-5 hours. If yogurt is not thick enough, extend the standing time. Remove from oven and refrigerate.

Limeade Dressing

⅓ cup frozen limeade concentrate (thawed)

⅓ cup honey
⅓ cup salad oil

With rotary beater, mix all ingredients. Serve on fresh fruit. Yield: 2 cups

Jack's French Dressing

2 medium onions, chopped fine
2 teaspoons savory salt
½ teaspoon ground cloves (optional)
½ teaspoon garlic salt
¾-1 cup sugar
½ teaspoon paprika
½ teaspoon dry mustard

4 tablespoons Worcestershire sauce
2 cups oil
1 tablespoon prepared horseradish
1 cup vinegar
1 (14 ounce) bottle tomato ketchup

Mix all dry ingredients first. Add Worcestershire sauce, oil, horseradish, vinegar and ketchup. Put in 2-quart jar with tight lid. Shake 2 minutes. Keep refrigerated.

Mayfair Dressing

1 medium onion, quartered
1 heaping teaspoon Accent
1 teaspoon fresh ground pepper
1 (2 ounce) can rolled ancho-anchovies with capers

1 clove garlic
½ cup oil
¼ cup prepared mustard
2 eggs, unbeaten
1 cup oil

Combine onion, accent, pepper, anchovies, garlic and ½ cup of oil in blender. Cover and run until well blended. Add the eggs and 1 cup of oil and run again until very well blended. Yield: 2 cups

Note: Flat fillets of anchovies and 1 teaspoon capers may be substituted for the rolled anchovies.

Pesto Sauce

2 cups fresh basil leaves, lightly packed, stems removed
½ cup olive oil
3 tablespoons pine nuts
3 garlic cloves, peeled and sliced

¾ teaspoon salt
⅔ cup freshly grated Parmesan cheese
3 tablespoons freshly grated Romano cheese
¼ cup soft butter

Blend basil, olive oil, pine nuts, garlic and salt in a food processor until smooth. Transfer to a bowl and beat in cheese and butter until well mixed. Makes 6 servings with fettucine or spaghetti.

Taco Sauce

3 quarts raw tomatoes,
  peeled, cut into chunks
2 green peppers, chopped
1½ cups onion, chopped

3 cloves garlic, chopped
½ cup brown sugar
¼ cup crushed red pepper or 1
  teaspoon cayenne pepper

Combine above ingredients in large Dutch oven and cook over medium heat for 30 minutes. Seal hot. Yield: 6-7 pints

Refried Bean Dip

2 cups refried beans
1 cup (about 4 ounces)
  Cheddar cheese, grated
½ cup green onion, including
  tops, chopped

¼ teaspoon salt
3 tablespoons taco sauce

In a pan or heatproof pottery, mix refried beans, cheese, onion, salt and taco sauce. Cook, uncovered, over low heat, stirring, until heated.

Serve warm with tortilla chips.

Relish

3 apples, cored but not pared
2 dill pickles
1 onion

¼ cup sugar
½ cup vinegar

Grind apples, pickles and onion together. Add suagar and vinegar mixing well. Let stand overnight. Yield: 1 pint

Marinade for Cornish Hens

½ cup onion, chopped
½ cup soy sauce
2 tablespoons brown sugar
2 tablespoons sesame seed
2 tablespoons oil and butter
½ teaspoon salt

2 teaspoons lemon juice
½ teaspoon pepper
½ teaspoon fresh ginger,
  thinly sliced
2 tablespoons sherry wine
2 tablespoons pineapple juice

Mix ingredients for marinade. Pour over hens and marinate for several hours; drain and stuff with a favorite dressing. Roast hens in a covered barbecue unit for 1¼ hours, or until tender, basting with marinade every 15 minutes. Yield: 2 cups marinade (enough for 6-8 birds)

Salsa Verde

To prepare the tomatillos:

Remove husks, wash and cut in half. Place into a saucepan with enough water so that tomatillos will not scorch while cooking. Water should cover about ¼ of the tomatillos. Bring to a boil, reduce heat, cover pan and simmer approximately 10 to 15 minutes or until tomatillos are cooked and soft. Blend in a blender just until nicely chopped.

For each 2 cups of blended tomatillos add the following ingredients:

2 to 4 pickled jalapeno or serrano chiles, stems and seeds removed, minced
1 small onion, finely chopped
1 clove garlic, minced or mashed
½ teaspoon salt, or to taste
1 tablespoon fresh minced cilantro or 1 teaspoon dried cilantro

Place in a covered container and refrigerate. If salsa is too thick, add a little of the water used to cook the tomatillos, or juice from the jalapenos.

Sweet, Crispy Pickle Slices

4 quarts medium-sized cucumbers
6 medium onions, sliced
2 green peppers, chopped
3 garlic cloves
⅓ cup salt
5 cups sugar
1½ teaspoons turmeric
1½ teaspoons celery seed
3 tablespoons mustard seed
3 cups vinegar

Slice cucumbers. Do not peel. Slice onions. Chop green peppers. Combine the cucumbers, onions and green peppers with garlic and salt. Cover with cracked ice. Mix and let stand for 3 hours. Drain thoroughly. Combine sugar, seasonings and vinegar and pour over cucumber mixture. Heat in a saucepan just to boiling. Pour into hot, sterilized jars and seal.

Dill Pickles

10 cups water
6 cups white vinegar (5%)
1 cup pickling salt
1 teaspoon pickling spice
½ teaspoon alum

2 bunches fresh dill
1 garlic clove
1 hot pepper
  Pickling-size cucumbers

Combine water, vinegar and salt. Bring to a boil. In each quart jar place pickling spice, alum, dill, garlic and hot pepper. Clean cucumbers and pack in jars (if large, slice lengthwise or crosswise for hamburger dills). Pour boiling pickling sauce over cucumbers and seal. Yield: 9 quarts

Dandelion Wine

2 quarts dandelion blossoms
1 gallon water
4 oranges

4 lemons
4 pounds sugar
1 cake yeast

Wash dandelion blossoms and bring to a boil in water. Cover and simmer for one hour. Strain and put liquid into a crock. Add the juice and the chopped rinds of oranges and lemons. Stir in the sugar and crumble in the yeast. Let stand at room temperature for one week. Strain. Allow liquid to stand at room temperature for fermentation for 4 to 6 weeks. Stir every day. Strain, fine (clarify by filtration) and decant into bottles.

DANDELION

CONTRIBUTORS

Jeanette Abrahamson
Enid Ackerman
Betty Aide
Lydia Albrecht
Jeanne Allan
Bea Alm
Corynne Anderson
Francis Anderson
Gary Anderson
Judy Anderson
Marcia Anderson
Clare Angell
Carol Arenstein
Ingeburg Arnold
Ricki Arnold
Jean Bailey
Gladys Bain
Emma Bair
Jane Bair
Jean Ballantyne
Esther Barneck
Marilyn Barnicle
Pam Barsness
Esther Bauer
Joyce Bauer
Arlo Beattie
LaVonne Beattie
Esther Beazley
Bernie Beierle
Janet Beltran
Caryl Bennett
Jeanne Benrud
Lucille Berg
Lorraine Berger
Jane Bibelheimer
Pat Bigornia
Lynne Bigwood
Roberta Bishop
Judith Bodmer
Duane Bohrer
Marlana Bohrer
Eleonore Bollinger
Jan Bond
Helen L. Booth
Carol Bothun
Norma Boutrous
Mirian Boyd
Joan Bratley
Ella Lippert Broschat
Mary Ann Brosnahan
Alane Brosseau
Lois Brown
Shirl Brunsoman
Anne Bucklin
Sigrid Bucklin
Louise Burke
Betty Siros Burns
Joan Gunness Burns
Bill Butcher
Dina Butcher
Nan Campbell
Willa Carlson
Lydia V. Carriedo
Barbara Carson
Eloise Carson
Carol Cashman
Marilyn Christianson
Audrey Cleary
Marlene Clemens
Signe Snortland-Coles
Virginia Coughlin
Yvonne Cronquist
Marion Crouse
Floyce Cummings
Bonna Cunningham
Betty Dacar

Ada Dahl
Vivian Dahl
Vaso Daniolos
Anne Dashiell
Lynn Dashiell
Marilyn Davis
Eileen DeKrey
Stephanie Delmore
Anna Delvo
Charlie Demakes
Carol Dilse
Aggie Dobowey
Margo Dockter
Janet Doerner
Mary Kay Doerr
Lois Dolan
Marlys Dotseth
Marilyn O'Leary Duffey
Joni Duemeland
Lova Dyer
Diane Dyk
Cheryl Eastgate
Janet Eberle
Mary Ann Eckroth
Millie Eckroth
Monica Eckroth
Edible Bean Growers
  Assn. of ND & MN
Louise Edwards
Deb Egeland
Alice Eider
Jane Ellis
Lois Engler
Lois Erdmann
Lori Faiman
Beverly Farrell
Diane Farrell
Esther C. Farrell
Gareth Fay
Harriet Feist
Sue Feland
Margaret Fiechtner
Shelley Flaget
Gary Flagg
Lyla Flagg
Kathy Fortman
Carolyn Frank
Craig Fransen
Loris Freier
Wilma Freise
Doris Fricke
Betty Froeschle
Phyllis Gackle
Brita Gardebring
Helen S. Gately
Kathryn M. George
Peggy Giese
Carolyn Gilbert
Nancy Gill
Verna Gimbell
Barbara Glore
Dottie Glore
Mary Goldberg
Mary Golden
Helga Gonzalez
Suzi Gorelick
Connie Gray
Dean Grebe
Lorraine Gregware
Jean Grindberg
Fran Gronberg
Olivia Gross
Marilyn Grotewold
Marilyn Gundlach
Mary McCannel Gunkelman
Bonnie Hadland

Sis Hadley
Avis Hagen
Kathe Hall
Esther Hample
Helen Hanisch
Lois Hanson
Mary Ann Hanson
Florence Hauer
Anita Hafermehl
Mitsuko Heinitz
Betty Heinrich
Darrel Hildebrant
Beth Hill
Mrs. Martin Hill
Rosemary Hill
Jo Hilzendager
Winnie Hoersch
Bertha Holt
Ellie Hook
Merry Hook
Patti Hopkins
Fran Hopper
Mary Elle Hunter
Grace Indseth
Dorris Iverson
Peg Jack
Marlene Jacobson
Alvera E. Huber Jaeger
Ruth Jakes
Adele Johnson
Barbara Johnson
Button Johnson
Colleen Johnson
Donella Johnson
Emily Johnson
Judy Johnson
Eunice M. Jones
Mona Jordon
Linda Juhala
Christine Murray Kauk
Mary Beth Keller
Jean Kiesau
Dorothy Kinnard
Jan Kipp
Lorene Kirsch
Edie Kjos
Ginger Klein
Harriet Klein
Deborah R. Korsmo
Bonnie Kosir
Mrs. Paul Kraenzel
Father Thomas Kramer
Yvonne Kroll
Emma Kwako
Shirley Lacher
Pat Lahr
Barbara Larson
Beth Larson
Jane Lauer
Gloria Legrid
Joan Leifur
Hilma Lein
Rose K. Leingang
Rosa Lewis
Betty Lindelow
Rita Lindemoen
Patricia Lidstrom
Grace Link
Donna Lommen
Mary Lommen
Susan Loyd
Evelyn Lundberg
Susan Lundberg
Dorothy Lussenden
Alvina Luyben
Doris Lydeen

Mary Magill
Betty Maher
Dolly Makelke
Charlotte Makelky
Janice E. Manchuso
Margie Martin
Joanne Mason
Susanne Mattheis
Ruth May
Jan Mayer
Drinda McCormick
Carol McCullough
Vicki McGurren
Sonja Melby
Angie Stein Melland
Ray Meyer
Marian E. Mezoff
Lois Michels
Alice Miller
Betty Miller
Helen Miller
Wilford L. Miller
Ginny Mittelberg
Sue Mollison
Adeline Montague
Florence Montz
Vita K. Moore
Dorothy Sweetser-Morrissey
Edna Moses
Brenda L. Murray
Surekha S. Murthy
National Beef Cookoff
Lillian Nayes
Dottie Neils
Delight Nelson
Florence Nelson
Goldie M. Nelson
Jean Nelson
Joan Nelson
Joann Nelson
Karen Nelson
Pat Nelson
Pat Ness
Rosalinda Newell
Vi Nicola
N.D. Egg Board
N.D. Governor's Residence
N.D. Lamb Growers Assn.
N.D. State Wheat Commission
N.D. Sunflower Council
Mrs. Del Nystedt
Marlene Okeson
Barbara Olson
Carolyn Olson
Jean Olson
Marcia Olson
Sally Oremland
Peggy Ormseth
Marlys Orser
Vallerie Otto
Gerry Patchen
Carolyn Patterson
Cecelia Paul
Margaret Payne
Suzie Pearce
Joanne Pearson
Judy Pederson
Betty Perry
Dell Petersen
Bev Peterson
Connie Peterson
Diane Peterson
Dolly Peterson
Helen Hedden Peterson
Sarajane Peterson
Lou Pfeifle

212

Darlene Porsborg
Cy Puetz
Peggy Puetz
Pamela Pulkrabek
Elaine Qual
Becky Quanrud
Ted Quanrud
Tija Ramos
Jean Ray
Red River Edible
 Bean Growers Assn.
Red River Valley
 Potato Growers Assn.
Lora Redington
Mrs. Jack Reese
Sue Reeves
Rose Reinbold
Fran Renner
Irene Renz
Lois Richmond
Erna Riskedahl
Ann Robb
Corrine Rockstad
Gerry Rockstad
Mrs. W.G. Roesch
Millie Ross
Eleanor Roswick
Bonnie Rothenberger
Stan Rothenberger
Florence D. Ruff
Martha Rule
Cathy Rydell
Francis Sagsveen
Betty Samuelson
Stelle Sande

Sally Sandison
Darlene Sandvold
Ellen Sanford
Katherine Satrom
Joyce Sauer
Heidi Saueressig
Peggy Schaaf
Kay Schindler
Shari Schlosser
Geneva Schnell
Ann Schuetzle
Elaine Schultz
Jane Schulz
Julie Schwartz
Geogiana Seay
Charlene Seifert
Phyllis Senechal
Barbara Severin
Eran Severn
Mink Shalhoob
Gail Shank
Brenda Shark
Gertrude Shark
Elsie Shaw
Honey Shaw
Shirley E. Shaw
Phyllis Shields
Vesper Shirley
Patricia Shorma
Mildred Simle
Jean Simpkins
John Simkins
Janie Sinner
Margaret Sitte
Nancy Skaret
Beverly Slotten

Birgit Smeenk
Dorothy Smith
Adeline Snortland
Nellie Solberg
Helen Sorlie
Joy Sorenson
Bonnie Staiger
Ruth Stark
Clara Stein
Janice Steinle
Janice Steinwand
Jane G. Stewart
Teri Fay Storhaug
Bill Stradinger
Kay Strothman
Wanda Sturlaugson
Paula Swanson
Kathy Sweere
Lois Swenson
Nancy A. Swenson
Don Switzer
Cecelia Tannehill
Phyllis Tarnasky
Aldeen Taylor
Mary Tello
Peggy Thakor
Linda Thomas
June Thompson
Jan Thon
Cindy Tierney
Arlys Timian
Nell Torvik
Karen Traeholt
Corliss Trom
Gwen Tucker Bradley
Anne Ulmen

Mike Unhjem
Elaine A. Vanderscoff
Shirlee E. Van Erem
Shirley Velander
Joan Von Rueden
Joseph Vuolo
Lee Waldschmidt
Betty Warner
Lillian Wass
Ruth M. Watson
Joan Gregware Wattles
Melva Weber
Susan Wefald
Barbara Western
Sybil Wezelman
Gerridee Wheeler
Irene Whitney
Audrey Whittey
Marge Wickert
Phyllis G. Wigen
Dee Wildfang
Rita Willer
Bonnie Wilson
Joan M. Winbauer
Susan Ramig Wischmeier
Jean Wolf
Karen Wolf
Mary Ellen Woodmansee
Yes Virginia
Carole Youngs
Josephine E. Zahn
Dick Zajic
Karen Zajic
Judy Zanin
Irene Zuger
Mary Zuger

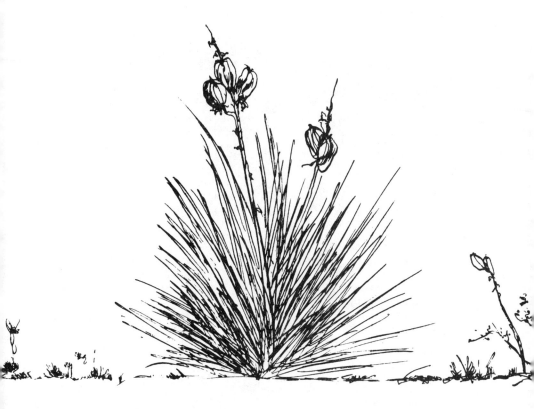

INDEX

A

B

214

216

D

E

F

G

H

I

J

The Prairie Collection Cookbook

Bismarck Mandan Symphony League
Box 131
Bismarck, North Dakota 58502

_____ Books at $17.95 each . $ _____

Postage and handling $2.50 each $ _____

N.D. residents add 5½% sales tax

    at $.99 per copy $ _____

                   Total $ _____

Make checks payable to:
The Prairie Collection Cookbook

Purchaser: _____

Address: _____

Phone number: _____

Ship to: _____

_____

_____

Direct wholesale inquiries to the above address.

The Prairie Collection Cookbook

Bismarck Mandan Symphony League
Box 131
Bismarck, North Dakota 58502

_____ Books at $17.95 each . $ _____

Postage and handling $2.50 each $ _____

N.D. residents add 5½% sales tax

    at $.99 per copy $ _____

                   Total $ _____

Make checks payable to:
The Prairie Collection Cookbook

Purchaser: _____

Address: _____

Phone number: _____

Ship to: _____

_____

_____

Direct wholesale inquiries to the above address.